STREETWISE

SMALL BUSINESS
TURNAROUND

STREETWISE

SMALL BUSINESS TURNAROUND

Revitalize Your
Struggling or
Stagnant Enterprise

by Marc Kramer

Adams Media Corporation
Holbrook, Massachusetts

Published by Adams Media Corporation
260 Center Street, Holbrook, MA 02343

ISBN: 1-58062-195-3

Printed in the United States of America.

J   I   H   G   F   E   D   C   B   A

Library of Congress Cataloging-in-Publication Data
Kramer, Marc.
Streetwise turnaround / by Marc Kramer.
p.   cm.
ISBN 1-58062-195-3
1. Small business—Management. 2. Success in business.
3. Corporate turnarounds. I. Title.
HD62.7.K73   1999
658.02'2—dc21   99-28137
CIP

This publication is designed to provide accurate and authoritative information with regard to the subject matter covered. It is sold with the understanding that the publisher is not engaged in rendering legal, accounting,
or other professional advice. If legal advice or other expert assistance is required, the services of a competent
professional person should be sought.
— From a *Declaration of Principles* jointly adopted by a Committee
of the American Bar Association and a Committee of Publishers and Associations

Illustration by Eric Mueller.

This book is available at quantity discounts for bulk purchases.
For information, call 1-800-872-5627.

Visit our exciting small business Web site: www.businesstown.com

CONTENTS

PART I: MAPPING OUT YOUR STRATEGY

PART II: IMPLEMENTING YOUR STRATEGY

PART III: PREPARING FOR THE FUTURE

Acknowledgments

I would like to thank my wife Jackie and my two daughters, Ariel and Sydney, for their understanding and support as I wrote this book.

I want to thank my friends who assisted in the editing and provided feedback for the content of this book: Dr. David Krasner, Gary Samartino, and Mark Talaba.

Throughout the book are interviews with experienced professionals, and I would like to thank those people for the time they took in answering my questions: Neal Colton, Sam Fredericks, Steve Goodman, Ash Liliani, Bill Macaleer, Jim Matour, Mike Miller, Abbe Miller, Nido Paras, Jay Star, and Rob Weber.

I am grateful to my editor, Jere Calmes, and my publisher, Adams Media, for the opportunity to write this book.

Preface

Turning around a small business is a gut wrenching experience akin to getting into great shape. One day you are a fine tuned 180-pound star athlete and ten years later you weigh over 220 pounds and can't run twenty yards without being out of breath.

You didn't get out of shape overnight; it happened over a period of time. You stopped going to the gym on the days you weren't playing tennis. Over time you stopped going to the gym completely because you were playing tennis. Then you cut down the number of days you played tennis until you weren't playing anymore.

Before you die of a heart attack, you realize you need to exercise and lose weight and begin to get in shape all over again. To get back into peak condition, you don't start going to the gym and playing tennis for the same amount of time and at the same level you did ten years ago. First you work with your doctor to develop a diet and exercise program you can live with because a crash diet will only solve your problem temporarily.

Turning around a company is like getting back into shape. The reason your business got out of shape is because you stopped doing the little things right that made you a success in the first place. You became full of yourself. In your mind, no one was better or smarter. In the beginning you hired employees who brought ideas and intensity to the business, but as they left for other opportunities or you failed to keep your promises, you didn't upgrade your personnel or provide better opportunities.

I have personally been involved in managing four small company turnarounds and have worked with numerous troubled businesses. The first time I was involved in a turnaround was in 1984. I went to one of the big chain bookstores and asked the manager what book he would recommend reading. He suggested former Chrysler chairman Lee Iacocca's book, *Iacocca: An Autobiography.*

Although the story was great and the book was well written, I was managing a thin-margin, $2 million, twenty-employee retail business. I didn't have the luxury of being able to let go of 20,000 people, close a few factories, or tell my suppliers to give me better discounts and forget some of my debt or you will never get paid. And I didn't

> Turning around a company is like getting back into shape.

employ enough people to ask the government for a low-interest rate loan.

I began reading such magazines as *Success* and *Inc.* and clipping out company turnaround story articles. When the articles didn't provide enough information, I bought books on how to write business, marketing, operations, and sales plans and books on how to raise money and work out problems with your creditors and so forth.

Each time I got involved in a turnaround situation, I went to the bookstore and looked for books on the subject. Heads of large multibillion dollar companies wrote the only books I could find. The last turnaround I managed, the founder of the business said if he could have found a book that walked him through the steps of restoring his company's health he might not have needed to hire me. At the least he would have known what to do and expect instead of relying on someone else to save his business.

Right after I finished my last turnaround, a friend called me to have lunch and told me her business was in trouble and she wanted to fix the problems herself. She asked if I could recommend anything to read on the subject. I went to the various on-line bookstores and couldn't find anything that would walk a business owner through the processes one goes through when fixing a sick company.

I began to write my own book and shared it with friends whose businesses were either in dire straits or who felt uneasy with how their business was operating. These friends gave me their input and some hired me to coach them through their problems.

When I wrote to publishers about my book only a handful were interested in developing such a book for small business. Those who were interested couldn't believe such a book didn't exist until they did their own research.

I was fortunate to work with Adams Media and have my book be a part of their Streetwise series. Adams Media is only interested in books that provide practical solutions. This book walks you through every step my clients and I have had to go through to fix and keep our companies from ending up in Chapter 7 or 11. In my opinion, the last option for a small company should be to file for Chapter 7 or 11. Below is an interview with a very experienced bankruptcy attorney,

> The founder of the business said if he could have found a book that walked him through the steps of restoring his company's health he might not have needed to hire me.

Neal Colton, who explains the steps, circumstances, costs, and the personal ramifications of filing for bankruptcy.

Neal Colton graduated from the University of Pittsburgh (A.B. 1965); Columbia University Graduate School of Business (M.B.A., 1967); and Temple University School of Law (J.D., 1970). Mr. Colton is a senior partner at Cozen and O'Connor, one of Philadelphia's most prestigious law firms, and chairman of its Insolvency, Bankruptcy, and Restructuring Group. Mr. Colton is a member of the American Bankruptcy Institute and has been certified as a Business Bankruptcy Specialist by the American Bankruptcy Board of Certification. He is listed in *The Best Lawyers in America*.

When should you think about filing for bankruptcy?

Bankruptcy (particularly Chapter 11) is a tool. Accordingly, in the event of:

A. Violation of debt covenants
B. Loss of a major customer
C. Product liability claims/litigation
D. Failure of major customer (write-off of receivables)
E. Significant operating losses
F. Pending foreclosure
G. Catastrophic contract commitments

> The objective is to avoid waiting until it is too late to save the business.

bankruptcy should be considered. The objective is to avoid waiting until it is too late to save the business because the problems cannot be rectified with the resources available at the time of the bankruptcy filing.

What are the bankruptcy options?

For a business—primarily Chapters 7 and 11. Chapter 7 is a liquidation—the business ceases operation, a trustee is appointed, and everything is sold at public sale. There is no way to save a business in Chapter 7. In Chapter 11, there is an effort to reorganize—address the business's problems and correct them. Alternatively, in

Chapter 11, it is possible to sell business units or the entire business at a private sale, subject to approval by the court and the creditors.

How do I know which one to choose?

Customarily, if there is a glimmer of hope, the business will file a Chapter 11 petition. There is a time when that is not advisable, however. For example, if there is no reason to believe that losses, which are experienced before the bankruptcy, cannot be stemmed after the filing, then there may be a diminution in value of the business by keeping it going. Such a decision is substantially detrimental to all constituencies, including the owners. This is because the owners often have personal guarantees, and if the business is worth less after a failed Chapter 11, then the guarantee obligation to creditors will increase.

How should you go about selecting a bankruptcy attorney?

In most instances, through a referral from someone trusted by the owner/manager of the business (assuming that the individuals don't have prior personal experience!). The business owner should inquire about the attorney's experience generally in representing businesses in a restructuring environment. Further, it may be relevant to know whether the attorney has had prior experience with the particular industry of the troubled business. Also, it is crucial to inquire about the number of conflicting demands on the attorney's time, the staff that will work on the matter, the attorney's hourly rates, and any possible conflicts.

What is the difference between a good bankruptcy attorney and a bad one?

Generally, a good attorney will be "accomplished." See what he or she lists as academic and professional achievements. Where has the attorney practiced law? Does the attorney have a business background? Can he/she read and analyze financial statements? Do you believe that the attorney is committed to you—and cares? Are you given the attorney's home telephone number?

> The business owner should inquire about the attorney's experience generally in representing businesses in a restructuring environment.

What organizations could point me in the direction of a good bankruptcy attorney?

None. Many organizations will provide names, but no organization really endorses an attorney.

How much should I expect to spend in legal fees when filing for bankruptcy?

Fees depend on complexity and contentiousness. A business bankruptcy (Chapter 11) can run anywhere from $50,000 to $500,000 or more.

What control do I have over my business when filing for bankruptcy?

There is a substantial loss of control when a bankruptcy petition is filed. The proceeding is "judicial" and the judge must approve major decisions. In addition, unsecured creditors often are permitted to form a committee, which participates in proceedings before the court, and other parties get to state a position to express opinions and oppose the business's requests.

> There is a substantial loss of control when a bankruptcy petition is filed.

Can I lose my home, personal bank account, and possessions?

Yes, if you have personally guaranteed business debt or you have engaged in using the business to meet personal expenses, at which point creditors might argue that you have subjected all of your assets to business debts.

If I file for bankruptcy will I ever be able to get credit and bank loans to restart my current business or start a new business?

Yes. Credit and bank loans often are very easy to get after bankruptcy if you have been discharged from all of your prebankruptcy debts. If you have current income and no debts, lenders will be very enthusiastic about you as a borrower if you can satisfactorily explain your prior business problems and how they will not re-occur.

Now that you have read Mr. Colton's advice on bankruptcy, do you still think that is the best option for you? In my opinion and experience, filing for bankruptcy is the last course of action any size company wants to take, especially a small company with little spare cash to spend on attorneys. In the appendix are sample forms for filing Chapter 7 bankruptcy and dissolution of the corporation and Chapter 11 forms for reorganizing the company with the oversight of the courts. Please contact your state bankruptcy court to fully understand the laws that govern bankruptcy in your state.

Rather than spend the money on attorney's fees, you might consider bringing in an expert to either assist you part-time or to take over running your business day to day.

I would advise taking the following twelve steps and reading the rest of this book so you and your management team can decide what you can and can't do, based on your skills and experience, and focus on getting your business back on track.

Write a business plan.

Step One: Write a business plan
Step Two: Write an operating plan
Step Three: Write sales and marketing plans
Step Four: Look for expenses to cut
Step Five: Reorganize and re-energize management and the employees
Step Six: Communicate organizational changes and challenges to employees, vendors, and clients
Step Seven: Communicate financial problems and provide solutions to banks and taxing authorities
Step Eight: Audit existing clients to find out how the company is perceived
Step Nine: Add to or replace existing professional advisors
Step Ten: Add to or replace existing board members
Step Eleven: Decide whether to raise new capital or sell the business
Step Twelve: Evaluate your future role in the business

This book walks you through each step and provides you with real-world, small-company examples of what other companies have done to put themselves back into a position to succeed. If there is a market for your business all you need to do is stay calm and not get overwhelmed by the enormity of having to fix your business.

Everyone goes through ups and downs because it's part of the business cycle.

There are three keys to success:

1. Keep your expenses low, your quality of employees high
2. Provide employees with opportunities to fail, learn, grow, and succeed
3. Focus on keeping your customer happy and your margins healthy

Let's get started on helping you get back to and exceed the level your business was in. If you have any questions and I can be helpful, please e-mail me at marc@kramercommunications.com.

> Everyone goes through ups and downs because it's part of the business cycle.

Mapping Out
Your Strategy

Summary of Part I

This section will help the business leader with the crucial tasks of:

- Understanding the ten steps to turning around a business
- Developing a new business plan
- Identifying an outside professional to re-establish the business

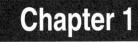

Chapter 1

Steps for Turning Around a Company

"Show me a man who cannot bother to do the little things and I'll show you a man who cannot be trusted to do big things"

—LAWRENCE D. BELL (1894–1956)
American helicopter manufacturer

The majority of the books written about corporate turnarounds, such as *Mean Business* by former Scott Paper, Inc. chairman and CEO Albert Dunlap, are written by executives who have fixed Fortune 500 companies. These individuals have the ability to cut large numbers of employees, tap pension funds and banks for infusions of capital, and sell off enormous assets to raise cash and decrease debt.

Although not demeaning the accomplishments of these people, few small and midsize companies can make such dramatic changes. These businesses can have a difficult time getting a line of credit from a bank, typically don't have meaningful assets to sell to increase the company's cash position, and can't afford to lay off large numbers of people.

There is another category of books written by business consultants that focus on financial and accounting issues. Unfortunately, many of these books deal with only the half the problem an executive faces in a turnaround, and none of them provide examples of how to write business plans to raise new capital or marketing/sales plans to increase sales. They also don't address the people management issues and the mistakes the leaders make.

I have spent my career turning around and starting small companies and have found that both offer unique and sometimes very painful challenges. To accomplish corporate turnarounds successfully you need a great deal of energy, self-confidence, resiliency, and the ability to maintain a positive mental attitude every day. Your employees, shareholders, and family look to you for leadership and stability.

Business leaders who find themselves in a turnaround situation are initially afraid and likely to question whether they have the skill to fix their company. They might even feel worthless and sorry for themselves. Unfortunately, those feelings can't last long or they'll affect the energy and ability that is needed to turn the ship around.

Before discussing how to recognize that your company needs to be fixed, and how to fix it while maintaining control, let's review some information on business bankruptcies and failures published in a 1997 Small Business Administration report (available on the SBA Web site in February, 1998):

> They also don't address the people management issues and the mistakes the leaders make.

According to the Small Business Administration, business failures are up 16.6 percent from 1986 to 1996. Business bankruptcies increased by 5.3 percent during 1996, rising from 50,516 in 1995 to 53,214 in 1996.

Why did I share this information? First, to let you know that if your business is in trouble, you aren't alone. Second, I hope those numbers will scare you into taking a positive action.

How Do You Know You're in Trouble?

Companies usually don't find themselves in trouble overnight. It happens over a period of a few months to a couple of years.

How do you know your company is in or is coming close to being in dire straits? Here is a simple list of symptoms:

- Sales are decreasing in a growing market
- Current customers are leaving for reasons that are in your control
- Clients complain their calls aren't being returned
- More client projects are over budget
- Profits are declining and expenses are going up
- Employees are telling each other, and, unfortunately, customers, they aren't sure of the company's direction
- Employees are telling management they don't feel they are being led
- Employees are coming in late and leaving early
- Employee monthly meetings stop taking place and good employees start leaving
- Employees stop trusting management
- Employees are beginning to bicker over small things
- Management meetings that used to be weekly are happening whenever people feel like getting together
- Management isn't working as a team
- The company can't afford to pay its taxes
- The company is falling behind paying its vendors

Companies usually don't find themselves in trouble overnight.

If, after an honest assessment, you recognize these symptoms and realize you are in trouble, then you need to take the following steps to get your shareholders, employees, and yourself out of trouble.

Ten Keys to Performing a Successful Turnaround

This book is focused on how to turn around a small company or division of a larger company. Leadership is faced with innumerable problems. Some are large and some are small. The best way to tackle these issues is to break them down into ten categories and focus on them. Below are the ten keys to performing a successful turnaround:

> Company managers must be able to handle adversity and willing to work long hours.

1. The top executive must be strong, decisive, and a good communicator
2. The business, marketing/sales, and operating plans must have a narrow focus that everyone in the organization understands and can support
3. Company managers must be able to handle adversity and willing to work long hours
4. Employees must be willing to make sacrifices and work more than forty hours per week
5. The company must have a strong, experienced board of directors or advisors
6. Company vendors need to be flexible regarding payment for services and supplies
7. The company's bank loan officer has to understand the company's business and believe in its future
8. Everyone in the company must be dedicated to quality
9. The marketplace needs the company's product/service
10. Management must hire accountants and lawyers who understand their business and have dealt with companies that need to be turned around

The ten keys for turning around a company can also be viewed as ingredients for running a successful company. However, they aren't necessarily the ingredients needed to start a company. I have seen many companies started by people who have great sales or technical skills, but they aren't good business people.

Existing management doesn't have to be removed if they take responsibility and are willing to make immediate changes to fix the company. Unfortunately, more often than not, existing management thinks it is doing all of the right things but fails to recognize that the company is in trouble. I have been involved with entrepreneurs who talk themselves into believing they are doing all of the right things. They believe only a few adjustments need to be made and the company will be fine. They don't take stock in themselves, their managers, their employees, their product/service, or the way they do business. They refuse to honestly ask themselves if each of the aforementioned areas was working as well as it could be.

Turning around or fixing a company doesn't take tremendous brainpower. It requires common sense, decisiveness, honesty among all parties who are involved, and an understanding that things must change for everyone to be successful. Success for employees and owners is never really about money; it's about doing a job well and getting repeat business. The money will come if the company is successful.

> Turning around or fixing a company doesn't take tremendous brainpower.

Ten Steps to a Successful Turnaround

To implement the ten keys in a successful turnaround, you have to perform, in order, the following ten steps. Owners of small- and medium-size businesses have successfully used these steps.

Step 1: Write business, sales/marketing, and operation plans

We will go into greater detail about the value and structure of a business plan in Chapter 2, but for the purposes of this list we will talk about the importance of written plans. Rarely do companies who write and maintain plans on an annual basis get into trouble. Plans chronicle the good and bad of the past and set a vision for the future.

Investors, management, and employees all need to know what the company's future plans are. They need to see where they fit in, how they can help, and to share suggestions based on their expertise that will help the company succeed.

Step 2: Meet with key personnel and a board of directors or advisors

You must get the key people in the business together to have a no-holds-barred discussion on how to fix the company. Don't go into the meeting without a plan of your own. People lose confidence in leaders who lack a plan and vision for their business. The key in this type of meeting is to be self-assured, open-minded, and flexible.

Step 3: Revise plans

After listening to key executives in the business, revise and ask key executives to review the plans a second time before presenting them to the board of directors and employees.

Step 4: Meet with employees

Have a company meeting, admit that there are things wrong with the business, and discuss how management plans to fix it. Provide employees with a copy of the company business plan and ask for their input. For an established business, this step demonstrates that careful consideration has been given to the development of the business.

Step 5: Meet with customers

Rumors of your imminent demise are swirling around the business community. Key customers are becoming nervous and some are even looking for new vendors. Don't stick your head in the sand. Inform your customers about your situation and tell them how you plan to correct it. Be reassuring, but not deceitful.

> Have a company meeting, admit that there are things wrong with the business, and discuss how management plans to fix it.

Step 6: Meet with vendors

Company vendors get very nervous when they hear "on the street" that one of their customers is having trouble. Sometimes word travels faster than you can thoughtfully alert the appropriate people about your problem. With that said, you need to develop a prepared statement outlining the problems and how you plan to deal with them. You will receive plenty of concerned telephone calls. Respond quickly and thoughtfully to all of them.

Step 7: Contact tax authorities

If you can't pay your local, county, state, and federal taxes, notify the authorities. Tax authorities will work with you. You'll be on much better terms with them than if you fail to pay and have it appear as if you are trying to avoid your obligation.

Step 8: Contact your bank

If you have loans or a line of credit, call—don't write—your loan officers and tell them you need to meet in person. Give them the bad news followed by your plan of action. Appear confident and reassuring.

> If you can't pay your local, county, state, and federal taxes, notify the authorities.

Step 9: Keep only employees who are essential to the business

Figure out which employees you can let go without damaging your business. Nobody likes to let people go, but for the business to survive you want to keep only people who are bringing in, making, or servicing sales.

Step 10: Cut unnecessary costs

Make a list of all your expenses and eliminate what you don't need. You need to buy time in order to fix your problems, and cutting expenses is a good way to buy "financial" time.

Chapter 2

Writing a Business Plan

"No plan can prevent a stupid person from doing the wrong thing in the wrong place at the wrong time—but a good plan should keep a concentration from forming"

—CHARLES E. WILSON (1890-1961)
Chairman, General Motors Corporation and
U.S. Secretary of Defense

> A business plan should be a realistic view of the expectations and long-term objectives for a business.

Few people who start a business have not heard of the concept of writing a business plan. Many business people think you only write a business plan if you are planning to raise money. However, this is a narrow view of how a business plan should be used. The purpose of a business plan is to lay out a road map that management, employees, and investors, if they are needed, can follow to make sure the business is going in the right direction.

You wouldn't build a house without architectural plans because selecting the wrong layout, ground, and building materials could result in a house that falls on top of you after you move in. Well, a business plan is the architectural blueprint for your business.

A business plan should be a realistic view of the expectations and long-term objectives for a business. It provides the framework within which it must operate and, ultimately, succeed or fail. For management or entrepreneurs seeking external support, the plan is the most important sales document that they are ever likely to produce as it is key to focusing the company and to raising capital. Preparation of a comprehensive plan will not guarantee success in raising funds or mobilizing support, but lack of a sound plan will—almost certainly—ensure failure. Also, a formal business plan is just as important for an established business, irrespective of its size, as it is for a start-up.

While preparing a satisfactory business plan can be painful, it is an essential exercise. The planning process itself forces managers or entrepreneurs to understand more clearly what they want to achieve and how and when they can do it. Even if no external financial assistance is needed, a business plan can play a vital role in helping to avoid mistakes or to recognize hidden opportunities.

A formal business plan serves four critical functions:

- helps management or an entrepreneur to clarify, focus, and research the development and prospects of their business or project;
- provides a logical framework within which a business can develop and pursue business strategies over the next three to five years;

- serves as a basis for discussion with third parties such as shareholders, taxing authorities, banks, investors, etc;
- offers a benchmark against which actual performance can be measured and reviewed.

Just as no two businesses are alike, so also with business plans. As some issues in a plan will be more relevant to some businesses than to others, it is important to tailor a plan's contents to suit individual circumstances. Nonetheless, most plans follow a tried and tested structure, and general advice on preparing a plan is universally applicable.

The Importance of Planning

Robin Weber, a graduate of the Wharton School of Business, spent five years turning around a small electronics company outside of Philadelphia. He is a proponent of developing business plans. When Mr. Weber was brought in as president, the company had thirty-five employees, $1.8 million of revenue, and was losing money. The company manufactured specialty electronic components called connectors that were used in small electronic devices. One-third of the company's sales was with one customer in a low-margin business.

Within five years, company sales were running at a $5–$6 million rate and the company was profitable and moving into new markets. They still had one major customer that accounted for one-third of sales, though it was high-margin business.

Did you write a business plan to turnaround your company?
Yes. It was one of the first things that I did.

Did you write an operating, sales and/or marketing plan?
The business plan was fairly detailed and took on much of the look of an operating and sales and marketing plan. Mostly one document.

> Nonetheless, most plans follow a tried and tested structure.

How important is writing a business plan when trying to fix a company?

Essential. It is used primarily to get the management team, and the company as a whole, behind a vision for the company. Second, it helps to establish the key priorities that everyone signs up to.

What kind of skills and experience did you look for in the attorneys and accountants you hired?

Initially, we had attorneys and accountants. Since we were venture capital backed, and needed to plan for an eventual exit for the investors, we changed attorneys and accountants to firms with experience in M&A and IPO. We chose Morgan Lewis and Bockius and PriceWaterhouseCoopers.

What was the most difficult problem you had to deal with and how did you deal with it?

The management team was not ideally suited to the needs of the company, so immediate changes had to be made. The company had a bonus program for employees that paid out even if cash flow did not support it—that had to be changed while maintaining high morale.

What kind of role did your board play in helping you fix the company?

The board had to be supplemented with outside industry experts before it reached its optimal position. Once the new board was in place, we were able to look at big-picture, long-term strategic opportunities. A board member introduced us to a key customer in a key industry. This new customer affiliation was intensely interesting to a potential acquirer. So, this one board member had a key role in helping get the company sold.

What skills should board members have in a turnaround?

Ideally, one or more individuals from the industry. They will add big-picture thinking, which will go far in moving the company ahead. Other entrepreneurs on the board are extremely helpful, as it

> The management team was not ideally suited to the needs of the company, so immediate changes had to be made.

gets lonely at the top for the CEO and it's good to have someone to talk to about issues.

Did your clients know you were in financial trouble?

No. We were able to continue to deliver quality products on time, so no clients knew.

What role did your bank play, and is it better to use a large or small bank?

Our bank, Meridian, was very patient and supportive. They continued to renew lines of credit and allowed slack on our term loans. They came in, learned about our situation (we gave them a copy of our plan), and were very supportive.

Did you ever have days when you wondered whether you were the right person to fix the company?

Yes. I was especially new at leadership and managing people. There had been attempted coup d'etats, employee injuries, fires, and every imaginable thing go wrong.

What is the most important lesson you learned?

Develop a vision, get the right team in place, get the right board in place, and move forward forcefully. Any sign of weakness will be disastrous—as will not having the right team and board. If you go in to a turnaround, demand full control of the situation.

Developing a business plan

The following sections discuss the preparation of a strategic plan as well as present ideas for preparing an outline and detailed business plans.

Preparing an Outline

A typical business plan starts with a brief introduction on the background and structure of the plan. The main body of the plan, which expands on the subjects brought up in the introduction, follows this. The final parts of the plan are the financials, exhibits, and

> Develop a vision, get the right team in place, get the right board in place, and move forward forcefully.

any other supporting information not found in the main body of the plan.

A short outline (two to three pages) can provide a very useful foundation on which to base a much more detailed and comprehensive business plan.

Before any work commences on writing a plan, identify the plan's audience. With this knowledge, you can then determine content requirements and level of detail. Then, map out the plan's structure (i.e., its contents). The plan shouldn't be more than twenty-five pages. Identify all the main issues to be addressed and ask your managers to review the outline to make sure nothing is missing.

Prior to developing an outline, you should clearly identify the current status, objectives, and strategies of the existing business. Correctly defined, these can be used as the basis for a critical examination to probe existing or perceived strengths, weaknesses, threats, and opportunities. This then leads to strategy development covering the following issues, which are discussed in more detail in the plan itself:

- Vision
- Mission, objectives and goals
- Values
- Sales, marketing, and hiring strategies
- Competition
- Income and expense projections

The first step is to develop a realistic *vision for the business*. This should represent a picture of the business in three or more years time in terms of its likely physical appearance, size, activities, and so on. Make sure your vision is simple and clear; some venture capitalists have their secretary's screen business plans, and if the secretary can't understand the plan, the venture capitalist never sees it.

The nature of a business is often expressed in terms of its *mission*, which indicates the purposes of the business, for example, "to be the leading kidney food company in the United States." A statement along these lines indicates what the business is about and is

> Prior to developing an outline, you should clearly identify the current status, objectives, and strategies of the existing business.

infinitely clearer than saying, for instance, "we're in the food business" or worse still, "we are in business to make money" (assuming that the business is not a mint!).

It's very important that every employee knows the mission of the company so they can do everything in their power to make the company a success. If employees are clear on the mission, they can help sell the company in formal and informal settings. Also, some people confuse mission statements with value statements–the former should be very hard-nosed while the latter can deal with softer issues surrounding the business.

The third key element is to explicitly state the *objective* of the business in terms of the results it needs/wants to achieve in the short and long term. Aside from presumably indicating a necessity to achieve regular profits, objectives should relate to the expectations and requirements of all the major stakeholders, including employees, and should reflect the underlying reasons for running the business.

The next element is to address the *values* governing the operation of the business and its conduct or relationships with society, customers, employees, and so on.

Next are the *strategies*–the rules and guidelines by which the mission, objectives, and so on may be achieved. They can cover the business as a whole–including such matters as diversification, organic growth, or acquisition plans–or they can relate to primary matters in key functional areas, for example:

> The third key element is to explicitly state the objective of the business in terms of the results it needs/wants to achieve in the short and long term.

- the company's internal cash flow will fund all future growth;
- new products will progressively replace existing ones over the next three years;
- all assembly work will be contracted out to lower the company's break-even point.

The next topic to address is *goals*. These are specific interim or ultimate time-based measurements to be achieved by implementing strategies in pursuit of the company's objectives (for example, to achieve sales of $3 million in three years).

The final elements to cover are the *programs*, which set out the implementation plans for the key strategies.

It goes without saying that the mission, objectives, values, strategies, and goals must be interlinked and consistent with each other. Most companies don't articulate this in writing, and this is a huge mistake. Board members, employees, and investors need to know your plan to comment and assist in the company's success.

Preparing a Detailed Plan

You should identify any shortcomings in the concept and gaps in supporting evidence and proposals. This will facilitate an assessment of research to be undertaken before any drafting commences. Business plans in turnarounds must be written quickly and concisely—the writer can't focus on perfection. The reason the plan must be written quickly is because turnaround companies are usually in dire financial straits and don't have the time to wait for the perfect plan.

It's important to remember that the plan is a road map for getting you back on course to prosperity. Events and situations will cause you to change plans, sometimes in midstream. Don't worry about that; just keep moving forward and issues will resolve themselves or you will see a better solution.

External help and guidance in preparing a business plan can be extremely valuable. Outsiders who understand your business may provide valuable insights and suggestions, so don't let your ego and insecurities get in the way of soliciting the best possible advice. If outside help is used, the authors must ensure that the resultant plan remains their own and not that of their advisers.

The following suggestions will help you create a quality plan:

- The most important and difficult sections to prepare relate to marketing and sales, as these can make or break not only the business plan but also the business itself!
- The financial projections are likely to be straightforward, but decide on a sensible level of detail regarding the time horizon.
- Consider using a personal computer and a financial modeling package for the projections. Microsoft Office comes with financial spreadsheets and financial modeling options. Two

> It's important to remember that the plan is a road map for getting you back on course to prosperity.

other good software packages designed to assist with business plan writing are Plan A (from Internet Capital Bulletin Board, Inc.) and Plan Write (from Business Resource Software, Inc.). Both packages ask the user a series of questions, which the user types in. When the user finishes answering all of the questions, a formal business plan with financials is provided.

- When drafting the plan be positive, but realistic, about the business's prospects and explicitly recognize and respond honestly to shortcomings and risks.
- The management section of the plan is crucial. It should demonstrate the management's experience, balance, ability, and commitment. If a new venture is involved, then management is likely to be its only real asset. Consider formation of a management team or strengthening management as part of the plan. Remember that the fate of the company is not in the product but in the management team.
- Avoid unnecessary jargon, economize on words, and use short, crisp sentences and bullet points. Always check to make sure all words are spelled correctly. When there are significant issues, break the text into numbered paragraphs or sections and relegate detail to appendices.
- Get a qualified outsider to review your plan in draft form. Be prepared to adjust the plan in the light of the reviewer's comments.
- Support market and sales projections with market research. Ensure that there is a direct relationship between market analysis, sales forecasts, and financial projections. Assess competitors' positions and possible responses realistically.
- Restrict the level of detail on product specifications and technical issues.
- Be realistic about sales expectations, profit margins, and funding requirements. Ensure that financial ratios are in line with industry norms. Do not underestimate the cost and time required for product development, market entry, securing external support, or raising capital. Consider the possibility

> Avoid unnecessary jargon, economize on words, and use short, crisp sentences and bullet points.

of the halve-double rule: halve the sales projections and double the cost and time required.

- If looking for external equity, be realistic about the value of the business, risks involved, and possible returns, and be sure to indicate possible exit mechanisms. Put yourself in the shoes of an investor and remember the golden rule—he who has the gold makes all the rules.

This advice applies more to turnarounds than start-ups and existing businesses. Most people who invest in turnarounds are sometimes referred to as "bottom fishers." They see value in the product/service and believe that the company is either mismanaged or the entrepreneurs running the business didn't do appropriate financial planning.

- Only address matters of real substance and major significance. Feel free to change the suggested structure to suit the business and where the business is in its life cycle. When writing an outline plan, allow between a one-half and two pages per section.

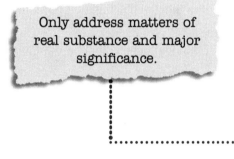

Only address matters of real substance and major significance.

Sample Small Manufacturing Company Business Plan

The following subsections present guidelines for and snippets from a sample business plan. The examples included here could be readily expanded to become a complete business plan. The level of detail would have to be expanded. Ideal page lengths for a straightforward but comprehensive plan are given in parenthesis. Note the importance of marketing and sales in terms of the suggested number of pages. Relegate detail to accompanying appendices.

Executive Summary (one to three pages)

Introduce the plan. Explain who wrote it, when, and for what purpose. Give contact details. Underline the most important statements so the reader hones in and remembers them. Sometimes it is easier to write the executive summary last after you have put all of the other parts of the plan together. On the other hand, a business associate of mine likes to write this part first because it allows him to see an overview of the entire business.

Sample Executive Summary

Opening

Dr. David Kroll, chairman of Health Foods, Inc., has sold specially prepared food for diet constrained individuals. The company, which has been in severe decline over the past two years, has identified a need for shelf-stable foods for kidney patients. This market was identified through surveying of existing and prospective customers. Dr. Kroll believes focusing the company on this market can produce sales of $50 million within three to five years and make HF profitable again.

History

Realizing his company was failing, Dr. Kroll commissioned a study on the health food needs of kidney patients and found the following:

- no microwave-ready food met their medical needs;
- kidney patients (or their spouses/parents/children) have to prepare each meal separately;
- food for kidney patients is usually bland.

From the study, Dr. Kroll concluded kidney patients wanted a prepared meal that met the scrutiny of the American Kidney Association but would require no refrigeration and could be taken to work in a briefcase or handbag. He thought creating an appetizing shelf-stable food for kidney patients would solve that problem.

Dr. Kroll sent out a survey to 100 of his patients to test his concept. Twenty-two percent of the respondents said they would buy the product for a price between $3.50 and $4.00 and would buy five products a week on average. Based on the results of the survey, Dr. Kroll decided to launch Gourmet Delights—"The Healthy & Tasty Alternative for Kidney Patients."

> He thought creating an appetizing shelf-stable food for kidney patients would solve that problem.

Profit and Loss Projections

SALES	YR1	YR2	YR3	YR4	YR5
Income	$5,000,000	$10,000,000	$20,000,000	$40,000,000	$50,000,000
Expenses	$6,000,000	$5,000,000	$10,000,000	$20,000,000	$25,000,000
Profit/Loss	($1,000,000)	$5,000,000	$10,000,000	$20,000,000	$25,000,000

Competition

Campbell Soup Company is the only major food company developing frozen products for this market. Campbell's products are also for people with high blood pressure and other medical concerns that require a special diet. Campbell's products haven't hit the market, but management believes Campbell's entry validates the market.

Philip Ford, president of the American Kidney Association, based in Alexandria, VA, commenting on Campbell's efforts, thinks potential is great. "There are several attractive things about this— first, it's not a drug," said Ford, who has worked with Campbell's. "Second, it works. Third, it's convenient."

> The company's product strategy is simple.

Product Strategy

The company's product strategy is simple. To insure quality and strict adherence to the American Kidney Association standards, HF will collaborate with a dietitian from the University of Pennsylvania whose specialty is kidney patients. There will initially be five types of entrees: pasta, meat, fish, poultry, and vegetarian. This will provide enough variety on a weekly basis for consumers not to be bored with the selection. Limiting the number of entrees initially developed will allow HF to speed its entry to the market. This is consistent in approach with other proven-successful food product introduction strategies.

Manufacturing

Quality will be insured because of the vast experience of the company's manufacturing partner, Land O'Frost, who has been in the food processing business for over forty years.

Marketing Strategy

HF plans to market its products through five channels:

- Multilevel network marketing augmented by newspaper advertising
- Internet
- Direct mail
- Selling through specialty food stores
- Joint ventures with pharmaceutical companies and associations

In management's opinion, multilevel marketing using kidney patients to sell the product is the most cost-effective and best way to insure a quick sales ramp up. There will be a great trust factor from the start. The product will be promoted and sold by doctor practices and pharmacies. A kidney specialist created the business and the food is appetizing and nutritionally complete.

The process for marketing the product is as follows:

Step One:
- Send 20 samples of each of the five products to 100 physician practices that handle a minimum of 50 kidney patients.
- Develop a Web site to sell the product on-line.

Step Two:
- Advertise in the *Philadelphia Inquirer* and *Pittsburgh Post Gazette* for distributors of the product. Each distributor will be required to buy $500 to $1,000 worth of the product. The number of distributors will be limited to 100. Pennsylvania has 1.1 million kidney patients.
- Advertise in medical magazines such as *Health Forecast* and *Two-Types*.
- Send press releases to regional newspapers in both major Pennsylvania cities.

> There will be a great trust factor from the start.

Step Three:
- Once the product is shown to be successful in Pennsylvania, then we will look for distributors in other major cities, and advertise and send samples to doctor offices in those cities.
- The next state/region to focus sales on will be Florida followed by New York, Boston, Baltimore-Washington, and Los Angeles.

Capital Required and Exit Strategy

Healthy Foods is looking to raise $1 million in the first round for 40 percent of the equity of the company. HF plans to be acquired by a large food company within five years.

Mission and Objectives (one to two pages)

The mission statement allows the reader to know what the business is trying to accomplish. A client of mine once asked five non-executive employees, each from a different department, what they thought the mission of the company was. Each had a different response. The company can't be successful unless everyone is on the same mission.

This same executive asked his top three managers what they thought were the company's objectives. Much to my client's disappointment, the only objective they were all in agreement with was that the company wanted to make money.

There are two questions management must ask itself as it develops its mission and objectives:

- What are the central purposes and activities of the business?
- What are its major objectives, key strategies, and prime goals?

The mission statement should be clear and easy for everyone in the company to understand and remember. A sentence or two should capture the essence of the company's reason for existing.

Following the mission statement should be the objectives of the company. Objectives are centered around financial and market share

> The mission statement allows the reader to know what the business is trying to accomplish.

goals. In most cases, financial goals are more meaningful than market share, unless you are in a niche business such as selling surgical gloves to hospitals.

In the example below, Dr. Kroll contacted the American Kidney Foundation and found out how many people had kidney problems and needed special diets, then estimated how many of them would buy his product.

Sample Mission and Objectives Statement

The mission of the company is to provide quality-prepared microwaveable foods to individuals with kidney problems so they are freed from the task of preparing their own food. HF will offer a variety of entrees to meet their special nutritional requirements and, in doing so, make meal planning easier, more convenient, and less stressful.

HF's plan is to develop unique entrees and related foods focused on kidney nutrition, and to market these products both domestically and abroad.

Objectives
There are two sets of objectives:
Short Term: 1997–1999

- To raise $1 million to finance initial product acquisition and marketing costs.
- To recruit quality management to build a world-class food company.
- To develop quality, microwaveable, shelf-stable entrees.
- To set up distribution channels and perform sample marketing.
- To attain name recognition in the kidney community via targeted marketing efforts and dissemination of educational information.
- To reach $20 million in sales.

> Offer a variety of entrees to meet their special nutritional requirements.

Long Term: 2000–2003
- To expand penetration into international markets with the help of overseas distributors.
- To expand product line to include side dishes, desserts, and snacks.
- To develop other forms of recurring revenue such as additional product lines targeted to other niche markets.
- To reach long-term revenue goals of $52 million within five years.
- To go public or be bought by a larger company.

Company History (one to two pages)

Summarize achievements and performance (financial, sales, technical, etc.) to date. Introduce the stakeholders in the business. This is the easiest part of the plan to write. You tell the reader which employees played a significant role in the business, the company's past revenue, and past technical achievements if there are any.

> Introduce the stakeholders in the business.

Sample Company History

Health Foods Inc. was launched in 1993 to provide healthy food alternatives for individuals with special medical needs. Dr. David Kroll family physician, and Jacqueline Kadoch, a ten-year consumer food product manager for Campbell Soup Company, started the company.

The company's sales have grown from $50,000 in 1993 to $2 million in 1997. The geographic area HF has covered to date is the eastern seaboard of the United States. Due to increased market access through the Internet, HF is now selling product all over the world through their Web site. The company has copyrights and trademarks on ten different products.

The staff has grown from the two founders to twenty-five full-time employees. There are ten people in the research and development department, two outside salespeople, three telemarketers, three order fulfillment people, a company controller, an office manager, and a receptionist.

Product/Service Description (one to two pages)

Keep descriptions short and confine them to broad groups. Explain briefly what makes them special.

Sample Product/Service Description

Health Foods Inc. has developed a shelf-stable diet food appropriate for kidney patients. The five meals, which are each 8 ounces, are:

- Pasta with vegetables
- Pasta with chicken
- Chicken with white rice
- Chicken with vegetables
- Fish with white rice

Profile of Target Market(s) (one to three pages)

This section should address size, segments, trends, and user/customer profiles. This can be found by looking at industry publications, contacting the research departments at Big Five accounting firms who specialize in a particular field, contacting college professors who have done research on the industry, and speaking with trade associations who provide programs and trade shows to the industry. The best tool for finding information from the aforementioned sources is the Internet, and the best search engine is at dejanews.com. This search engine was designed to be used by people doing intensive research on a particular subject.

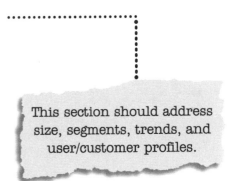

This section should address size, segments, trends, and user/customer profiles.

Sample Market Profile

Customer Profile

This section should provide insight into the scope of our target market and the potential for future growth:

According to The American Kidney Association, there are currently 8 million Americans with some type of kidney disorder and 80 million worldwide. The following is important statistical information from a 1993 AKA study:

- Two percent of all Americans have some type of kidney problem; 40 percent take prescription drugs through injections, 49 percent use oral agents, and 10 percent use a combination.
- 51 percent are women and 49 percent are men.
- 55 percent are over age 65.
- 2 percent are children under 19.
- 10 percent are of the African American population.
- 10 percent are of the Hispanic American population.
- 6 percent are of the Anglo-Saxon population.

> According to the American Kidney Association, the following are long-term complications of uncontrolled diabetes:

According to the American Kidney Association, the following are long-term complications of uncontrolled diabetes:

- Cardiovascular disease is 2 to 4 times more common.
- Cardiovascular disease is present in 75 percent of kidney-related deaths.
- The risk of stroke is 2.5 times higher in people with diabetes.
- Kidney disease is the leading cause of new cases of blindness among adults 20 to 74 years of age.
- Kidney patients account for more than 50 percent of the lower limb amputations in the United States. From 1989 to 1992, the average number of amputations among diabetics was 54,000.

Competition (one to two pages)

There are primary and secondary competitors. The competition section of a plan should comment on a competitor's strengths and weaknesses. The same sources you used to find information on the market can be used to find information on competitors. If you are competing in only one geographic area, you should contact your local chamber of commerce and review their membership directory and membership archives for stories written about your competitor.

The competition section of a business plan is very subjective. The writer needs to be honest about the strengths of his competitors so as not to take for granted the competitor's ability to win and hold onto business.

The best search engines for finding information on competitors are Alta Vista, Yahoo, Excite, and Lycos. These search engines provide information ranging from competitor Web sites, if they have one, to articles written about the company and posted on the Internet.

Sample Competition Section

Until recently, the kidney food market was largely ignored by the food industry. Currently there are two major competitors to HF:

Large Competitor
The entrance of Campbell's Intelligent Cuisine marks the first foray of a large food company into the kidney food arena. Their product line will consist of 41 frozen TV-dinner style meals such as an egg sandwich for breakfast, chili and stew for lunch, pasta and chicken for dinner, and pretzels and cookies for snacks. Buyers must purchase seven days of meals and one daily snack for $79.95, which includes shipping and handling. This comes out to $3.50 a meal.

The products will be shipped to customers in dry ice via U.P.S. Campbell's has announced launching this line this year, but there are no numbers to report. Steven Galbraith, investment analyst for Sanford C. Bernstein & Co. Inc. in New York, thought shipping meals overnight directly to buyers was "bizarre" and wasn't sure the products would be a big winner.

Small Competitor
A small competitor is A.R. Kidney Supply Company in Deerfield Beach, Florida. They have created a frozen food line of 14 separate entrees called Long Life Cuisine. Users must buy a 12-day meal plan for $99.99, which includes shipping and handling. This works out to $8.33 per meal. Each entree has a vegetable and a desert.

> The entrance of Campbell's Intelligent Cuisine marks the first foray of a large food company into the kidney food arena.

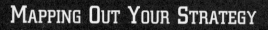

Competitive Advantage:
HF's competitive advantages are:

- *Product Selection.* Initial product development centered on the use of microwaveable shelf-stable entrees that can be transported nationally and worldwide, with lower transportation costs than frozen food items. These products generally have a shelf life of approximately 12 to 18 months.
- *No Refrigeration Required.* HF's clear advantage over Campbell's Intelligent Cuisine is that our shelf-stable product does not require refrigeration, while still maintaining outstanding flavor. We believe this significant convenience will engender customer loyalty to our products.
- *Goodwill.* In an effort to gain goodwill and word-of-mouth referrals, HF intends to provide educational information to our diabetic clients. This will likely take the form of suggestions on proper eating habits, information on current advances in the treatment of diabetes, and tips to help maintain a healthy lifestyle. This information can be disseminated directly with our food items, and can even be presented as a daily tip-of-the-day on our Internet Web page.

> HF intends to provide educational information to our diabetic clients.

Marketing Strategies and Sales Plans (two to three pages)

The marketing strategies section needs to answer the following questions:

- How will the business market its products/services and sell them to customers?
- What sales will be achieved in its main markets?
- How will it deal with competitors and what will be the associated costs?

Management needs to take a bottom-up approach to developing this part of the business plan, which will be the basis for an expanded marketing and sales plan (discussed later in the book). The marketing plan is driven by who will buy the product, at what price they are willing to pay, and the volume they are willing to purchase. In some cases, geography plays a role, such as in a regional medical equipment rental business or local brewery.

Once management has established its target market and surveyed potential customers, then it will know how to promote and sell to the market. For example, companies that develop Web sites of $25,000 or more know that advertising in the commercial section of the phone directory or in the local newspaper is a waste of money. Decision-makers are usually the vice president of marketing/sales and management information systems, and their selection process revolves around hearing speakers at conferences, reading articles in industry publications, and advertisements in specialty publications focused on the reader's industry.

The same sources of information used for developing the target market would be used in this section as well. Another source of information for validating your strategy would be to look at what competitors do and what others in a similar business do in other parts of the country.

Sample Marketing Section

HF will look for the least expensive way to market the products to conserve capital and test the marketplace. The cost of buying supermarket and pharmaceutical store space (i.e., slotting cost) is high and may be cost prohibitive and unnecessary in the beginning. We intend to focus our efforts primarily on the end users of our products (kidney patients) rather than a blanket marketing approach.

Multilevel Network Marketing
The best and most cost-effective way of selling this line of microwaveable foods is to find kidney patients who are experienced salespeople and have them buy and resell the product in their region. They would buy a case(s) of each entree and resell them direct to kidney patients in their region. We believe they can be a

> Another source of information for validating your strategy would be to look at what competitors do and what others in a similar business do in other parts of the country.

very successful because people with similar conditions know other people with the same condition and there is a high trust factor.

The Internet

We plan to establish a Web site that will include an electronic brochure containing product descriptions, pictures, prices, and ordering information (including transactions via the Internet). We intend to advertise our Web site on our packaging, in our direct mailings, and via participation in diabetic discussion groups. Additionally, a tip-of-the-day will be provided, containing practical advice for meeting the daily challenges facing diabetics. Occasionally, HF will sponsor experts to directly respond to clients' inquiries and participate in diabetic discussion groups. Another marketing effort will involve a lottery whereby each 100 orders (for example) would be markedly discounted or receive a pertinent bonus. As this medium develops, we expect to utilize the expanding technology to help further our growth and development.

> As this medium develops, we expect to utilize the expanding technology to help further our growth and development.

Direct Mail

Utilizing mailing lists, we will market our products directly to kidney patients, health professionals treating kidney disease (including family physicians, internists, endocrinologists, and dietitians), health food outlets, diabetic specialty stores, and airlines. We believe this strategy will maximize our exposure while limiting our overall costs.

Specialty Food Stores

Initially, the product will be sold only through network marketing and the Internet. Once the product has some success, which should be by the end of Year Two, then we will approach health food stores.

Co-Marketing

We plan to approach medical companies that develop and manufacture drugs and medical devices for kidney patients to co-market our products with theirs. In addition, managed care companies will be solicited to incorporate our products into their promotions to kidney patients. This would generate goodwill for these companies and greatly expand exposure for us.

Additional Exposure

Another avenue for exposure includes the participation of representatives of HF at kidney fairs at hospitals and American Kidney Association functions.

Product Distribution

Order fulfillment will be handled by Express Technology, which specializes in phone response and order fulfillment. Express is also being used to create and maintain the company's Web site, which will allow users to order products. They are located in Downingtown, Pennsylvania, and have 25,000 square feet of warehouse space.

Advertising:

Initially, HF will launch its line in Pennsylvania and buy newspaper advertisements in the *Philadelphia Inquirer*, *Pittsburgh Post-Gazette*, *Harrisburg Patriot*, *Allentown Call*, and *Lancaster Intelligencer*. The ads will be one-eighth of a page in size and will have the following information:

- An 800 number that allows people to buy direct from the company. As distributors are signed up, HF will provide their names and telephone numbers;
- A description of the product offering;
- On-line endorsements from kidney patients and doctors;
- An endorsement from the American Kidney Association.

As sales increase, HF will buy radio and television time.

> Doing a plan will make you think things through.

R&D and Technology (zero to two pages)

If relevant, explain progress, plans, and resources, and highlight any technological advances. This section is not applicable to many businesses. For technology-based businesses such as biopharmaceutical, food, electronics, and specialized product manufacturing, management doesn't need to provide in-depth information.

This section can speak to the resources needed to upgrade the company's current products, technological advances in the industry developed by university researchers and competitors, and what the company needs to do to stay competitive and increase profits. There are three good places to start to research this information. The search engine www.webcrawler.com will pull up all related Web sites on any subject. Another good search engine is www.altavista.com, which locates chat rooms and specific information on a topic. Also check university libraries, which can also be accessed through the Internet.

> The focus of this section of the business plan is HF's short-term and long-term product goals.

Sample R&D and Technology Section

Because HF subcontracts its manufacturing, its only concern is that the subcontractor keeps current with the latest technology. HF's head of production will do site inspections of subcontractors and visit potential new subcontractors to make sure the current subcontractor's price and quality are fair and meet the needs of HF.

The focus of this section of the business plan is HF's short-term and long-term product goals:

Short-Term Goals

Our short-term focus is on providing 5 to 10 core entrees of a variety of foods, all containing ingredients consistent with dietary recommendations for kidney patients. Kidney dietitians will be recruited to create these unique entrees, with recipe selection contingent upon production limitations, cost, price, and palatability.

Long-Term Goals

As sales increase and cash flow improves, the product line will be expanded to accommodate entrees containing a variety of calorie levels, which will further help our clients meet their individual nutritional needs. Eventually, breakfast, lunch, dessert, and snacks will be added to help round out our product line.

Additional long-term strategies focus on the expansion into other niche markets in the prepared food arena. This will include the following:

- Products low in salt that target the vast number of individuals with hypertension.
- Products low in protein to target the estimated 20 million individuals with kidney disease (studies have shown that a low protein diet can help slow the progression of kidney disease).

Management believes our marketing strategies as outlined are ideal for capturing those largely ignored niche markets in the prepared food arena.

Manufacturing/Operational Plans (two to three pages)

This section should cover how the company plans to improve distribution and service activities and/or manufacturing. The people responsible for these areas of the business should supply this information. Benchmark your company against the industry by contacting trade associations and consulting firms that follow your industry and produce reports on best practices for the industry.

Another good source is contacting universities who produce graduates that go to work in the company's industry, because the faculty at those universities probably have researched the industry and written papers on best manufacturing and operational practices.

The American Association of Executive Directors has a Web site (www.asae.org) which assists the user in finding the appropriate trade association, consulting firms, and academics that follow an industry.

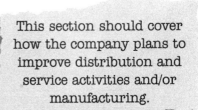

This section should cover how the company plans to improve distribution and service activities and/or manufacturing.

Sample Manufacturing/Operations Plan

An experienced shelf-stable food manufacturer will assist in developing and will manufacture HF's products.

The process from concept to actual packaged product takes six months and is as follows:

Step One: Kidney dietician works with the food development people at O'Brian Foods.

Step Two: A sample batch of 15 to 30 of each product is developed and tasted by a small audience.

Step Three: Product is finished; packaging company takes pictures of each product and designs a package.

Step Four: Package is created and O'Brian Foods makes 35,000 of each product.

Step Five: Product is shipped to an order fulfillment house, Impac Technologies.

Management (one to two pages)

This section introduces the executive management team. Include only information that is relevant to the business.

> Include only information that is relevant to the business.

Sample Management Information

Chairman/CEO—Dr. Kroll is the founder of HF, a former *Inc.* Entrepreneur of the Year, and is in the Entrepreneurs Hall of Fame at the University of North Carolina. He earned his medical degree at the University of Iowa and an undergraduate degree from New York University. Dr. Kroll has treated over 1,000 kidney patients during his career.

Executive Vice President—Jacqueline Kadoch, a graduate of Yale and University of Pennsylvania's Wharton School of Business, has ten years experience in food marketing experience with Aloette Foods and Mrs. Smith's Foods.

Director of Production/Development—Donald Ellis is in charge of all HF production. Donald graduated from Temple University and has fifteen years of food production experience with ARA, Inc.

Manager of Sales—Thad Young, a graduate of Pennsylvania State University with degrees in food marketing, oversees network marketing sales for HF. He worked for nine years for Johnson Foods in sales and marketing.

Funding Requirements (one page)

If applicable, summarize funding requirements, possible sources, likely terms, and, for investors, the projected return on their investment. Although this section appears before the financials, it is actually the last section written in the plan. There are two reasons this section is written last.

- You have to determine what your income and expense projections are, which in turn determines how much money you need to borrow or raise.
- Once you determine how much money you need, you may have to sell an equity interest in the business to raise the needed capital because you may not be bankable. Understanding your financial requirements allows you to determine how much of the company you are willing to sell for the appropriate amount of money.

Sample Funding Requirements

HF is looking to raise $1 million for 40% of the common stock of the company. The money will be used as follows:

PERCENTAGE	USAGE
25%	Marketing
30%	Product development
20%	Repaying long-term investor debts
25%	Cash cushion

HF management believes this infusion of capital will allow the company to become a dominant kidney health food arena world-wide. HF believes that when gross sales are between $15 to $20 million, the company will either go public or be purchased by a larger food company.

> Once you determine how much money you need, you may have to sell an equity interest in the business to raise the needed capital because you may not be bankable.

Management believes that a $25,000 investment, which represents 2,000 shares or 1% of the company's common stock, will be worth $100,000 in four years. This represents a 400% return on equity. Management believes this number is realistic based on two studies done by a Big Five accounting firm on determining the future value of niche market food companies. The studies state that niche food companies:

- Are usually bought for one times gross sales.
- If able to go public, historically have sold for 15 times net income before taxes.

Financial Position and Projections (two to three pages)

Use simple tables to present key financial projections, such as summary profit and loss (P&L), cash flows, balance sheets, and key ratios. Include the detailed analyses in appendices. I highly recommend that you use a spreadsheet application on a personal computer to develop your financial statements. It makes the job much easier and allows you to change figures and quickly see results when trying different "What If?" scenarios.

Small Retail Store Business Plan

The following plan was developed in order to raise money from banks, private investors, and an economic development organization.

> Use simple tables to present key financial projections, such as summary profit and loss (P&L), cash flows, balance sheets, and key ratios.

Smith's Men's Stores Business Plan

Executive Summary

According to an April 6, 1998 article in *Forbes*, "What male shoppers want are ways to purchase quality men's clothes without spending a lot of time in a store shopping." A July 21 *Men's Health* article states there are two issues that are keeping male shoppers from making more purchases. The first is time and the second is convenience.

Smith's Men's Stores, which was started by Harry Smith in 1951 in the small Pennsylvania town of Coatesville, has been scraping by. At one time, Smith had 10 stores and because of financial problems the company is down to three. Harry Smith's son, Harry Jr., has come to the realization that the only way to save the family business is to leverage Internet technology.

Solution

Smith's Men's Stores recognizes that affluent male shoppers who buy a variety of casual attire are spending less time shopping in person at department stores and more time shopping by way of the Internet.

Smith's Men's Stores believes that it can increase in-store sales through the use of the Internet by offering discounted products real time and on-line and having a live salesperson assist shoppers find the products they are looking for.

How It Works

Smith hired a technology company to develop a video technology that doesn't require the end user to download software and has audio capability. For the user this means that they don't have to download any software or use a particular browser to view a site to hear audio and view video. Smith's Men's Stores would invite shoppers to buy discounted products from name department stores that they know and trust and receive the assistance of a personal shopper, who would steer them to other products.

Example

A man goes to the Smith's Men's Stores site looking for a suit. He sees on the home page that Smith's is having a sale on Ralph Lauren suits, which would normally cost $500, for $150. Before the buyer pays for his suit a live shopping consultant would ask the shopper if he needed shirts, shoes, ties, and other accessories. The buyer would tell the sales consultant that he might need a pair of shoes and a couple of shirts and would ask if there are any discounts for those products. The buyer would be shown related discounted products by the shopping consultant who would make buying recommendations, close the sale, and thank the buyer for coming to their store.

How Smith's Men's Stores Makes Money:

Smith's Men's Stores will have three sources of revenue:

- Establish a "personal relationship" with buyers and know the buying profiles and habits of its customers. Through knowing their customers buying habits and interests, Smith's Men's Stores can let customers know when products of interest are in by e-mail.
- Sell advertising to manufacturers that Smith's Men's Stores carries.
- Sell customer profiles to companies whose products are in the department stores.

Five Year Financial Projections:

REVENUE	YR1	YR2	YR3	YR4	YR5
Storefront Rent Revenue	$ 500,000	$ 2,750,000	$ 6,050,000	$ 13,310,000	$ 29,282,000
Advertising/Total Pg. Per Yr/1000	4,950,000	9,090,000	16,692,545	30,653,583	56,291,126
Sponsorships	120,000	264,000	580,800	1,277,760	2,811,072
Total	$ 5,570,000	$12,104,000	$23,323,345	$ 45,241,343	$ 88,384,198
Total Expenses	$2,893,600	$4,028,580	$5,838,686	$8,615,298	$18,799,660
Profit (loss)	$2,676,400	$8,075,420	$17,484,659	$36,626,046	$69,584,538

Capital Requirements

Smith Men's Stores intends to raise $1 million for 40 % of the common stock equity of the company. The capital invested will be used to promote and market the site to shoppers.

Exit Strategy

Smith's Men's Stores would look to sell their entire business—Internet and free standing stores—to a large retail chain.

Company Mission and Technology Description

Mission

Smith's Men's Stores's mission is to provide shoppers with a "personalized interactive shopping experience" by providing shoppers substantial discounts from major name brand manufacturers and buying assistance from "live" shopping professionals.

Technology Description

There are three types of technology that Smith's Men's Stores will utilize to make the shopping experience fun and lucrative.

Video Compression and Deployment

Smith's Men's Store's software developers have developed proprietary software that is unique and the first of its kind in that it allows for cross-platform and cross-browser deployment and viewing of video without the necessity of downloading special software.

Search engine

Customers will be able to type in the types of clothing and their sizes and a search engine will find what they are looking for and show pictures and prices of the products they are searching for.

E-mail

Smith's Men's Stores will use e-mail integrated into a database that will tell customers when items of interest are on sale.

Company Background

Harry Smith, Sr., started Smith's Men's Stores in 1951. Smith, a World War II veteran, thought suburban and country men needed a quality men's store to buy suits, overcoats, hats, and shoes when dealing with business people from Philadelphia and Baltimore. He knew that men in Chester County, located approximately 30 miles west of Philadelphia, wanted to appear sophisticated so the city businessmen wouldn't underestimate or try to take advantage of them.

Harry Smith, Jr., the current president of Smith's Men's Stores, took over the stores from his father in 1980. At its height, the company had 10 stores located in three counties that surrounded Philadelphia.

Mr. Smith joined his father, Harry, Sr., after graduating from Penn State University with a degree in business.

As regional malls and large chain stores invaded Smith's Men's Stores region, Mr. Smith's chain has survived because of his marketing creativity and his willingness to use technology. Smith's Men's Stores was the first retailer to use fax machines to alert male shoppers about special sales and was the first chain in their region to have a tea for wives of male shoppers to promote clothing lines.

Current State of On-line Shopping:

Intelliquest Information Group stated in an April 16, 1998 article in the *Wall Street Journal* that 62 million Americans use the Internet and almost 200 million people worldwide use the Internet. Twenty-three percent of the homes in the United States, according to the same article, are connected to the Internet.

Jupiter Communications 1998 On-line Shopping Report states there are 16 million consumers shopping at retail sites today, and they project the number of on-line shoppers will grow to 45 million by the year 2001. International Data Corporation projects consumer on-line shopping will grow from $5 billion to $59 billion by the year 2001.

Buyer Profile Statistics

According to an April 16 *Wall Street Journal* article, the following statistics apply to Internet users and usage:

- 74 percent of all Internet users are over the age of 18. The average age for Internet users is 37
- 90 percent of all Internet users have at least a 28.8 modem
- 31 percent have a college degree
- 58 percent of all users are male
- $55,000 is the average income of an Internet user. People making $75,000 or greater make up 18 percent of the users

According to an April 6 article in *Forbes*, the following information builds a strong case for the future of on-line shopping.

- 40 percent of all retail sales are being transacted after traditional stores close
- 55 percent of consumers say they are looking to the Internet to save them time when shopping

Current State of On-line Retail

There are only a handful of small clothing chains using the Internet to promote their business, and those chains only provide information on what the stores sell and their locations. Only a handful of name brand department store chains have an Internet presence:

- Bloomingdale's
- Dayton
- Hudson
- JC Penney
- Kmart
- Macy's
- Nordstrom's
- Wal-Mart

All of the above department stores have setup on-line catalogs. The catalogs feature pictures and descriptions of products. The only interactivity, with the exception of Nordstrom's, is the selection and purchase of a product. Nordstrom's allows the user to connect by way of e-mail to a personal shopper who will assist the buyer in finding the right products to purchase.

Success Stories

Is on-line shopping a passing fad? That question is asked every day in the media. The following companies have demonstrated that consumer electronic commerce is just beginning to take off.

- QVC, the world's largest television shopping network, built a Web site to sell the products people bought through their television show on cyberspace. Within two years, QVC is selling over $50 million through their Web site, and they project that number to hit $500 million within the next three to five years.
- Dell Computer, one of the largest computer sellers in the world, began selling computers on-line three years ago and today sells $700 million to consumers over the Internet.
- CDNOW, the world's largest on-line seller of musical CD's, was started by two brothers three years ago. Their revenue has grown from $500,000 to a projected $60 million in 1998.

Mr. Smith believes that men will shop more because of the convenience of using the Internet and that when they come to pick up their purchases they will see impulse and other sale items, which will increase in-store purchases.

Launch and Content Strategy

Smith's Men's Stores plans to run a direct-mail campaign and advertise on regional cable television to drive traffic to its stores. Mr. Smith said they would also run advertisements on other local Web sites and pay the owners of those sites a commission on each sale.

Potential Partners

According to Tom Dyer, head researcher for the Small Retailers Association, there are 8,800 men's stores in the United States. Each store is approximately 2,000 square feet on average and brings in $2 million. Forty percent of most retailers' sales are made from Thanksgiving to Christmas.

Smith's believes that it will be important to partner with Internet access service providers, movie theaters, sports facilities, regional newspapers, and cable operators to promote and drive traffic to the Smith's Men's Stores site. The companies Smith's is in discussions with are as follows:

Davis On-Line

The leading Internet access provider will put a picture of Smith's Men's Stores's home page in every bill and have an advertisement on the Davis home page that will take them to the Smith's site.

Chester County Cable

The leading cable television provider will do live home shopping shows from one of the three Smith's locations and put coupons for discounts in their monthly bills.

Sports World

The largest indoor sports facility would put signs on the courts and ice rinks in its facility promoting Smith's.

World Cinemas

The largest national movie chain would run advertisements on its movie screens while movie watchers waited for their movie.

Chester County Publishing

Smith's would run advertisements in the largest regional chain of newspapers, which extends into adjacent counties. Smith's would also be the exclusive men's store on CCP's Web site.

Revenue Source

Smith's Men's Stores will have three sources of income:

- Advertising. Smith's will receive cooperative advertising money from clothing manufacturer commissions on the gross revenue of each department store site.
- Clothing Sales. Sales of the various clothing and shoes being sold in the stores.
- Data. Sales of information on the buying habits of men to clothing manufacturers.

Managing Risk

Smith's Men's Stores, unlike other retailers, won't be buying any clothes and shoes up front. Manufacturers will have to provide stock on consignment. Smith's will only target upscale, small manufacturers who have a hard time negotiating with big department stores and national retail chains.

Risk for the department store is minimized by the fact that they don't have to make any significant Internet technology investment and can piggyback on their existing bricks-and-mortar and advertising investments. Smith's Men's Stores will also provide the electronic commerce software that connects to their existing merchandise and customer database.

Potential Advertising and Database Customers

Accessories and Jewelry
- Charles Rogers
- Citizen
- Fendi
- Gucci
- Louis Vuitton
- Movado
- Timex

Clothing
- Ellis
- Franklin's
- Moore's
- Sam's
- Twilight Clothes

Shoes
- Adams
- Daulton's
- Schmidt's
- Universal Footwear

Site Content

Smith's Men's Stores will take one of its stores and have it televise live sales on various products. The personal shoppers will come on-line with the customer and visit different departments in the store by way of mounted video cameras. The cameras will provide the buyer close-ups of different products to choose from. The buyer can elect to buy the product "real time" on-line or have the item held at the store for twenty-four hours.

There will be "live interactive" sections of the site where the following will take place:

- Mavens of fashion will talk about the latest clothing trends.
- Sportswear consultants will discuss the best sports attire for fishing and other sports.
- Authors of cosmetic books will give insight and advice on how to improve one's appearance.
- Consumer technology gurus will speak about various consumer electronic products.

Marketing of Smith's Men's Stores

Smith's has and will continue to advertise in the newspaper. The focal part of Smith's marketing will be to use the Internet. In addition to the aforementioned Internet plans, Smith's plans to become more aggressive and do the following:

Networking

Each Smith's salesperson and manager will be responsible for joining at least two organizations. The purpose of joining those organizations is to increase Smith's visibility and attract new customers.

Public Relations

Smith's has sponsored local little league teams in the past. Smith's will now sponsor and co-sponsor regional business events that will raise the store's visibility and enhance its image.

Competitive Analysis

Management's view of competition focuses on three stores: Bennett's, Goldine's, and Men's World. Two of the three are larger and better financed than Smith's. A younger man who is a very aggressive self-marketer owns the smallest one. The following is a breakdown of Smith's competitors:

Background on Competitors

Bennett's

This is the largest department store in the region. Unlike Smith's, their focus isn't purely on men's fashions, but because they cater to everyone in the family they are perceived as a one-stop shop for the entire family. They have very experienced buyers and a good name in the community. Their weakness is that they have huge personnel turnover in the men's department because they don't pay a commission on top of an hourly wage. Not having consistent salespeople hurts them in developing customer relationships, which is important in order to get to know someone's taste.

Goldfine's

The founder of Goldfine's started his business at the same time as Smith's. Although they are larger, they aren't perceived as having a good mix of products, and many of their products are outdated because they haven't hired younger people to make buying decisions.

Men's World

They are run by an aggressive former Goldfine's employee, Steve Zucker. What Zucker lacks in money to invest in advertising he makes up for in networking. He and his people are very involved in a variety of organizations, which helps in building awareness and developing relationships that lead to sales. We should follow their lead in having more employees involved in regional organizations. Their only negative is that they mostly sell trendy attire, which appeals to a smaller, younger audience. Over time, Men's World could become our biggest competitor because Zucker will see he is not fully serving the men's community the way it needs to be served.

COMPETITORS	BENNETT'S	GOLDFINE'S	MEN'S WORLD	SMITH'S MEN'S STORES
Years in business	15	40	5	40
Number of employees	100	50	10	22
Number of stores	1	5	1	2
Only men's stores			x	x
Good product mix	x			x
Good customer service	x	x	x	x
Quality merchandise	x	x		x
Clean store		x	x	x
Good location	x		x	x
Open seven days			x	
Quality sales	x		x	x
Advertises in newspaper	x	x	x	x
Advertises on radio	x	x		
Advertises on television	x			
Has a Web site				x

Management

Chairman/CEO

John Smith, a graduate of Bloomsburg University with a degree in business administration, has a quarter of a century of retailing experience.

Duties
- Develop the company's future vision
- Develop the overall marketing strategy
- Meet and greet customers

Direct Reports
- Accounting
- Sales

Sales Manager

Mary Wilson, a graduate of Philadelphia College of Textiles, worked ten years for Jones of New York, a major manufacturer and retailer of men's clothing.

Duties
- Hire and train in-store salespeople
- Oversee development of the business's Web site
- Assist president and store buyer in selecting products

Direct Reports
- Sales personnel
- Marketing assistant
- Computer systems administrator

Capital Sought and Uses:

The capital will be used for general purposes and to hire experienced executives to develop each business line.

Financials:

	Yr1	Yr2	Yr3	Yr4	Yr5
REVENUE					
Slotting Fee Revenue	$ 12,000	$ 22,000	$ 48,400	$ 106,480	$ 234,256
Product Commission Sales	800,000	1,056,000	1,393,920	1,839,974	2,428,766
Sponsorships	10,000	22,000	36,300	53,240	73,205
Total	**$ 822,000**	**$ 1,100,000**	**$ 1,478,620**	**$ 1,999,694**	**$ 2,736,227**
EXPENSES					
Salaries	325,000	350,562	469,413	514,694	564,421
Taxes & Benefits	81,250	87,641	117,353	128,674	141,105
Travel	8,400	10,560	13,068	14,375	15,812
Telephone	8,400	37,800	63,000	106,200	485,000
Rent/Utilities	25,000	31,562	88,263	95,429	103,229
Marketing Support	40,000	44,000	73,150	129,965	241,962
Business Supplies	6,000	7,000	7,000	7,000	7,000
Business Equipment	180,000	273,000	354,900	461,370	599,781
Internet Connection	5,000	5,000	5,000	5,000	5,000
Professional Services	10,000	12,000	14,400	17,280	20,736
Packaging	200	242	293	354	429
List Acquisition	600	660	726	799	878
Shipping	500	578	667	770	890
Warehousing	10,000	13,200	0	0	0
Miscellaneous	30,000	33,000	36,300	39,930	43,923
Total Expenses	**730,350**	**906,804**	**1,243,533**	**1,521,840**	**2,230,166**
Profit (Loss)	**91,650**	**193,196**	**235,087**	**477,854**	**506,061**

	Yr1	Yr2	Yr3	Yr4	Yr5
REVENUE					
Product Promo Fees	12,000	22,000	48,400	106,480	234,256
No. of Products	10	20	40	80	160
Cost Per Product	1,200	1,100	1,210	1,331	1,464
Product Sales	800,000	1,056,000	1,393,920	1,839,974	2,428,766
No. of Customers Per Year	2,000	2,400	2,880	3,456	4,147
Avg. Sale Per Customer Yr.	400	440	484	532	586
Sponsorships	10,000	22,000	36,300	53,240	73,205
No. of Sponsors	10	20	30	40	50
Avg. Price Per Sponsor	1,000	1,100	1,210	1,331	1,464
EXPENSES					
Management Salaries	220,000	198,000	217,800	239,580	263,538
President	1	1	1	1	1
Annual Salary	75,000	82,500	90,750	99,825	109,808
Sales Manager	1	1	1	1	1
Annual Salary	60,000	66,000	72,600	79,860	87,846
Head Buyer	1	1	1	1	1
Annual Salary	45,000	49,500	54,450	59,895	65,885
Controller	1	1	1	1	1
Annual Salary	40,000	44,000	48,400	53,240	58,564
Administrative	30000	66000	72600	79860	87846
Annual Salary	30,000	33,000	36,300	39,930	43,923
No. of Administrators	1	2	2	2	2
Warehouse Personnel	50,000	55,000	90,750	99,825	109,808
Annual Salary	25,000	27,500	30,250	33,275	36,603
No. of Warehouse People	2	2	3	3	3
Web Site Personnel	25,000	31,562	88,263	95,429	103,229
Content Coordinators	1	1	1	1	1
Annual Salary	25,000	27,500	30,250	33,275	36,603

	Yr1	Yr2	Yr3	Yr4	Yr5
Programmers	0	0	1	1	1
Annual Salary	0	0	55,125	60,638	66,701
Clerical Assistance	0	1	1	1	1
Annual Salary	30,000	31,500	33,075	34,729	36,465
Taxes & Benefits (% Salary)	25%	25%	25%	25%	25%
Travel (Per/Person Per Yr.)	1,200	1,320	1,452	1,597	1,757
Tele/(Per/Person Per Yr.)	1,200	1,260	1,323	1,389	1,459
Rent/Utilities	25,000	25,000	25,000	25,000	25,000
Square Feet	5,000	5,000	5,000	5,000	5,000
Cost per Sq. Foot	5	5	5	5	5
Marketing Support	40,000	44,000	73,150	129,965	241,962
Newspaper	25,000	27,500	55,000	110,000	220,000
Direct Mail	5,000	5,500	6,050	6,655	7,321
Cable Television	10,000	11,000	12,100	13,310	14,641
Bus. Sup. (PP Per Yr)	1,000	1,000	1,000	1,000	1,000
Bus. Equip. (PP Per Yr)	30,000	39,000	50,700	65,910	85,683
Internet Con.	5,000	5,000	5,000	5,000	5,000
Prof. Services (Legal, Acct.)	10,000	12,000	14,400	17,280	20,736
Packaging	200	242	293	354	429
No. of Boxes	100	110	121	133	146
Avg. Cost Per Box	2	2.2	2.4	2.7	2.9
List Acquisition	600	660	726	799	878
No. of Lists	1	1	1	1	1
Cost Per Acquisition	600	660.0	726.0	798.6	878.5
Shipping	500	578	667	770	890
No. of Items Shipped	100	110	121	133	146
Avg. Cost Per Shipment	5	5.3	5.5	5.8	6.1
Warehouse Equipment	10,000	13,200	0	0	0
No. of Shelves	10	12.0	0.0	0.0	0.0
Cost Per Shelf	1,000	1,100	1,210	1,331	1,464
Miscellaneous	10,000	12,000	14,400	17,280	20,736

Time Table/Launch Schedule:

Time Table	Launch Schedule
Months 1–2	Develop the Web site
Month 2	Select a small market of customers to test site
Month 3	Fix any problem with the site
Month 4	Advertise the site in the test market
Months 5–7	Attract sponsors
Months 8–10	Survey users
Months 11–12	Update content

Chapter 3

Writing the Operating and Launch Plan

"You cannot run a business, or anything else, on a theory."

—HAROLD S. GREEN (1910-1997)
Chairman, ITT Corporation

Professional football coaches call it a game plan. In the business world it's called a product launch plan, regardless of whether the business provides a product or a service. Next to the company's business plan, a launch plan is the second most important document the organization will create. Every turnaround I have worked with lacked a product launch plan. In turning around any enterprise, management needs to work out the details on how it plans to relaunch its product or service.

A good launch plan will contain the following:

- Description of the product/service
- Creation and development of the product/service
- Marketing strategy
- Cost of development
- Price of the product/service
- Personnel involved and their duties

Many businesses do no preplanning to see what obstacles they have to overcome. The management of such businesses instead believes in gut instinct. One of my clients told me, "plans are for sissies; real entrepreneurs go by gut instinct." This entrepreneur, who told me that business plans are unnecessary, provides me with the perfect story to illustrate why planning is important.

This person, whom we will call Jim Smith, was a master promoter. In one year he turned around a mall with which the last three management teams had failed. No one I have ever met had more charm and personality than Jim did.

He believed so much in his ability to promote businesses that he was sure anything he would operate would be a success. One day he met someone who told him that if he built an antique center he could make a lot of money. This man told him that the county he was in was the antique center for the state and had more antique dealers than just about any county in the United States.

Jim personally liked and collected antiques and dollar signs were flashing in his eyes. He asked the man how big a center would he need to build and how should the facility be designed to attract antique dealers. The man offered his suggestions.

> A launch plan is the second most important document the organization will create.

Jim told his assistant manager to call an architect and have them design this new antique center. The architect and building contractor said it would cost $250,000.

Jim's assistant manager was a bright twenty-five-year-old named Bob Stein. Bob had done some research in various business magazines about starting a business venture and told Jim he read in *Inc.* magazine that writing a business plan would be prudent and could save them from an embarrassing situation if the project didn't make financial sense. Bob told Jim that this would be a huge cash drain and, if the facility didn't make money every weekend, it could bankrupt the company.

Jim said he knew what he was doing and that both of them would make money. The facility was built and the first weekend was a success, which put a gloating smile on Jim's face. Unfortunately every week thereafter the number of tenants in the facility shrunk to the point that only 30 out of 118 booths were filled.

Jim believed that turning up his charm several notches and increasing advertising expenditures would turn things around. Finally, after another miserable month, Jim decided to take a week's vacation. During that time, Bob went and visited other antique centers.

He found out that antique facilities clustered together like car dealerships and fast food restaurants. They fed off of each other. If Jim had listened to Bob and prepared a business plan, they would have known how the industry operated and probably would not have built the facility. Within six months Bob was out of a job because Jim couldn't afford to keep him, and within two years Jim went bankrupt.

Below is a sample launch plan, with explanations for each section. The company, Investment Management Network, was a marketing communications firm that worked with retail money managers. Over a period of time, the field became very crowded with similar types of firms and margins were squeezed to the point that the business became unprofitable. The management of the company decided it had to remake its services into products that could be sold over the Internet. The key elements and questions mentioned in the beginning of this chapter are touched on throughout this plan.

> Facility shrunk to the point that only 30 out of 118 booths were filled.

INVESTMENT MANAGEMENT LAUNCH PLAN

Open Statement
Explanation
From the start you want to set the readers expectations. This part should be short and concise.

Purpose of this document
This launch plan describes the Internet strategy and implementation program for the products articulated in the business plan.
Explanation
This section lets the reader know what to expect in the plan. Investors read the launch plan to understand the entrepreneur's strategy. Employees read it to understand what expectations are being set.

Overview
The three vertical investment communities (plan sponsors, pension consultants, and investment managers) are described below in terms of their site content. The "anchor" products, noted in each navigation bar, are the revenue drivers and primary "traffic magnets" within each community. Anchor products, like an anchor tenant in a mall, will be the primary traffic draw. The anchor products are described in more detail in the business plan. The information on each site is designed to engage members, enhance the community's functionality, and foster personal/business relationships among members.

The Design Strategy
Generate Traffic (create awareness)
We will generate awareness of the site and its contents through powerful marketing overlays (for example, our publication) and "anchor products" (for example, sales and marketing research) as described in the business plan.

Own Plan Sponsors and Pension Consultants (concentrate traffic)
Plan sponsors and consultants are the groups that provide the "golden egg" for the investment managers (the group with the money and ultimate check writers). If we can own plan sponsors and consultants,

we will, by default, own the investment managers. To use an analogy, if these Web sites were cyber grocery stores and we could attract plan sponsors and consultants to regularly browse in their respective stores, then investment managers would be willing to pay handsomely for distribution (shelf space).

Keep Them Coming Back (lock in traffic)

Products and information on each site will be designed to reward the visitor's time spent at the site. Visitors will always feel their time has been well spent and will be surprised by the quality of insight and practical benefit they gain. To further spur revisits, anchor products and other critical information will be time sensitive. Additionally, an ongoing targeted marketing effort (public relations, advertising, direct mail, etc.) will continually enhance "top-of-mind" awareness and stimulate revisits. Finally, the interactive nature of the content will foster relationships among members, help us develop member-generated content, and expand the community's functionality and value for its members.

Technical Partners

We will look to use Jameison Capital companies, such as Vertical Group, to develop our initial Web sites and databases, Icat for on-line commerce, and Dejanews to find news related to the interests of the community.

Product Description

Explanation

This section provides the details of what the product will look like and contain. Having a section like this allows employees to re-evaluate what is being offered and how it can be improved.

One of my clients was a large consumer products company that had run into bad times. They decided to shift their business from brick-and-mortar stores to selling through the Internet. Initially, they didn't develop a design for what the look and feel of the site should be. This ended up costing the company an extra $100,000 in development costs and caused them to be late getting to the market.

In this example, Investment Management Network is explicit in what the content of the site should be.

Product Design For Each Web Site

Plan Sponsor On-line

Navigation Bar
- Peer News
- Money Manager News (anchor product: "on-line publication")
- New Products
- Seminars/Events
- Research
- Library
- Chat Room
- Employment Opportunities

Descriptions of Navigation Bar
Peer News
- Investment issue of the month: A different plan sponsor discusses an important issue and how he plans to deal with it. Over time, we will create a valuable library of materials and information that we can catalog and offer in print form.
- New plan sponsors: Profiles of individuals who have changed the plans they are managing or have succeeded their boss in running their retirement fund.

Money Manager News (anchor product)
- Money Manager Profiles: This section will provide investment philosophies and processes, plus buy and sell strategies, for the top 1000 money managers. In our first six months our goal will be to post the profiles of the top 250 money managers. Any manager will be able to post new information or correct existing information anytime. There will be a video and audio interview featuring a walkthrough of each firm on the site and interviews with key management personnel.
- New Firms: Names and descriptions of new firms being launched or existing firms that are re-emerging as successful organizations.
- Mergers: Names of firms that are merging and the background of the acquiring firm.
- Portfolio Manager Changes: Portfolio managers who are leaving one firm for another.
- Sales Executive Changes: Sales executives who are leaving one firm for another.

New Products
- Micro Cap: Name of firm, description of product, process, investment philosophy, portfolio construction, management team, and buy/sell discipline.
- Fixed Income: Name of firm, description of product, process, investment philosophy, portfolio construction, management team, and buy/sell discipline.
- Small Cap: Name of firm, description of product, process, investment philosophy, portfolio construction, management team, and buy/sell discipline.
- Mid Cap: Name of firm, description of product, process, investment philosophy, portfolio construction, management team, and buy/sell discipline.

Seminars/Events
- AMISE: Dates for seminars, conferences and accredited classes.
- AMIR: Dates for seminars, conferences and accredited classes.
- IMI: Dates for seminars, conferences and accredited classes.

Research
- Proprietary Investment Studies: White papers written about new investment theories, concepts, and techniques. (Money managers should be more than willing to supply us with this research, since they know plan sponsors and pension consultants will be reading it.)
- Peer Surveys: Surveys that shed light on challenges, successes, and other interesting insights from the plan sponsor peer group. Additionally, surveys may include topics such as how many plan sponsors are looking for new products to invest in, how many plan sponsors are looking to change managers, and how many plan sponsors are using the Internet to evaluate money managers.
- Money Manager Interviews: Interviews on new products that are being developed and insights into the stock market and different investment classes.

Library
- Synopses of new investment books provided by the publisher and the ability to order books at a discount on-line through a partnership with Amazon.com.
- Synopsis of articles pertinent to money management with links to publications such as *Pension and Investments*, *Money Management Newsletter*, and so on.
- Archival retrieval capability for commercial and academic publications. We will use Dejavu.com technology.

Chat Room
- Weekly Discussions: Topics will be presented and discussed on-line.
- General Discussion: Every day plan sponsors can talk about concerns and problems and get feedback and insight from their peers.
- Taft-Hartley: Discussions related to concerns and problems about union pension plans.
- Public Plan: Discussions related to concerns and problems about public state government, county, and municipal pension plans.
- Corporate: Discussions related to concerns and problems about corporate pension plans.
- Endowments and Foundations: Discussions related to concerns and problems about endowment and foundations.
- Healthcare: Discussions related to concerns and problems about hospital systems.

Employment Opportunities
- Resume Posting: Plan sponsors looking for new positions can post their "coded" resumes.
- Job Posting: Plan sponsors looking to fill positions can write job descriptions.

Marketing Plan

Explanation

Every launch plan needs a section on how the company plans to market their product. Rather than spending money on newspaper advertising, Investment Management Resources is putting out its own newspaper to promote its product lines. You will notice there is an explanation for the concept, how it will be implemented, and how it will pay for itself over time. There is nothing vague or left to the imagination.

Marketing Product

Publication

Concept

To attract traffic to the site we will create a monthly tabloid newspaper that profiles successful money managers and includes other valuable investment information. This newspaper will be mailed free of charge to plan sponsors, pension consultants and investment managers. The publication will encourage readers to visit the relevant Web sites to access even more useful information and insight. It will increase awareness and attract traffic to the various sites. Importantly, this publication will be used to generate advertising revenue and be a stand-alone profit center. This publication will contain substantive information on individual portfolio managers, surveys of the industry, articles on the latest technology, and other critical insights that will be of value to the institutional investment community.

Implementation

We are speaking with Jack Ryan, the former editor of the *Chester County Business Journal* and Mike Thomas, the former editor of *Business Times*, about their possible interest and recommendations regarding potential editors and writers.

Revenue Sources

To build traffic, this publication will be a key source of revenue as noted in our business plan. The revenue sources are summarized below and described in some detail latter in the document.

In addition to display advertising (which was noted in the business plan), there are other sources of revenue than those described in the business plan. They are as follows:

Paying Columnists	$120,000 annually
Special Advertising Sections	$480,000 annually
Home Page Advertisements	$216,000–$288,000 annually
Corporate Reports	$216,000–$288,000

Display Advertising Rates

1998 Black-and-white advertising rates for frequently used sizes

ISSUES:	1x	6x	12x	19x	26x
140"(2 pages)	$13,720	$12,810	$11,690	$10,920	$9,840
80" 10,440	9,920	9,280	8,840	8,280	
70" (1 page)	6,860	6,405	5,845	5,460	4,970
40" 5,220	4,960	4,640	4,420	4,140	
24" 3,384	3,228	3,036	2,904	2,736	
15" 2,167	2,070	1,950	1,867	1,762	
10" 1,445	1,380	1,300	1,245	1,175	

Color Rates

Four-color process: Extra per page over space costs $4,438; extra per spread $6,210.

Matched colors: Any color from the Pantone Match color system, excluding Dayglow and Metallic. Extra per page over space costs $1,947, extra per spread $3,362.

Standard colors: Extra cost per page space costs $1,409, extra per spread $2,347.

Mechanical Specifications

Advertising Space Size 140" (Tabloid Page Spread); 10 col. x 14"80" (Junior Page Spread); 8 col. x 10" 70" (Tabloid Page); 5 col. x 14" 40" (Junior Page); 4 col. x 10" 24"; 3 col. x 8"15"; 3 col. x 5" 10" (Horizontal); 3 col. x 3 1/3" 10" (Vertical); 2 col. x 5"; Column width is 2"

Production Requirements

Black and white advertisements: Supply right reading, emulsion-side down film negatives to exact size ordered. A velox or dylux must accompany film and indicate trim, bleed, and center marks. Recommended line screen 100.

Color advertisements: Supply one piece per color, right reading, emulsion-side down film negatives to exact size ordered. A velox or dylux must accompany film and indicate trim, bleed, and center marks. Recommended line screen is 133.

Issue Dates and Closing Dates

MoneyManager.com has 12 issues a year. Closing date for placing an advertisement is 12 days preceding date of publication, except during holiday weeks when earlier closing applies. Covers close 30 days preceding publication date.

Paying Columnists

How It Works

Each firm pays $2,000 an issue to write a column on issues pertaining to the money management field. The participating firm will be allowed to write up to 500 words. Their e-mail address and telephone number will appear at the end of the column.

Potential Income

The income potential is $10,000 an issue and $120,000 for the year.

- Potential Columnist Advertisers
- Accounting
- Legal
- Marketing
- Technology
- Telecommunications

Special Advertising Sections

How It Works

We will select 10 winners in an asset class each month. The selection will be based on overall performance. Each portfolio manager's firm will be encouraged to buy a $4,000 advertisement, which includes a banner ad in the on-line version.

Potential Income

If all 10 winner firms buy a special $4,000 advertisement to congratulate their portfolio manager, the income from the special sections will be $40,000 per issue and $480,000 per year assuming we run this feature monthly.

- Best Micro-Cap Managers
- Best Small Cap Managers
- Best Mid-Cap Managers
- Best Large Cap Managers
- Best International Managers
- Best REIT Managers
- Best Alternative Investment Managers
- Best Bond Managers
- Best Firm Under $1 billion (rated on overall performance and quality of service)
- Best Firm Between $1 billion and $5 billion (rated on overall performance and quality of service)
- Best Firm Between $5 billion and $20 billion (rated on overall performance and quality of service)
- Best Firm Over $20 billion. (rated on overall performance and quality of service)

Home Page Advertisements

There will be a section for money management firms and banks and insurance companies with money management arms to advertise their Web sites. The section will feature the home page and URL.

How It Works

There will be 12 home pages in this section. We will scan in participating company's home pages. There will be a static page on the on-line site that will have a hot link to the actual site.

Potential Income

Firms will be charged $1,500 to $2,000 per issue to display their Web sites and will have to buy a 6- or 12-month contract.

Term of Contract	Amount	Potential Income
6 months	$2,000	$288,000
12 months	$1,500	$216,000

Corporate Reports

Every public company wants to entice money managers to take positions in their company. They speak at investor conferences to enhance their chances of being noticed. All are interested in receiving coverage from brokerage houses and individual money management firm analyst.

How It Works

There will be room for pictures of 12 annual reports. Under the annual reports will be the name of the investor relations person, telephone number, Web site URL, and the industry the company is in.

Potential Income

Firms will be charged $1,500 to $2,000 an issue to display their annual reports and will have to buy a 6- or 12-month contract.

Term of Contract	Amount	Potential Income
6 months	$2,000	$288,000
12 months	$1,500	$216,000

Joint Ventures

Explanation

When writing a launch plan, you should consider potential partners who might benefit through your distribution channel. You often see fast food companies partnering with movie companies to promote and sell products related to a new movie. The fast food companies know their customers are interested in certain movies, and they know that at a certain price point they can increase in-store sales through the partnership.

Joint Ventures

The company could take each of their reports/publications and offer them on-line and take a percentage of the sales. Below are organizations that provide non-competing reports that could be offered on the company Web site.

- Eager & Associates
- Frank Russell
- Global Investment
- Greenwich Associates
- *Investment Management Weekly*
- *Money Management Newsletter*
- Money Market Directory
- Nelson's Directory

Pricing

Explanation

Determining how to price a product and what is included in the price can be very difficult. Few of my clients have ever launched a product whose initial price and features remained the same over the course of the launch planning. Usually when management views it on paper it ends up adding and subtracting both price and features. A written launch plan provides a vehicle for making these adjustments in a disciplined manner.

The client in this example looked at what other competitors were charging and discounted his initial price to ease the path to consumer acceptance. My client realized that if he charged too little, no one would buy the product because they would assume the value would be small. He also knew if he charged too much, customers would compare his product to products that they perceived to be of similar nature or value. As a final step, the client chose five potential buyers and asked them if the product at this price point was within their budget and would they buy the product at this price point.

Pricing

For Money Managers

On-line Public Relations Program

Cost: $15,000/Year

Includes:

- One banner ad (for 1 month) on the Plan Sponsor and Consultant Web sites
- Posting year-end/quarterly reports to the Plan Sponsor and Consultant Web sites
- Posting firm/portfolio manager profile to the Plan Sponsor and Consultant Web sites
- Posting firm research to the Plan Sponsor and Consultant Web sites
- One "thumbnail profile" on the firm/management team in our Plan Sponsor/Consultant publication

Sales & Marketing Research

Cost: $15,000/Year

Includes:

- Access to 250+ individual plan sponsor needs profiles "scouting reports" for prospecting, lead qualification, and sales strategy development
- Quarterly hard copy reports plus daily updated information on the Money Manager site
- Aggregate survey results showing summary trends and plan sponsor needs information
- On-line sort/search capability
- Free access to all information on the Money Manager Web site.

On-line Advisory Board (Test Marketing Program via an On-line Panel of Experts)

Cost: $7,500 annual access fee plus project fee for each research project undertaken

Includes:

- Exclusive access (limited to 100 investment firms)
- 50 "thought leaders" that will provide real-time feedback on anything a money manager may want to subject to market testing including: new product concepts, sales/marketing presentations, and investment strategies.
- The ability for a money management firm to tailor their selection of respondents
- A summary report of all results, implications, and recommendations

Interactive Sales & Marketing Tools

Video/Web Video Streaming

Cost: $50,000 ($12,000/year hosting charge after the first year)

Includes:

- Full production of a 7-minute video providing a tour of the firm and portfolio management team
- Inclusion of the video stream in our on-line Money Manager library located on the Plan Sponsor and Consultant Web sites for 1 year
- Video packaging/design

CD-ROM Development

Cost: $25,000

Includes:

- Full production of a CD-ROM providing a tour of the firm and portfolio management team
- Inclusion of the CD-ROM stream in our on-line Money Manager library located on the Plan Sponsor and Consultant Web sites for 1 year
- CD-ROM packaging/design

Note: In order to produce the CD-ROM, which will be used for marketing purposes, the customer must have us produce a video first, which initially is used for the video library and will be adapted to the CD-ROM format.

For Advertisers (money managers and other suppliers)

Publication Advertising

Display Advertising Rates

1998 Black-and-white advertising rates for frequently used sizes

Issues:	1x	6x	12x	19x	26x
140"(2 pages)	$13,720	$12,810	$11,690	$10,920	$9,840
70" (1 page)	6,860	6,405	5,845	5,460	4,970
24" (1/4 page)	3,384	3,228	3,036	2,904	2,736

Note: The display rate will include a banner advertisement for one month on one of the three Web sites.

For Plan Sponsors

Access to Plan Sponsor Web site community
Cost: free access (objective is to generate traffic).
Includes:

- Peer News
- Money Manager News
- New Products
- Seminars/Events
- Research
- Library
- Chat Room
- Employment Opportunities

For Pension Consultants

Access to Consultant Web site community
Cost: free access (objective is to generate traffic).
Includes:

- Peer News
- Money Manager News
- New Products
- Seminars/Events
- Research
- Library
- Chat Room
- Employment Opportunities

Launch Timetable

Explanation

The timetable section describes what types of people will be needed, who will be involved and what needs to happen to make the launch a success. This is where the proverbial rubber meets the road. If the timetable for the launch plan isn't well thought out, the business will certainly be staring at disaster.

Before the popularity of the Internet, a business associate of mine launched a venture where novice investors could find comprehensive investment information. This person opened up a facility and advertised in certain key business publications. When only a few close friends used his service, he decided to ask some of us if we would like to be on his company's advisory board to help him figure out how to make the venture a success.

He gave each of us a copy of his business, marketing, sales, and operations plans, but there was no plan for how the business would be launched. The company had no one in charge of informing the media about his unique venture, no one in charge of setting up speaking engagements for the president, and no one to drive membership. The founder thought word of mouth and advertising his unique concept would be sufficient, but it wasn't. Management has to think through all of the details of a product or service launch before beginning to sell or valuable time and money will be wasted.

Launch Timetable

Company Infrastructure
- Get Funding Approved (Dec. '97)
- Office space (Dec. '97)
- Accountant/Attorney (Dec. '97)
- Incorporate (Jan. '98)

Milestone
Infrastructure in place by early Jan. '98.

Personnel
- Hire secretary/admin assistant (Jan. '98)
- Hire administrative assistant, Al Braverman (Jan. '98)
- Hire chief information officer, Jim Leggo (Jan. '98)
- Hire sales executive, Lauren Tonya (Feb. '98)
- Hire research director, Kathy Welch (Feb. '98)
- Hire editor (Mar. '98)

Milestone
Core team in place by Mar. '98.
- Hire Webmaster (Jun. '98)

Web Site Development
- Identify specific site content and develop a working blueprint (Jan. '98)
- Finalize site "blueprint" (Feb. '98)
- Begin technical design (Feb. '98)
- Begin to develop content (Feb. '98)

Examples:
Industry News
1997 Money Manager year-end reviews
1997–98 Investment research papers/studies
"Flash" Plan sponsors needs surveys
1998 conference/seminar calendar
Sales and marketing tips
Public company/IPO profiles
Supplier directory
Employment opportunities

Launch Web sites

- Basic community information (Apr. '98)
- On-line publication/manager profiles module (Apr./May '98)
- Sales and marketing research module (Sep. '98)
- On-line advisory board module (Dec. '98)

Publication (Manager Profile Information)

- Collect firm profile information for publication (Jan. '98)
- Write/organize initial publication (Jan.–May '98)
- Edit copy (May '98)
- Print first edition (Jun. '98)

Milestone
First mailing of publication (May/Jun. '98).

Sales and Marketing Research

- Design information collection strategy/questionnaire (Jan–Feb '98)
- Collect the information (Mar '98–ongoing)
- Edit/organize the information (May–Jul. '98)
- Layout/print hardcopy version (Sep. '98)
- Mail hardcopy version (Oct. '98)

Milestone
Launch Web version of sales and marketing research (Nov. '98).

On-line Advisory Board
- Complete list of board members (Mar. '98)
- Link advisory board members into the Web site (Apr. '98)

Milestone
Sales & Marketing
Get 10 "seed" clients (presell by Apr. '98).

Morgan Stanley	Miller Anderson
SEI Investment	Chartwell
Delaware Management	Turner Investments
GE Capital	Rittenhouse
Invesco	T. Rowe Price

Write press release and meet with influential editors (Apr./May '98)
- Develop sales presentation (Jan. '98)
- Begin face-to-face selling program (Feb. '98)
- Develop marketing brochure (Feb./Mar. '98)
- Develop direct mail piece(s) (Jun. '98)
- Develop print ad(s) for *P&I* (Sep./Oct. '98)

Milestones
- 3 seed clients (Mar. '98)
- 6 seed clients (Apr. '98)
- Direct mail teaser (May '98)
- 10 seed clients (Jun. 98)
- PR article (Jun. '98)
- Print ad in *P&I* (Sep. '98)

Chapter 4

Hiring an Outside Turnaround Specialist

"A professional is a man who can do his best at a time when he doesn't particularly feel like it."

—ALISTAIR COOKE (1908–)
journalist and broadcaster

Joe Jackson was an entrepreneur's entrepreneur. He took big risks, lived on the edge, and worked many hours to make his marketing/communications business a success. For years the business comprised five or six full-time and two or three part-time people. The business did quality work and made money, but it hadn't grown to the level Joe had aspired for it.

Then an opportunity came up with one of their clients, a large public company, to put together all of the marketing materials for all twenty-one divisions. Joe's company had never handled more than two projects at a time for any one client, and although his people didn't have the experience to handle such a large client, Joe accepted the opportunity. He went to his bank and showed them his contract and asked for a large line of credit. The bank reviewed the contract and told Joe it was nervous about agreeing to his request because the contract could be canceled with thirty days notice.

> Joe said he would be willing to put up his house and any other asset to make the bank feel comfortable.

Joe said he would be willing to put up his house and any other asset to make the bank feel comfortable. After quick deliberation, the bank gave Joe a $1 million line of credit. Joe immediately began hiring people to staff up for the new business. He opened a West Coast office to be more accessible to the client's divisions in California.

As Joe was hiring people, buying equipment, and taking on new leases for office space, the new client said that the scope of work wouldn't be as great as initially thought, but would grow. Joe's business, which once comprised just five full-time people, now had twenty-five full-time people, two offices, and a slew of new equipment leases to support his new hires. Joe didn't want to unwind his business. He was an optimist and, in his opinion, a great salesman. He would just work twice as hard, hire some salespeople, and bring in enough new business to cover expenses until the public company's business began to gear up.

Joe's salespeople went after large companies that had large contracts, which was the opposite of what the business had gone after before. When the new salespeople didn't bring in business within thirty days of their arrival, Joe fired them and replaced them with new salespeople. After a while, word got out that Joe had unrealistic expectations about how long it took to get business, and good salespeople refused to work for him. The only people who would work for him were inexperienced or poor salespeople.

The new hires began to get nervous about the lack of business and some were contemplating looking for new jobs. Over a period of six months Joe's surplus of cash disappeared and was quickly being replaced by a variety of debts that ranged from taxes to run-of-the-mill business expenses.

One of his oldest employees suggested closing down the West Coast office and letting go some of the new people. Joe ignored the advice, and when the employee became more aggressive in her suggestion of how to reduce debt, Joe told her if she couldn't support his decision she should leave.

At the end of each quarter, Joe had his accountant review his bookkeeper's work and make sure everything was in order. At the end of the third quarter of the year, Joe's accountant told Joe he was technically in violation of his agreement with the bank, which stated that the company had to have a positive net worth and the ability to keep paying its bills. Joe's accountant told him that the business was technically bankrupt and he needed to do something quick.

A group of managers requested a meeting with Joe and told him that they had lost confidence in his leadership and that if he hoped to save the company he needed to bring in someone else to run the company. Joe acquiesced and through his accountant and lawyer met with prequalified candidates. Within one year of the date the new president was hired, the debt was wiped and the company was profitable.

Many business leaders are like Joe. They are good at starting a business or maintaining one that has already been started, but aren't good a fixing a seriously ill business. They often don't have the experience, skills, temperament, or willingness to do what is necessary to correct the problem.

An outsider who has no attachments to the people or investment in the past needs to be brought in. In Joe's case the new president moved quickly to close the new office, let go of people who weren't billing clients, work out payment schedules with vendors and taxing authorities, and refocus the business on the types of clients that made the business a success in the past. Initially Joe

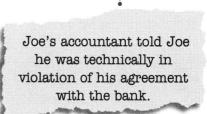

Joe's accountant told Joe he was technically in violation of his agreement with the bank.

MapPing Out Your Strategy

was resistant to all of the changes the new president wanted to make, but he weighted it against the loss of his business and all his personal assets.

Finding a Specialist

There are many ways of finding quality professionals to assist you in fixing your business. In large metropolitan areas, there are listings in the telephone books for turnaround specialists.

Professional Referrals

The first place to start when looking for a qualified turnaround specialist is by contacting your accountant, banker, lawyer, or financial planner. All four of these professionals have worked with clients who have had business troubles at one time or another and some of those clients have probably engaged a professional to assist them in fixing their business.

Large international accounting firms have in-house experts that work with all sizes of companies. Banks have internal groups called "work out departments" that work with troubled companies in order to protect the bank's investment in the company. The work out departments have a list of professionals they have worked with in the past and are glad to make introductions between their clients and these professionals.

> The first place to start when looking for a qualified turnaround specialist is by contacting your accountant, banker, lawyer, or financial planner.

Chambers of Commerce

Strong, involved chambers of commerce always know which members are doing well and which are having problems. The chambers are often contacted by members who are in trouble and looking for a referral to someone who can assist them in fixing their business. If the chamber doesn't have a direct contact, they will contact members who they know have engaged professional help in the past and ask them if they would be willing to share their experiences and contacts with a member who is having business problems.

Trade Associations

A troubled business owner can contact Turnaround Management Association (541 North Fairbanks Court, Suite 1880, Chicago, IL 60611, (312) 822-9700, www.turnaround.org. This association has a list of qualified professionals that work with troubled companies.

A business owner can also contact his national trade association and ask for a list of individuals and management companies that work with troubled companies.

Qualifications of a Turnaround Specialist

There are many people who profess to be general turnaround specialists, and their sole expertise is in looking at a balance sheet and figuring out what expenses to cut and how to reorganize debt and bank loans. Certainly, this skill and knowledge is important, but it is only part of the answer. It is also the easiest part of the fixing a company.

Understanding of Industry

Understanding how to manage people and build sales is important, as is understanding the industry the business is in. The value of understanding the industry is that the new president doesn't have to spend time being educated about the business and will bring contacts and ideas on how to fix the business.

> Skill and knowledge is important, but it is only part of the answer.

Turnaround Experiences

Don't hire a manager who hasn't suffered through adversity and hasn't successfully turned a business around. Many times companies hire competent, successful managers, but the manager has never worked with a sick company. They haven't worked with employees who have lost faith in themselves, vendors who are screaming to be paid, and clients who are reconsidering giving additional business to the company. Knowing what to say and how to respond to each constituency can make all the difference in the beginning, and if you can't control the major issues initially then the business will not survive.

Expertise

Not every situation calls for a manager who understands the financial, management, and sales issues. In fact, it is hard to find someone who has proven above-average results in all areas. If your major problem is consolidating debts and reorganizing bank loans, then a financial specialist may be all that is needed. In the case where the business leader is terrific with numbers but is a poor communicator and leader, then an expertise in managing people is essential.

Compensation Requirements

Turnaround specialists that work for large management firms are either paid by the hour or by the project. For a small company this may not be financially feasible. Small management firms and independent consultants are more flexible and are willing to take a combination of cash, equity, and cash bonus based on performance. If you are hesitant about having an outsider holding equity for fear they would sell their equity to someone you wouldn't approve of, you can design the contract so that you have first right of refusal to buy their stock back.

> Small management firms and independent consultants are more flexible.

Utilizing a Part-Time Specialist

If you are using a part-time specialist, you need to develop a written scope of work you expect them to do and a time period in which you expect them to accomplish their tasks.

Duties

Assign them duties and give them authority to carry out those duties. Make sure your expectations and their ability to deliver are in sync. All too often the owner has a set of expectations that aren't based on reality, especially when bringing on someone part time.

There are three effective uses of a part-time specialist. The one with the greatest impact is the specialist that focuses on working with outside vendors to develop new payment terms and payment schedules. The second best use of a part-time specialist is to develop a sales and marketing plan and work with the sales team to execute that plan. The third best use of a part-time specialist is as an advisor to the business leader on what they should do and how they should do it, someone to bounce ideas off of.

Hours

If you are using a part-time specialist for working with outside vendors and the bank and developing sales and marketing plans, you will want to engage them for twenty to thirty hours a week for one to three months depending on the complexity of the business and its problems.

Compensation

Negotiate with a part-time specialist and see if he or she will take a combination of cash and stock options and/or cash bonuses based on performance. Remember, you want to conserve as much cash as possible so the business will survive.

Hiring a Full-Time Specialist

A full-time specialist should be engaged when the business leader and/or its board of directors decide that new top leadership needs to be put in place.

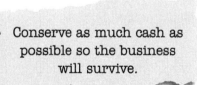

Conserve as much cash as possible so the business will survive.

Duties

The new leader will be responsible and accountable for all facets of the business.

Hours

A full-time turnaround specialist knows that a minimum of a fifty- to sixty-hour work week is expected until all of the problems are under control and the company is once again profitable.

Control

There can be no question that the specialist is in complete control of the business. No one can be hired or fired or one penny spent without the approval of the specialist. A lot of business owners naturally have a difficult time with this concept, but the specialist needs this level of control to be effective. In regards to check signing authority, the business owner can require two signatures on every check over $1,000 so he can monitor and approve expenditures.

Compensation

Most small firms and individual turnaround specialists require cash compensation plus cash bonuses based on performance and warrants/stock options in the company. There is no set rule on stock options, but usually they range from 5 to 15 percent of the company's stock.

There is no set rule on stock options.

Final Comments

Take a long look in the mirror and evaluate your own skills. If your business looks as if it coming into or is having problems that your skills and abilities can't fix, don't be ashamed or afraid to bring in help. You have a responsibility to your employees, their families, your vendors, and customers to do what is best for the company. If that means replacing yourself or one of your managers, regardless of relationships and ego, you have to do it.

Implementing Your Strategy

Summary of Part II

This section walks business leaders through implementing their plans:

- **Ways to rebuild morale and attract and retain employees**
- **Building sales through creative marketing**
- **Learning to hold the line on expenses and negotiate debt**

Managing People in a Turnaround

"There's no way you can have consistent success without players. No one can win without material. But not everyone can win with material."

—JOHN WOODEN (1910–)
Former UCLA Bruins basketball coach

Managing people in a start-up is relatively easy because everyone is excited about the challenge of growing something new. People are willing to stay late and work for low pay because they believe the rewards will be worth the time and effort. A stable environment has challenges such as motivating people and picking the right management to take the company to the next level.

In a turnaround, people can feel beaten, abused, unappreciated, and lacking in direction. Their anger and disappointment will probably be focused at management. People aren't interested in hearing that they need to work harder and longer and make financial sacrifices. They believe they have done all of that and it hasn't gotten the company anywhere. Worse yet, usually the best people are either considering leaving or have left.

If you are currently managing a company that finds itself in the position of having to be turned around, you feel as though the world is crashing down on you. Fear and indecision probably paralyze you. You don't know in whom to confide because you don't want to look weak.

This chapter will focus on the successes and mistakes two of my clients made as they worked on fixing their companies. Unfortunately, most of us learn more through mistakes than success.

> You feel as though the world is crashing down on you.

Rebuilding Morale

Sometime in a professional's management career, leaders go through a period where nothing they do seems to work. They can't understand why this is happening to them. At first they believe things will begin to turn themselves around, but eventually they start to lose confidence in themselves. Before long, they think they are failures.

This is what happens in organizations that are mismanaged. People throughout the organization begin to doubt themselves and those around them. They feel inadequate. Instead of getting in early and staying late, people do just the opposite. Friends who are interested in joining the organization are told to stay away. Everyone begins to think and view the company as the Titanic of their industry.

The following are ten steps used by one of my clients to rebuild their employee's confidence in themselves and the organization.

1. Hold a company-wide meeting where different employees are singled out for their successes. This demonstrates to other employees that successful people surround them.
2. Admit to management's past mistakes and talk about how management and employees are going to fix them together. People join small companies because they like to know they are having an impact, that what they say and how they feel matters. Leaders need to acknowledge that.
3. Meet with each employee individually to find out what they think needs to be done to get the company back on track and how management can help them with their job.
4. Send notices about new sales and post compliments received from clients. This allows employees to be proud of their accomplishments without having to tell everyone themselves what a good job they are doing.
5. Learn your employees' strengths and weaknesses and set them up to succeed. All too often management gives employees directives that are beyond their abilities, and when the employees drown in the failure, management wonders why.
6. Compliment employees regarding their work in front of their clients. Nothing makes someone feel better than being complimented by his or her boss in front of a client.
7. Promote from within. Nothing demonstrates the quality of talent better than promoting existing employees. It makes a statement that management believes the talent already exists within the organization.
8. Let go of people who aren't pulling their weight or aren't team players. Handling employees is like raising children. If one child sees another child getting away with something, they won't respect their parents and then management has chaos. Admittedly, that isn't always possible. In many technology companies, the company might have someone who has a specialty that is hard to find, and management needs to keep them until a replacement can be found.

> Send notices about new sales and post compliments received from clients.

9. Let employees know when management has taken and implemented a suggestion from the ranks. It shows that management values employee input.
10. Encourage risk and reward innovation. If the risk taker makes a mistake, remind them of all the chances other managers took that failed. Tell them that if management didn't have confidence in their judgment, they wouldn't have let them take the risk at all.

Rebuilding morale takes time and patience. People don't lose their confidence overnight. It slowly erodes.

Recruiting

Recruiting the right employees for a turnaround can be difficult because the current employees often have a negative view of themselves and the organization. People who have come from a comfortable environment that hasn't experienced much upheaval are usually in for a major shock when walking into a turnaround situation. Many times they will panic and second-guess themselves.

The right type of person to be involved in a turnaround is someone who likes to take the last shot in a basketball game or come to bat with the bases loaded and down by three runs. These people thrive on pressure because they don't look at the situation as being one of pressure. They look at it as an opportunity to shine.

A friend of mine who specializes in turning around distressed business told me that his personal mental image was of himself as the savior of the franchise. He said he wanted to rip open his shirt in front of the employees so they could see the big "S" on his chest. He wanted them to cheer and say, "Thank God he's here!"

The supporting cast in a turnaround has to have similar mental images about themselves. They have to be mentally tough, entrepreneurial, and look at the situation as a puzzle that needs to be solved. There will likely be long hours and sleepless nights, so people have to have a high energy level.

> Recruiting the right employees for a turnaround can be difficult.

Developing a profile of the type of individuals the company needs to hire is the most important challenge management will undertake. Management can't afford many mistakes because of the current employees' morale and the company's financial condition.

To limit hiring mistakes, many of my clients use a product called Prevue Assessment developed by Profiles International in Waco, Texas. The product assists managers in evaluating potential hires. This is the only prehiring personnel assessment test on the market. I have found this test to be accurate, and it has helped to save organizations that I have run or consulted from making disastrous mistakes. The Prevue Assessment is the only human resource test that measures mental abilities, motivational interests, and personality characteristics. The assessment includes a series of questions to determine the likes and dislikes of an individual. You then match the results against the profile you have developed for the position you are trying to fill. Here is a short list of some of the assessment questions:

- "Do you enjoy working on your own?" In a turnaround, management needs people who are team-oriented and willing to work with others for the common good.
- "Do you look at issues as being black and white?" People who look at everything as black and white usually are not flexible, and management needs flexible employees in a turnaround because every day is different and roles and responsibilities change.
- "How do you handle stress?" For individuals who can't handle stress, a turnaround is no place to be. Until the company reaches certain milestones, every day feels as if you are teetering on the edge of a cliff.
- "Do you like a structured or unstructured environment?" The characteristic addressed by this question is a two-edged sword. Management needs people who are going to put structure into a chaotic situation, but management doesn't want people who can't go with the flow or believe there is only one way to accomplish something.

> Management needs people who are team-oriented.

- "How important is free time to you?" People who value their free time will become frustrated and unhappy in a turn- around because the company will require that they give some (or much) of it up. The right employees are ones who look at their job not as work but as their favorite hobby.
- "Can you handle multiple tasks or only one task at a time?" People who like to do one thing at a time may feel swamped and pressured when overloaded with multiple responsibilities and may eventually want to leave. Turnarounds are usually not the right environment for such people.

Once management has made a profile of the type of people it is looking to attract, then management needs to identify where they can find them.

Finding the Right People

Unfortunately, management just can't run a want ad that says, "Company in bad shape. Need good people to turn it around. Send resume."

The best way to find the right people is to contact in writing oth- ers who understand the company's situation, then follow up the letter with a telephone call. The letter should have a description of the types of people and positions management are looking to fill. Management can find leads to potential employees by contacting the following.

Current Employees

Employees are a great source of potential leads if they believe management is on the right track. Often the most successful new employees were ones that were recommended by existing employees. Current employees understand the culture and situation of the com- pany, and that is important to the success of the business.

Friends

Management's friends have probably become very familiar with the business over time and may know people who would be a good fit.

> Unfortunately, management just can't run a want ad.

Business Associates

Like management's friends, business associates are probably familiar with the business and may know people in the industry that are looking for a challenge.

Trade Associations

Trade associations are a good source for people who understand management's business. The downside to using trade associations is that fellow members may be aware of the company's problems and, hence, may be reluctant to interview or suggest someone else. Also, depending on the industry the company is in, these same people may feel it's better to have one less competitor. Whether management gets leads from fellow trade association members depends on their trust and confidence in management as individuals.

Company's Board of Directors/Advisors

This group understands the business and is usually well connected. They have a vested interest in bringing only quality candidates.

> The downside to using trade associations is that fellow members may be aware of the company's problems.

Accountants

The company accountant probably meets people all the time who are looking for new opportunities. They also understand management's business and sometimes can think outside of the box in terms of who would be a good fit.

Lawyers

The company lawyer is probably like your accountant in that he or she comes across capable business professionals looking for the right opportunity. They also have gotten a chance to know your business and can look for people who would fit your situation.

Sample Letter to Find New Employees

Below is a sample letter I have sent to people when I have looked for new employees:

Dear John:

I hope all is well. As you know, we are going through a difficult time, but I believe we are finally getting our ship in order and we need to fill some holes. We need a good salesperson and a programmer.

We are looking to pay the salesperson $25,000 plus a 10 percent commission and partial benefits. This person should have two to five years of experience, can work on their own, and isn't a big company type. They have to be willing to work long days, but the payoff can be a move up to management and possible stock options.

We know good computer programmers aren't cheap, but we don't have a lot of cash to layout. Our salary package is $40,000, plus bonuses based on this person saving us time on production and company administration, which could put them over $60,000.

Please call me, or have whomever you have in mind call me directly and tell them to use your name. I will call you to see if you have any questions, and thanks for your help.

Sincerely,
Marc Kramer
President

> We need a good salesperson and a programmer.

Retaining

Retaining good employees doesn't have to be difficult if management creates the right environment. People who enjoy their profession and like their fellow employees will endure a lot of pain, but management has to make adjustments so the pain eventually goes away. This section focuses on the mental and physical side of creating a better working environment. The section after this deals with the financial issues, which can't be overlooked.

Management, in most turnaround situations, will find that compensation is an issue. But the larger issue for employees is having some amount of control and input. People want to know they are being heard and that their ideas are being acted upon. Like any good relationship, your partner doesn't like to be ignored or have lip service paid to their ideas.

We touched a little on this in the Ten Steps to Improving Morale in the beginning of this chapter. Here are Ten Ways To Keep Good Employees and how to keep good people from leaving.

1. *Listen and learn.* The reason most companies get in a jam is that they don't listen to either their customers or their employees. In most cases, the employees are more in touch with what customers want than management. Don't assume management knows everything. Ask employees for their suggestions on how to improve their departments and the company overall. If management hears a recurring theme, act on it immediately and credit the employee at a company meeting and through company communications.

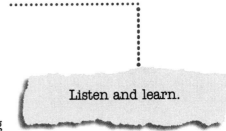

Listen and learn.

2. *Encourage fun.* Many of us spend more time at the office than we do at home, and, unfortunately, turnarounds require long hours. Allow employees to play computer games and do things that will relieve stress.
3. *Compliments.* People thrive on knowing that they are appreciated. Constantly let people know when they have done a good job.
4. *Free food.* Have a company lunch every month. It doesn't have to be elaborate. It can be sandwiches or pizza. When people work late at night, allow them to charge dinner to the company (but set a limit for the amount they can charge).
5. *Books and seminars.* Employees join a company to learn and grow. Buy books that will increase people's knowledge of the field and send employees to free or inexpensive seminars run by company vendors. All too often, employers want to chain employees to their desks. That sends the negative message that their personal growth isn't a concern of management.
6. *Toys.* Employees love to work with new technology, whether they are in production or other departments. They like to experiment with new technology such as desktop video conferencing, mobile telephones, etc. Although the company is

cash strapped, management can ask its vendors for demonstrations of their newest products.

7. *Empower employees*. Don't micromanage people. Encourage them to take chances and learn from mistakes. They will try harder, work longer, and care more. They will respect you and become more valuable.

8. *Promote from within*. Usually, no matter how small the organization, there are good people who have been overlooked for promotion into leadership positions. Management will find these people by just asking their colleagues.

9. *Honesty*. Being honest and confiding in employees is the most important thing management can do. Employees will follow their leaders through a burning building if they trust them.

10. *Time off*. If management sees that someone is tired or has worked a lot of overtime, give them time off with pay even if they have run out of vacation time. There are laws that require certain types of employees to receive financial compensation, but many companies who are cash strapped circumvent this law. Oftentimes employees will not make an issue of this, either to help the company or for fear of losing their job. It's important to do the right thing for the employee because it sends a positive message about the organization.

Promote from within.

Compensation Schemes

There are two things in a turnaround that cause a severe amount of butterflies in the management's stomach: laying people off and dealing with compensation for the remaining employees. We will discuss laying people off in a later chapter and cover compensation in this chapter.

Often when companies get into trouble, they ask their employees to take a pay cut but usually don't offer anything in return. Sometimes management will be involved in a situation where many of the best people are underpaid; then, there are other people collecting a paycheck who shouldn't on the payroll.

Let's discuss how to handle pay cuts, the acrimony associated with it, and what management needs to offer to keep people from running out of the building.

First, management needs to let employees know they are reducing their own pay or taking part of it to buy additional stock in the company. Once management has done that, here are some suggestions of what management can offer employees to make up for their reduction in pay.

Stock Options

Set aside a certain amount of stock in the company and give each employee a certain number of options based on seniority, amount of responsibility, and the importance of their position. The options will phase in over a period of time and will grow as the company grows. Management will need to have the company accountant or a business evaluation company set a price for the shares, and management should update that value every six months to a year. This will show the value of the employee's shares.

Phantom Shares

Management might not want to have anyone besides the founders and the company's investors hold any shares in the company for control reasons. Phantom shares work exactly the same as stock, but the employees never really own any equity in the company. The shares are valued the same way and management is responsible for redeeming shares that employees want to cash in. Management can allow other employees to buy those shares, but in the future, if the shares are worth something, the company will have to pay real money for those shares.

Profit Sharing

This is probably the most common form of providing extra compensation to employees. It provides incentive for everyone to work hard for the common good. The split between ownership,

> Management needs to let employees know they are reducing their own pay or taking part of it to buy additional stock in the company.

management, and rank and file employees must be equitable or sharing of profits becomes meaningless.

Bonuses

There are innumerable ways of structuring bonuses for employees. The key to the success of this program is being fair and having the money to pay them. Following are the types of bonuses management can provide to different types and levels of employees and terms on which management can base their bonuses:

> The key to the success of this program is being fair and having the money to pay them.

- Secretaries: Devising ways to make administration more efficient.
- Finance: Finding ways to cut costs and the ability to bring in receivables quickly.
- Service: Business retention.
- Sales: A combination of gross sales, margin, and quality of sales. Management doesn't want its employees to give away the company's products or services, and management doesn't want customers who are bad or slow payers.
- Marketing: Number of attendees at seminars they run, number of quality leads derived from trade shows they work, and quality of prospect appointments that lead to sales.
- Human Resources: Retention of quality employees. If they have done a good job of screening employees and the employee stays with the organization, they should be compensated for their good judgment.
- Assembly Line: Percentage of defective products. Use an industry benchmark and bonus based on beating the mark.
- Management: Combination of profits, retention of clients, increases in sales, retention of employees, and customer satisfaction.
- All Employees: Finding quality employees and customer leads that result in sales.

The goal is to have everyone focused on how to make the company a success and feel they are being rewarded for it. Whatever management pays out in bonuses, the company will get a return many times greater. However, it can't be stressed enough that, whatever program management sets up, management must follow through with it or the company will be worse off than having had no program at all.

Successful and Failing Leadership Practices

Below are examples of two clients of mine whose morale was low. One client made innumerable mistakes and eventually went out of business. I introduced the second client to the first client and he learned how to avoid the first client's mistakes.

> The company will be worse off than having had no program at all.

First Example

The first client invested in a three-year-old, thirty-five-person regional magazine company whose investors were in the who's who of the business community—people who had run large banks, real estate operations, advertising agencies, radio stations, and consumer products companies. The chairman of the company was a self-made millionaire who made his money in advertising. There were two magazines—one business and the other covering antiques.

The reason my client invested in this company was so he could be part of this group and, hopefully, so that other investment opportunities would come his way. He also knew something about publications from starting and running a newspaper. He liked the chairman and his son, who was in charge of one of the two publications.

Six months after he invested, the company wasn't making its projections and the investors were getting nervous. The company had a negative net worth of $1 million. He made suggestions on how to improve revenue and, based on his newspaper success and contacts from running one of the country's largest business associations, he was asked to come on as interim president/CEO. If he liked running the company and was successful, he could leave his current position as head of the trade association and devote full time to the magazines.

Without doing a lot of thinking and having supreme confidence in his abilities, he took on this daunting task. He had done two other turnarounds that had been successful, and he felt reasonably comfortable he could repeat that outcome with this company. However, he also realized that this turnaround was much more difficult than the other two because of the industry and the pressure put on by the people investing in it.

His first day started off great. He met with the employees, many of whom were aware of his past successes, and told them they were very talented, that the magazines had a lot of quality, and that his goal was to build a national chain and go public. He said he was going to write a new business plan and that they would all have input. He told them his door was always open and that he planned to interview each one of them to find out what was needed for the company to succeed.

A few days after his speech to the employees, one of the city's leading newspapers ran a front-page business section story about his appointment and speech. How they found out what he said is anyone's guess. He assumed one of his writers knew the writer of the story and leaked his comments. Morale was so high that the publisher of the business magazine wrote in his column that getting my client was like getting the first pick in the draft.

Unfortunately, my client's golden touch and common sense disappeared soon thereafter. Going forward, he made one mistake after another. Let me share with you The Ten Biggest Lessons he told me he learned. Then you will see from the second example another client who learned from those mistakes.

Lesson No. 1: "Take notes; don't type."

He met with just about every employee for a formal interview and typed into his computer as they were speaking. No one likes to be interviewed and have his or her thoughts quoted on paper. People have a hard time being upfront if they think there is any chance your notes can get into the wrong hands.

> He had done two other turnarounds that had been successful, and he felt reasonably comfortable he could repeat that outcome with this company.

Lesson No. 2: "Learn the internal politics."

My client, like the board of the company, thought there were synergies between the two magazines and that he could exploit them. He thought the publisher of one had strong sales skills and could oversee the combining of both magazines sales forces and sell both products together. The other publisher had strong editorial skills, and my client thought he could do the same on the editorial side. What my client didn't know coming in was the sales staff of the business magazine disliked the publisher with the sales skills, and that she had no interest in cross-selling.

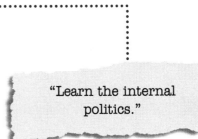

"Learn the internal politics."

Lesson No. 3: "Don't second-guess yourself."

When he first arrived he had a plan and he shared it with the two publishers, the chairman, the vice president of sales, and the chief financial officer. He asked for their input. The chairman looked at his son, who was one of the publishers, and he said it wouldn't work. At that point, he should have told management the board wants change and either jump on the train or get off.

Instead, he waffled and second-guessed himself. He was indecisive for the first time in his professional life. In a turnaround, everyone is looking to the leader to select a path. One of his board members gave him a great piece of advice when turning around a company: "It doesn't matter which path you choose, just pick one so everyone has something to focus on. You can always alter it."

Diverse opinions are welcome, but at some point the leader has to take ownership and make a decision. My client didn't do that, and all of the good will he built up before his arrival and during his first week was ruined. Who caused this calamity? My client took responsibility.

Lesson No. 4: "Always explain to survivors why others were let go."

Soon after he joined the company, my client had to lay off 10 percent of the workforce. Those he let go had been with the company from day one. Again, he made the mistake of not going with his instincts. He was advised by the chairman and both publishers to have a company meeting to announce he was letting some people go and to not allow the employees to ask questions. The people who were let go didn't hear it from my client, but rather from their direct superiors.

In a small company, the president should call the individuals into his office and tell them in person. If they are quality people, they should be offered assistance in finding a new position. The laid off employees should be regretfully told why people are being let go and allow them to vent their frustration. The only thing my client felt he did right was setup job interviews for the laid off employees.

Again, he looked like a misguided jerk, not someone that was going to lead these people to success.

> In a small company, the president should call the individuals into his office and tell them in person.

Lesson No. 5: "Be aware of managers who become labor lawyers."

My client had one of his most productive people getting ready to take maternity leave. He called three people into his office and asked them who could fill this role without bringing on an outsider, which would add to the company's expenses. The three people said that no one person could fill this person's shoes, but all three of them knew an aspect of the job and would be glad to pitch in.

He thought he had a solution, until the publisher of one of the magazines burst through his door and said it wouldn't work. My client asked why not. He said none of the three was being financially compensated for this extra duty and that they wouldn't do it. This was news to my client, and it was no time for people to ask for extra compensation. Double duty is expected in entrepreneurial and turn-around situations.

He knew this publisher was not going to agree with anything he proposed. He should have fired him for interfering. He then should have told the three employees that if they had a problem, to see him and that he expected them to help out during this crisis. You can't have employees acting as agents for other employees trying to get them more money when things are in bad shape.

Lesson No. 6: "Don't be afraid to ask employees questions."

My client liked to ask employees direct questions about why something was done. He was concerned that managers would cover up problems for fear of looking bad. Not surprisingly, this happens in businesses that aren't well run. The same publisher in lesson number five again came into my client's office and told him he just couldn't go around asking people questions. He said because my client was president, people were intimidated by him and didn't know what to say. Plus, there was a chain of command and he went around this person's superior.

The publisher then went to the chairman (his mother) when my client disagreed with him. The chairman sided with her son. Start worrying immediately when managers become concerned that you are speaking to their people directly. No manager at General Electric ever made a fuss when Jack Welch asked an employee a question. If they did, they are probably working somewhere else by now.

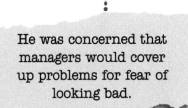

He was concerned that managers would cover up problems for fear of looking bad.

Lesson No. 7: "Be aware of head games."

If your strength is managing people, don't let anyone tell you otherwise. Unbeknownst to my client, his chairman was notorious for playing psychological games with her managers. Soon after he began working for her, the chairman told him people didn't like his management style and handed him a book on how to manage people. My client said he wanted to confront those people who are unhappy and see what adjustments he needed to make, if any. The chairman told him they would never be upfront with him and he had to take her word for it.

My client said his gut feeling was to ignore the chairman's suggestion, but he had always trusted older mentors. It took him four months to realize his chairman had a different agenda than he did.

Lesson No. 8: "Is anyone reading from the same book as me?"

My client was looking for a vice president of sales for one of the magazines and he had a very hot prospect. Everyone liked him and his background. However, the prospect decided not to join the company because, in his words, "you guys are the most dysfunctional business family I have ever met." If management seemed dysfunctional to him, my client could only guess how management looked to the employees.

To be successful, everyone has to sing from the same song sheet. It's the president's responsibility to make sure everyone was in sync or get rid of those who wouldn't go along.

> To be successful, everyone has to sing from the same song sheet.

Lesson No. 9: "Watch your back."

All day, every day, my client spent his time in closed-door meetings at each manager's office trying to drum up support for what he was trying to accomplish. Managers would agree with him in private but at full management meetings, they would throw their support to the chairman and her son.

The employees must have been sadly laughing to themselves as they saw him shuttle from one office to the next. They must have known that certain managers would say yes when they really meant no. It is best not to have private meetings, but instead hash things out in group meetings. Management must be seen as working on their problems together, not in separate groups.

Lesson No. 10: "Don't keep existing management."

The board of the company told my client to try to work with existing management. They felt the missing ingredient was someone who thought strategically, was creative, had strong sales skills with a proven track record, and an even keel personality could turn the company around.

Most times the reason businesses are in trouble is that the current management doesn't have the right skill sets or they are mismatched as a group. The company in this example had an odd collection of personalities that couldn't get along and didn't trust each other. My client should have demanded that the board allow him to let all or most of them go. Sometimes there are people who will flourish under new leadership.

Finally, he realized the best course of action was for him to find a new president who understood the magazine business and the collection of people in this company. If he couldn't do that, the board would have to demand all of top management's resignations. This could have been a major problem because the chairman and her son/publisher owned 45 percent of the stock and the other publisher owned 10 percent. It would have probably lead to litigation.

The chairman also owned another publishing company, and he asked its president if he would consider merging his publications with my client's and taking over the combined entity. The other company's president said he was interested. In a few weeks, the joint president took over, my client left, and the employees felt reinvigorated.

Second Example

The second example comes from a client of mine who was brought in to turnaround a regional multimedia company. I introduced this client to my first client because I thought the circumstances in terms of reporting issues and personalities were similar to the ones my first client experienced.

The founder of the multimedia company was a young entrepreneur who loved the multimedia field. She was a hard worker and a good judge of creative talent. Clients loved her, and she liked to take on the most difficult projects. Unfortunately, she didn't have the right personality or training to run a business. Below is a list of what employees told my client about the founder when he interviewed with them:

- She didn't know how to communicate with subordinates—there were no management meetings, and managers weren't asked or empowered to make changes.

> The chairman also owned another publishing company, and he asked its president if he would consider merging his publications with my client's and taking over the combined entity.

- There was no management structure and, therefore, no one for employees to go to about a problem or a suggestion.
- She was dictatorial. She sent employees nasty e-mails ordering, not requesting, them to do what she wanted.
- She was secretive. Employees like to know if the company is making money, if there will be bonuses forthcoming, and if not, why. Employees want to know how they can help the company reach its objectives. The founder never shared this information with employees.
- She was a micromanager. When she brought in a new client, she didn't empower the people in charge of the project to do what they thought was necessary to make the project successful. She didn't allow managers to take risks, so they could not grow professionally.
- She couldn't admit when she was wrong on major issues. She hated to admit to making mistakes.

> She didn't empower the people in charge.

By the time the founder brought my client in, a few of her best employees had left or were leaving. They had lost complete faith in her ability to lead and manage the company. When my client sat down with her, the founder said, "Sure the buck stops with me. I'm responsible because it's my business, but . . . "

She didn't really believe she was at fault for any of the major problems, especially morale. As we spoke further, she preceded to blame her partners, key employees, lack of capital, and so on.

If a leader wants to alienate his employees and lose total credibility, point the finger at everyone but himself and tell people they aren't working hard enough. Do that and you can be assured of losing the best employees and creating an aura of distrust and discontentment.

Leaders have to move fast to build credibility. Employees will automatically distrust new managers until they earn their respect and trust. To do that, managers have to listen and address the concerns of the employees through their actions, not just through words.

My client wrote a checklist of what he thought needed to be done immediately to rebuild faith in management and implemented it. The following were his Ten Steps to Stabilization.

1. *Interview employees.* My client met with employees to ask them what they thought needed to be done to make the organization successful. Most of them suggested getting rid of the owner, or at least getting her out of running the business on a day-to-day basis. The latter part was easy because she didn't really want to run the business. Other ideas, such as letting the production department rearrange their space, developing a database to track each project, and not moving project managers from project to project on a daily basis, were things they all had strong feelings about. My client told them they were empowered to make the changes they thought necessary.

2. *Open company books.* He offered every employee an opportunity to look at the company's books. They were allowed to see everything, except other people's salaries. After two weeks, no one ever asked to look at the books. Just knowing that the books were open for them to view was enough.

3. *Managerial input.* He asked employees who among them they felt could run the various departments, and my client then put those people in charge. If management can promote from within it should do so; it is a great morale booster to people who have lost confidence in them. Also, management may not have a choice but to promote from within. The company in this example was technically bankrupt; therefore, they didn't want to recruit someone who was in a stable environment and who could possibly be out of a job soon after their arrival.

4. *Company meetings.* My client held the first of many monthly company lunch meetings. He told the employees his door was open and that management, not the employees, had put

> My client told them they were empowered to make the changes they thought necessary.

the company in its current situation. His company meetings covered the following four topics:

- Company cash position
- Reports by managers
- Questions and answers from employees
- Naming an employee of the month

5. *First in.* My client made sure he was the first person in every morning and that he visited everyone during the course of the day. Everyone wants to know the boss is working just as hard, if not harder, than they are, and they want contact and reassurance that everything is going to be all right. You can't build rapport with people unless they see you and get to know you.
6. *Ask questions.* My client made sure everyone knew that he thought they could teach him a lot about the industry and that he could help them grow as professionals.
7. *Downsizing.* He decided which employees he had to let go. Once he made that decision, he told the remaining employees why he had to let those employees go and how he was assisting them in finding new opportunities. Never let people go in groups if it can be helped. If management does that, everyone starts to prepare their resumes for fear of when they will get the ax. Productivity basically drops to almost nothing and the company will soon fold.
8. *Communication.* He made sure the employees received the same information that the chairman did, such as the following:

- Productivity numbers by employee
- Productivity numbers as a company
- Accounts receivable and payable
- Cash on hand
- New clients

> My client made sure he was the first person in every morning and that he visited everyone during the course of the day.

9. *Praise employees.* He sent company-wide e-mails when some-one did something great. For example, one of the employees had the guts to tell their biggest client that they had to pay for changes or the company would be out of business. Management was afraid to tell the client this for fear of los-ing them. This employee rationalized that they wouldn't be around anyway if they continued to let this customer push them around.

10. *Empower employees.* Prior to his arrival, employees were afraid of being chewed out if they took a risk on a client's project that failed. He told employees that one of the reasons they weren't succeeding was because they weren't taking risks and that he would support them as long as he or their superior was informed in advance.

The employees, with no bonus or stock structure in place, stayed the course and attracted and retained other quality employ-ees. Because the debt was so cumbersome, my client decided to put the company for sale and in short order found two buyers. The employees are now part of one of the largest and most successful Web development companies in their region.

> They weren't taking risks and that he would support them as long as he or their superior was informed in advance.

How to Write a Marketing and Sales Plan

"Luck sometimes visits a fool, but never sits down with him."

—A German Proverb

Chapter 6

Writing a marketing and sales plan isn't just for Fortune 500 companies. Developing a well-thought-out marketing and sales plan is the best and quickest way to get a company out of trouble.

One of my clients thought a sales plan was photocopying names of companies from a regional business directory. He would then gather his salespeople and ask them to go after every company on the list. It was apparent to his salespeople that he had no strategy and their time would be wasted.

After he finished going through the list, I suggested he write a full sales/marketing plan so everyone's energies would be focused on the right prospects. He said he had no experience in writing such plans, so we worked together on developing a new plan.

> One of my clients thought a sales plan was photocopying names of companies from a regional business directory.

Marketing Plan Outline

My suggestion for a marketing plan is that it have the following twelve sections:

1. Executive Summary
2. Mission Statement
3. Competitive Advantage
4. Objectives
5. Sales Strategies
6. Marketing Services
7. Target Markets
8. Retention Program
9. Personnel
10. Competition
11. Launch Plan
12. Financial Projections

The following subsections describe each of the sections, and include examples.

Executive Summary

The executive summary is an overview of the plan that should be shared with everyone in the company. Everyone needs to know what the sales and marketing goals are and the plan for how they will be achieved.

Informed employees can sometimes help sales and marketing reach their objectives. A secretary at one of my client companies read her company's sales/marketing plan and realized that her brother's company would be an ideal client. She called her brother and asked him for the name of his marketing director and if her company could use his name in the introduction. He said yes and she reported to her boss that she had a contact that could yield potential business. Her boss passed the contact onto the head of sales and the company got a new client.

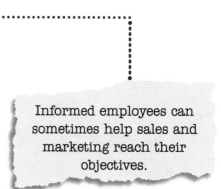

Informed employees can sometimes help sales and marketing reach their objectives.

Sample Executive Summary

American Vacuum Cleaner is a 200-person, 10-office private company that supplies commercial vacuum cleaners and vacuum supplies to Fortune 1000 companies. AVC is opening a Philadelphia office, where it hopes to generate $1 million in revenues within two to three years.

Purpose of Plan

This plan outlines a sales/marketing course that will allow AVC to increase its market share in the Greater Philadelphia Region.

History

The Philadelphia office of AVC is relatively new. The New York region serviced the Philadelphia region until the middle of 1996.

American Vacuum's Current Customer Base

Customers range in size from $1 million to billions in sales. They come from a variety of industries.

AVC's strengths and achievements include

- Highest number of sales for a purely industrial vacuum cleaner company over the last five years.
- Winning the prestigious Max Award for the best industrial-strength vacuum cleaner.
- Having the largest network of service groups throughout the United States.

Present

The Philadelphia office has only had one client—Ajax Machine Company— which bought five vacuums in 1997.

Goals

| Short Term: | Philadelphia AVC's goal is to bring in $1 million worth of new business by Year 2000. |
| Long Term: | Philadelphia's goal is to bring in $5 million in revenue by 2003. |

Mission Statement

The mission statement should describe the company's overall mission, but should focus solely on sales and marketing.

Sample Mission Statement

The mission of American Vacuum Cleaner is to be the leading provider and supplier of industrial vacuum cleaners and cleaner supplies in the eastern Pennsylvania, southern New Jersey, and Delaware regions. This means selling vacuum cleaners to medium-size and Fortune 1000 companies that have their own janitorial department and to janitorial companies focused on small- to medium-size businesses who outsource their cleaning needs.

The Competitive Advantage statement is crucial.

Competitive Advantage

The Competitive Advantage statement is crucial. It should address the clear competitive advantages that your company has over the competition. Competitive advantages can include better technology, quicker service, better quality service, wider coverage area, more experienced personnel, or cheapest price.

If you aren't sure what your competitive advantage is, ask your customers why they buy from you instead of the competition. Ask your salespeople why people buy from them instead of the competition.

Sample Competitive Advantage Section

American Vacuum has five competitive advantages, according to an independent customer survey:

- Longest lasting industrial vacuum cleaners
- Best industry repair response time
- Most elaborate warranty policy
- Best prices on vacuum cleaner supplies
- Easiest to use Web site for ordering vacuums and vacuum cleaner supplies

Objectives

The objectives of the region and/or company should be the same. The objectives should be developed by the management team and should be realistic. Objectives shouldn't be just centered on financial goals but should encompass personnel and other types of goals that will enhance a company's chances of being successful.

I had a client who told his management team that he forecasted the company would have $35 million in sales within five years. When asked how he arrived at that number, he said an investment banker he met at a conference said that $35 million would be the number his firm would need to see to take my client's company public. The number wasn't based on market opportunities or development of new products, just a number pulled out of the air by an investment banker.

> The objectives of the region and/or company should be the same.

Sample Objectives

Short Term: 1998–2000

Financial
- Develop $500,000 worth of new business in 1998.
- Develop $1 million worth of new business and develop $1 million from existing customers in 2000.
- Develop $3 million worth of new business and develop $2 million from existing customers in 2003.

Visibility
- Run six seminars that attract 180 new prospects.
- Appear six times in regional newspapers.
- Run a cleaning contest using AVC products.

> Hire two full-time maintenance people.

Personnel
- Hire two full-time former house appliance salespeople.
- Hire two full-time maintenance people.
- Hire one full-time secretary/office manager.

Long Term: 2003–2007

Financial
- Develop $6 million worth of new business and develop $3 million from existing customers in 2001.
- Develop $9 million worth of new business and develop $4.5 million from existing customers in 2002.
- Develop $13.5 million worth of new business and develop $6.75 million from existing customers in 2003.

Visibility
- Run 10 seminars per year that attract 300 new prospects.
- Appear 10 times in regional newspapers.
- Make the AVC competition a premier event for the cleaning industry.

Personnel
- Hire two more salespeople.
- Hire two more service people.
- Hire a full-time receptionist.

Sales Strategies

This section describes how you plan to sell your services/product. This section is developed by the head of sales and is based on the most successful sales techniques used by the company and competitors.

To find out your competitors' success secrets, read your trade journals and run advertisements for new salespeople. Often, your competitors' salespeople are looking for new opportunities because they might not feel appreciated, want a new challenge, or think they can make more money from a competitor who needs to improve their sales. When you interview these people, ask them to describe their sales process from start to finish. In this way, you can find out what successful organizations are doing.

Benchmarking this section of your plan against the best in your industry will improve your sales process and increase sales.

Sample Sales Strategies Section

The steps we will take to attract new customers are as follows:

First Step: Identify prospects. Identify the industries they are in and their geographic location should list prospects.

Second Step: Send letters to prospects. We will send a one-page letter to each prospective company along with our information packet.

Third Step: Make a telephone call. Each person who receives a letter from us will be contacted within 10 days of his or her package being mailed. The person following up will say the following:

"Good morning, I am Marc Kramer, a sales consultant in the Philadelphia office of American Vacuum Cleaner. I sent you a package last week and I wanted to make sure you received it. I would like to invite you to lunch to discuss your cleaning needs and see if we can be of assistance. What day and time would work for you?"

Fourth Step: Visit(s). When we visit target companies, we will be dressed in conservative suits and white shirts. We want to look professional and trustworthy.

> Benchmarking this section of your plan against the best in your industry will improve your sales process and increase sales.

Fifth Step: Proposal. We will send well-written proposals based on client needs and follow that up with a meeting to review the proposal and close the deal.

Marketing Services

This section provides information on how you will market the company to prospects and current customers. Writing or making blind telephone calls is an extremely difficult way to get sales. There are at least five sources you can speak with to try to get an introduction to a target company.

> Often, your vendor is selling his products to the same customers you have targeted and they have a contact within the organization.

- *Current customers.* Sometimes your customers have relationships with companies you are targeting because they either sell to them or buy from them.
- *Vendors.* Often, your vendor is selling his products to the same customers you have targeted and they have a contact within the organization.
- *Chamber of Commerce.* If your target company is a member of the local chamber of commerce, the chambers' staff should know someone in the organization and open a door for you.
- *Trade association.* If you belong to the same trade association, the trade association staff should be able to provide an introduction to the prospect for you. When I ran a trade association, many of our members were reluctant to ask us for an introduction. They didn't know if that type of request was appropriate. I told them that was part of the service they were paying for.
- *Accountant and lawyer.* One of your accountant's or lawyer's clients may be a target customer. If so, ask them for an introduction.

Don't be shy about using your network of contacts to open a door for you. If you are tactful and sincere in your approach, no one will mind you asking.

Sample Marketing Services Section

Marketing Package

- Brochure on products and services
- Client list
- Price sheet
- Client endorsement letters

Note: The package doesn't have to be crammed with material. We want people to actually read what we send and find it valuable.

Mass mailing to target audiences

- Postcards with Web site on it
- Letters to prospects with a copy of a client endorsement letter

Trade Shows

- Select Targeted Industries (For less targeted or general, drop off old brochures) ·····························

> Select Targeted Industries

Events to attend (Attended by decision makers and influencers)

- Chamber of Commerce luncheons and annual dinner
- Rotary luncheon and annual dinner
- Lions Club luncheon and annual dinner

Initial Sample Letter

John Smith
Head of Janitorial Services
AJAX Company
55 E. Lincoln Highway
Coatesville, PA 19320

Dear Mr. Smith:

I recently joined American Vacuum Cleaners as a sales consultant. I would like to show you how we can assist you in improving your work environment and saving you money. Our products are of the highest quality and our service has been highly rated in independent studies.

AVC is one of the largest sellers of vacuum cleaners and industrial cleaning products in the U.S. We started a quarter of a century ago and have 10 offices and 200 employees. AVC is privately held.

Enclosed is a package on our organization, descriptions of our products and services, and endorsement letters from some of our clients. I will call your office within the next week to discuss your participation in our seminar series.

Sincerely,
Marc Kramer
Sales Consultant

Success Seminar Series

Developing a quality seminar series will raise our visibility and put us in a position to bring and retain business.

Newsletter

We will develop a bimonthly newsletter that is in both electronic and paper form. The newsletter would provide new product, service, and cleaning information. AVC employees and clients will write the articles.

> AVC is one of the largest sellers of vacuum cleaners and industrial cleaning products in the U.S.

Target Market

This section provides a profile of target industries and the names of specific companies in each industry. Not every business can benefit from every service or product that is in the market. Most businesses believe their product/service can serve and are wanted by the masses, but in most instances that just isn't true.

For example, my father owns a one-man medical equipment firm in a small town outside of Philadelphia. One day he called me and told me a firm that develops Web sites contacted him and he wanted to know how he could benefit from this. The salesman told him he could reach new customers beyond the town he was in by having a Web site.

I asked him if the salesman quoted him a price for this service. My father said no, but said the salesman wanted to make an appointment to introduce himself and his company. Both the salesman and my father would have found the meeting a waste of time. My father receives most of his business through doctor referrals, and his market is a four-mile square radius of the town in which his store is located.

If the salesman had properly qualified my father's business, he wouldn't have called my father in the first place. Even if he wasn't sure of the size of my father's business, he could have eliminated my father from his prospect list by just asking him who he sold to, where his customers were located, and how he procured orders.

To make sure you are going after the right customers, make a list of everyone you would want to sell to. Ask yourself three question before contacting the potential customers:

- Do they need my product/service?
- Can they afford my product/service at the price I want to sell it to them?
- Am I covering too small or too large an area?

Take 10 to 20 percent of the list and contact them by telephone to see if they would be interested in your product or service. Whatever number of potential customers tells you they would be

> His market is a four-mile square radius of the town in which his store is located.

willing to buy your product at the price point you are suggesting, cut the number in half and that will give you a realistic picture of what your sales potential could be.

If you can afford to have an outside firm conduct a focus group with potential customers, you will be able improve your product offering and focus your energies on the right prospects. You should ask your prospect the following questions:

- Have you ever heard of XYZ Company, and what are your impressions?
- Who do you currently buy this product/service from?
- Who do you think provides the best product/service of this kind in this market place?
- What would cause you to do business with XYZ Company?
- How much would you be willing to pay for such a product/service?

> How much would you be willing to pay for such a product/service?

These are very important questions to ask. A friend of mine was running a CD-ROM game company and lamenting to me how disappointed he was in his sales. I asked him what impression the market had of his product. He told me they had never performed a customer or market survey. People were buying his games, just not as many as he had hoped.

I decided to visit a total of ten large and small stores in my friend's geographic area that sold CD-ROM games and ask the salespeople what they thought of the product. Only three out of ten stores had even heard of my friend's company. Two of the three who had heard of the company thought it had gone out of business. One out of ten actually sold the product.

I went back to my friend and told him what I found out. He was flabbergasted. He hired an expert in product marketing and his sales have improved.

Sample Target Marketing Section

Overall Profile:

A. Corporate:

- 25 or more employees
- Has a janitor or janitorial staff
- Spends $10,000 or more in vacuums and cleaning supplies

B. Janitorial Services:

- Ten or more employees
- Serves 20 or more accounts
- Spends $50,000 or more in vacuums and cleaning supplies

Primary Target Industries

Chemical & Petrochemical: Specialty lubricants, solvents, catalysts and reagents, plastic and other resins.

Target Companies

1. Arco
2. Betz Dearborn
3. DuPont
4. Henkels
5. Hercules
6. ICI Americas
7. PQ Corporation
8. Rohm & Haas
9. Sun Company
10. Sybron

> It is important to target your market rather than simply throw it in the water and see if it swims.

Traditional insurance companies that sell health and commercial insurance usually employ large numbers of people and traditionally outsource maintenance.

Target Companies:

1. Aegean
2. Aetna/U.S. Healthcare
3. AIG
4. Cigna
5. Chubb Group of Insurance Companies
6. Harleysville Insurance Group
7. Oxford Health Plan
8. Penn Mutual Insurance
9. Prudential
10. University of Pennsylvania Health System

> These companies either outsource maintenance or buy large quantities of cleaning supplies because of the need for keeping the facilities clean.

Biotechnology/Pharmaceuticals: Companies that develop and sell consumer drugs. These companies either outsource maintenance or buy large quantities of cleaning supplies because of the need for keeping the facilities clean.

Target Companies:

1. Astra Merck
2. Cephalon
3. Centocor
4. McNeil Pharmaceuticals
5. Merck DuPont
6. Merck & Company
7. Rhone Poulenc Rorer
8. SmithKline Beecham
9. United States Bioscience
10. Zeneca

Commercial banks: Contact the facilities managers.

Target Banks:

1. Bank of Boyertown
2. Commerce Bank
3. Downingtown National Bank
4. First Financial Savings Bank
5. First USA
6. First Union
7. Jefferson Bank
8. Mellon Bank
9. MBNA
10. PNC

Electronics companies: Many electronics firms either don't have facilities managers or they aren't empowered to make decisions regarding vendors and supplies. Therefore, we have to contact the chief financial officer, who is usually responsible for making such decisions.

Target Companies:

1. AMP
2. Ametek
3. CFM
4. Fisher & Porter
5. Integrated Circuit Systems
6. GMT Microelectronics
7. Liberty Technology
8. Mars Electronics
9. Phoenix Microwave Corp.
10. SubMicron Systems

Gambling houses: Contact the facilities managers.

> Many electronics firms either don't have facilities managers or they aren't empowered to make decisions regarding vendors and supplies.

Target Companies:

1. Bally's Park Place Casino Hotel
2. Caesar's Atlantic City
3. Claridge Hotel & Casino
4. Harrah's Casino Hotel
5. Resorts International
6. Sands Hotel & Casino
7. Show Boat Casino
8. The Grand
9. Tropicana Hotel & Casino
10. Trump Taj Mahal

Retention Program

Many companies take current clients for granted. They forget that their current customers already believe and support them. Telephone calls from clients can take days to be returned, unlike prospect calls that are returned right away. However, it is important to treat current customers as well as, if not better than, potential customers.

One of my clients was a trade association, and they were terrific at signing new members up, but they fell short in servicing the members. They had no program in place to make sure that current members felt that they were receiving value for their membership. I told my client that running a series of member breakfasts and lunches once a year would give his members an opportunity to let her know what they appreciate about the organization and what areas need to be improved. I also recommended having one person in the organization call each member company once every three months to make sure the member knew the organization was working in their interest and to make sure there were no problems.

My client followed this simple advice, and membership defections dropped by 80 percent in the first year the retention program was enacted.

> It is important to treat current customers as well as, if not better than, potential customers.

Sample Retention Program

Our client retention program includes the following steps:

- Contact our clients once a month to find out if they are happy with our service.
- Provide articles related to their industry.
- Invite new clients to meet with the AVC advisory board once a year.
- Host a yearly event as a way to thank clients.
- Buy four season tickets to the theatre to entertain big clients and solidify a long-term relationship.
- AVC's Web site will feature links to sites that have information related to the industrial cleaning industry.
- Provide semiannual, half-day technology and product updates.
- Solicit an annual formal review by each client. Half the clients will be interviewed in July and the other half in August. Each account executive will interview another account executive's clients to insure an impartial evaluation.

Personnel

Every executive agrees that the employee selection process and the ability to place people in positions in which they can succeed are as important as writing quality business plans. Unfortunately, the companies that find themselves in trouble don't take the time to think through the hiring process; instead, they're typically just looking to fill positions.

When discussing the filling of two sales positions, one of my clients told me to "just get a couple of bodies to fill the position." This client turned over his whole sales force once every six months. He didn't consider their experience, how they would fit into the company's culture, what types of skill sets they brought with them, and what size sales they were used to handling. He also didn't consider what the cost of training new people and lost opportunities were doing to his business.

> Solicit an annual formal review by each client.

Before hiring anyone, list the position's duties and responsibilities. Then write out what type of educational background, business experience, and skill set is needed for the position. Determine the salary and benefits package you are willing to offer and compare it to what other companies in your region are offering for similar positions.

Salary and benefits information can be obtained by contacting an international accounting or human resource firm. These firms run annual compensation surveys for every position in a company and provide data by region. You can also contact the local economist office of the Federal Reserve, which performs such surveys.

Delegate the responsibility of developing a position description to the manager to whom the new hire would report. Then ask other managers to review the description and make comments.

Sample Personnel Section

Account executives. We need to hire two people who have the following experience and skills.

Good verbal skills

- Three to five years of industrial cleaning product sales experience
- Minimum of a high school diploma
- Good verbal skills
- Dresses professionally
- Personable
- Team player

Receptionist/office manager. One of the most important positions because all clients and contacts interface with this person. Qualities we are looking for:

- Professional
- Well-spoken
- Organized
- Friendly

- High energy
- Willing to work more than 40 hours a week, which may mean staying late or taking things home
- Computer literate
- Minimal amount of supervision

Note: We want someone who can talk about the company intelligently if no one is available.

Competition

We have covered how to develop a competition section in a business plan in Chapter 2. There are three points we will stress here.

First, keep a file on each competitor, and every time you see an article or press release, pass it around to all of the appropriate people in the organization (sales, marketing, board of directors/advisors, and top management) so they know what the competition is doing. This will encourage you to constantly re-examine your sales, marketing, and product offering strategies.

Second, if you constantly read that your competition is getting a certain size or type of client, you will be able to determine if it makes sense to go after the same market. You can also use it as judo against your competitor when you're both finalists for a contract.

I had a client that noticed one of his major competitors was constantly getting pharmaceutical companies as clients. My client decided to stay away from pharmaceuticals and focus on the banking industry. This same client was in a final competition for a bank and reminded the prospect that the competitor was very knowledgeable about the pharmaceutical industry but didn't have any experience in the banking business. My client received the business.

Third, it gives you a good idea if you should target their employees in order to exploit the same market if you determine that is a market you want to get into.

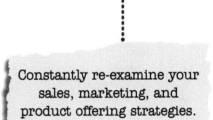

Constantly re-examine your sales, marketing, and product offering strategies.

Sample Competition Section
This section focuses on American Vacuum Cleaners' primary competitors and what their strengths and weaknesses are. This helps AVC better position itself with prospects and helps employees focus on what makes AVC unique.

Competitor	Strengths	Weaknesses
Jones Industrial Cleaners	Statewide Cash rich Experienced employees Good reputation Great client list Focused on Fortune 1000 companies	Expensive
Maxwell Vacuum	National Large middle-market client base Cash rich	Poor quality High employee turnover
Secondary Competitors	**Strengths**	**Weaknesses**
Act Cleaners	Quality staff Strong client list	Small staff Low margins
Core Corporation	Good products Good salespeople	Unfocused Poor service

Launch Plan

After putting on paper everything management believes it needs to do to be successful, management must develop a timeline for executing the plan. Writing a launch plan will keep the organization focused and moving forward. The president and/or chief operating officer should write the initial launch plan and have every manager review it to see if they can execute each part of the timeline.

Launch plans focus on dates, action items, and those who will carry out those action items. When reviewing the launch plan, management should verify they have the right staff and resources to succeed. Finally, management has to be realistic when reviewing and accepting the launch plan. If management is overly optimistic and the company doesn't come close to reaching its goals, employees will lose confidence in themselves and management. The trick is to develop a plan that is attainable but forces everyone to work harder and smarter than they did before.

Sample Launch Plan

This section describes how we plan to launch our marketing/sales program. The launch program is broken down by month and action items.

Month	Action Items
January	Approve sales/marketing plan.
	Run advertisement for two full-time sales executives.
	Run advertisement for one secretary/office manager.
	Line up joint venture partners for seminars.
	Send letters and packets to five companies on target list per week.
	Visit two target companies.
February	Hire two full-time sales executives.
	Hire one secretary/office manager.
	Select and approve topics for seminars.
	Send letters and packets to five companies on target list per week.
	Visit four target companies.
	Develop a semimonthly newsletter.
March	Run first event.
	Send letters and packets to five companies on target list per week.
	Visit eight target companies.
	Put together semimonthly newsletter.
April	Run second event.
	Send letters and packets to five companies on target list per week.

Line up joint venture partners for seminars.

	Visit eight target companies. Mail newsletter.
May	Run third event. Send letters and packets to five companies on target list per week. Visit eight target companies. Work on second edition of newsletter.
June	Run fourth event. Send letters and packets to five companies on target list per week. Visit eight target companies. Complete second edition of newsletter.
July	Run fifth event. Send letters and packets to five companies on target list per week. Visit eight target companies. Mail second edition of newsletter.
August	Send letters and packets to five companies on target list per week. Visit eight target companies. Begin planning for 1999. Begin third newsletter.
September	Run sixth event. Send letters and packets to five companies on target list per week. Visit eight target companies. Edit third newsletter.
October	Run seventh event. Send letters and packets to five companies on target list per week. Visit eight target companies. Mail third newsletter.

Visit eight target companies.

November   Run eighth event.
Send letters and packets to five companies on target list per week.
Visit eight target companies.
Begin fourth newsletter.

December   Run ninth event.
Send letters and packets to five companies on target list per week.
Visit eight target companies.
Edit fourth newsletter (the newsletter will be mailed in January).

Financial Projections

The final part of the plan is developing financial projections. Before management can enact its plan, it needs to determine what financial resources will be needed to accomplish the plan and what the projected results will be if the plan is successful. This is one section that management can't delude themselves about regarding what they can and can't afford.

The best tact to take is to overestimate expenses and underestimate income. Something always goes wrong that derails some part of the plan. A client I worked with projected getting three major projects from three new clients. One of those clients told them they would like to start in thirty days, but, unfortunately, the person in charge of the project was transferred and then her organization's mission was changed. The bottom line was that the project, which was projected to be 30 percent of my client's forecasted revenue, never came about.

Finally, break every expense down and see what can be eliminated. On the income side, cut your projects by 25 to 50 percent. A very successful client of mine drummed the following advice into his staff: "It's better to underestimate and overperform than overestimate and underperform."

> The best tact to take is to overestimate expenses and underestimate income.

Sample Financial Projections

Marketing Plan for Stein Media

REVENUE	YR 1	YR 2	YR 3	YR 4	YR 5
Revenue	$1,000,000	$3,000,000	$6,000,000	$9,000,000	$13,500,000
EXPENSE					
Manager	90000	94500	94500	94500	94500
Sales Executives	100000	105000	210000	210000	315000
Support Staff	25000	52500	52500	78750	105000
Tax and Benefits	146250	146250	146250	146250	146250
Packet Mailing	1500	1625	1750	1875	2000
Seminar Mailing	640	1536	1536	1536	1536
Seminar Cost	3000	3000	3000	3000	3000
CD-ROM					
Development Cost	25,000	0	0	0	0
Travel	18000	21600	42000	48000	75600
Telephone	3600	4500	9000	10500	16800
Memberships	5000	5000	5000	5000	5000
Total	$417,990.00	$435,511.00	$565,536.00	$599,411.00	$764,686.00
Profit Loss	$417,990	$2,564,489	$5,434,464	$8,400,589	$12,735,314

Partner	90,000	90,000	90,000	90,000	90,000
Pay Raise	1	1.05	1.05	1.05	1.05
Sales Executives	50,000	50,000	50,000	50,000	50,000
Pay Raise	1	1.05	1.05	1.05	1.05
No. of Salespeople	2	2	4	4	6
Support Staff	25,000	25,000	25,000	25,000	25,000
Pay Raise	1	1.05	1.05	1.05	1.05
No. of Consultants	1	2	2	3	4
Tax and Benefits	0.25	0.25	0.25	0.25	0.25
Packet Mailing	500	500	500	500	500
Postage	3	3.25	3.5	3.75	4
Seminar Mailing	200	400	400	400	400
No. of Seminars	10	12	12	12	12
Postage/fax	0.32	0.32	0.32	0.32	0.32
Seminar Cost	300	300	300	300	300
No. of Seminars	10	10	10	10	10
CD-ROM Development Cost	25,000	0	0	0	0
Travel	500	600	700	800	900
No. of People	3	3	5	5	7
No. of Months	12	12	12	12	12
Telephone	100	125	150	175	200
No. of People	3	3	5	5	7
No. of Months	12	12	12	12	12
Memberships	5000	5000	5000	5000	5000

How to Develop a Budget and Where to Save Money

"A penny saved is a penny earned."

—Benjamin Franklin

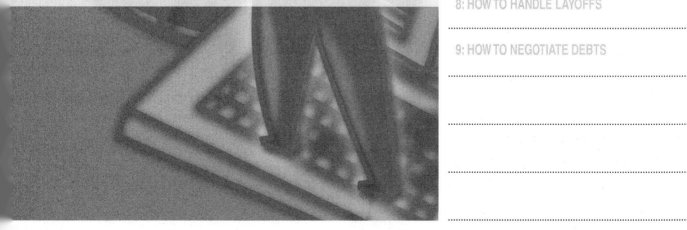

There are three reasons why companies get into financial trouble. First, they are under funded. Second, they spend money unnecessarily. Third, they can't sell enough products or services to make up for the lack of funds. Numbers one and three are the most common reasons for getting into financial trouble.

Business people who use their own money usually watch their company's expenses like hawks. The rare exception is the company founder who comes from a big company and is venture capital financed. These people can be dangerous to themselves and their company because they are used to large amounts of money being available. Here are two examples of companies that wasted a lot of money unnecessarily. Both were venture backed by large pharmaceutical companies.

The first company's founders used 3 percent of their capital to buy quality artwork because the founder said it put him in the right mood. The second company had an opportunity to buy an existing building three times the size of the building they were considering to rent. If they bought the larger building, they could have rented out the unused part of the building and basically used the building rent-free. Unfortunately, the founder opted to sign a ten-year lease for the rental building because it was ten minutes closer to his house and more architecturally pleasing.

Neither founder survived more than two years with the company they founded because the investors preferred management who viewed money as a scarce commodity.

> Unfortunately, the founder opted to sign a ten-year lease for the rental building because it was ten minutes closer to his house and more architecturally pleasing.

Ten Ways to Avoid Spending Money Unnecessarily

Here are ten ways to avoid spending money unnecessarily.

1. Develop a budget for each department.
2. Develop a list of what employees are allowed to purchase.
3. Know how much cash you have in the bank every day.
4. Read and approve each expense.

5. Stay on top of and try to collect as quickly as possible your accounts receivable.
6. Extend your accounts payable.
7. Barter for services and products.
8. Only buy things you absolutely need.
9. Ask every vendor for advice on how to save money on products you purchase from them.
10. Put out a bounty on internal savings by rewarding employees with 10 percent of whatever money they can save the company.

Sample Expenses to Reduce or Cut

Management must be diligent and well organized to ferret out unnecessary expenditures. The following is a list of unnecessary expense items that various clients of mine cut to save money.

Magazine Subscriptions. A client of mine once ran a company that had thirty employees and sixty-seven magazine subscriptions. Some people bought the same magazine twice. When she questioned them why they needed duplicate subscriptions, they stared at the floor and said so they wouldn't have to carry the extra paper in their briefcase. There are so many free subscription magazines available that this is one area you can save a nice amount of money. The company in this example was spending over $5,000 a year in magazine subscriptions, yet they couldn't afford to buy some much needed software and computers, which would pay for themselves by increasing productivity.

Telephone. The competition is so fierce that a company can always save money in this area, regardless of usage. One of my clients was paying fifteen cents a minute for long-distance charges from one of the top long-distance companies. He asked his controller to send out for bid their telephone bill. The result was a smaller company gave them a rate of nine cents, which translated into 40 percent savings; in this case the company saved $12,000 over the course of a year.

> Management must be diligent and well organized to ferret out unnecessary expenditures.

Mobile Telephone. This is an area that is widely abused, but usually unintentionally. A prudent client of mine told her employees that the company will only pay for calls to customers and prospects to tell them that they are running late or for some other emergency. As of the writing of this book, all the usage rates are basically the same, so the only way to save money is to instill discipline.

Leasing Companies. Most companies can't afford to buy all of the equipment they need to operate, so they lease equipment. Leasing is a very expensive form of financing. Shop around and look closely at three things before signing a lease: the rate of interest you are being charged, how much insurance they want you to carry or buy to protect their investment, and late penalties. Late penalties can sometimes cost as much as the lease itself. One of my clients decided to borrow money from his retirement plan, which he swore he would never do, and bought out the leasing contract he had signed because the interest rate he could pay himself was cheaper.

> Late penalties can sometimes cost as much as the lease itself.

Insurance. Every type of insurance policy should be reviewed and put out for quote each year. Insurers who have to pay out a lot of money to cover liabilities end up having to raise everyone's rates, even those who had no claim. Therefore, putting your insurance out for bid each year can guarantee the company paying the lowest premiums. If your company files none or just a few claims, another insurer will be glad to add your company to their pool and lower your premiums for lowering their risk.

Service Contracts. Service contracts usually aren't worth the money with the exception of copier service contracts. All of my client's experiences are that photocopiers breakdown often, and the service charges are usually exorbitant.

Memberships. Only keep memberships in organizations that have the potential to bring you business. Also, the only people who should be members initially are company salespeople. Watch out for duplicate organizational memberships and make sure someone is responsible for being the liaison between the company and the organization.

Many of my clients who were in financial trouble called organizations they wanted to join and asked them for reduced rates or requested to pay on a monthly basis. My clients told me it was rare they were refused this request.

Advertising. Unless the company is in retail, minimize or eliminate advertising. A client of mine who ran a large retail mall decided to eliminate advertising; the percentage of shoppers dropped by half within two weeks. One client of mine employed a simple advertising tracking system. He used the same coupon in each publication in which he advertised, but put a number in the corner of the ad to indicate which publication the ad came from. Once these coupons came back, my client was able to know which publications provided the best responses and was able to eliminate advertising in those publications whose responses were low or nonexistent.

Charity. Companies can be overwhelmed with solicitations from worthwhile causes. Unfortunately, management has to restrain itself and eliminate all but those important to one or two big clients. In a turnaround situation, even charity has to have a return on investment.

Business Supplies. Buy only what is needed and try to purchase things on sale. Have one person responsible for the supply closet; any person who wants a supply item must sign for it. This will give you valuable information on usage and who is using certain items.

One of my clients found that one person was using a lot of expensive computer disks. Their manager said they had to backup a project that required a lot of memory, and they could save the company a lot of money by erasing old disks used for former clients. My client asked why they weren't doing this already, and the manager said it was just a past policy of the former president to save everything. This requires a judgment call, but most times its best to reuse

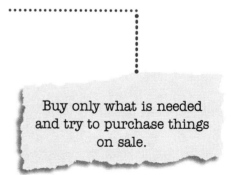

Buy only what is needed and try to purchase things on sale.

what you have unless you need to keep information for legal and/or contractual reasons.

Computers. Depending on the type of business you are in, you might not need a state-of-the-art computer system. Try upgrading what you have and make sure all equipment is being used to its fullest capabilities. One client's employees were so attuned to the company's financial situation that they started swapping parts out of old computers and reusing them. This saved the company a lot of money.

Travel. There are certain rules of travel people should follow. Never fly first class, unless the employee wants to pay the difference or has frequent flyer miles to cover the cost. If there are two airports within an hour to and hour and a half drive time, check which one offers the best rate. Flying to San Francisco from Philadelphia is 50 to 80 percent higher than flying out of Baltimore.

When attending a convention, always ask for the corporate rate at the hotel; never stay at the hotel booked by the convention. Usually hotels nearby a convention offer rates 20 to 50 percent below what a guest would have to pay for the convenience of staying in the convention's hotel. When visiting a Fortune 500 client, ask them for the hotel they use and if you can use their corporate rate. The savings can be significant.

When a company is in crisis mode, management needs to have every line item that represents $1,000 or more on a spreadsheet so managers can see where all of the company's money is going. Below is a sample of how to review expenses.

Check which one offers the best rate.

Breakdown Of Company Expenses Monthly and Yearly

	Position	Monthly	Yearly
Salaries		**39,168**	**470012**
Todd Thompson	Programmer	2,500	30,000
Jay Howell	Programmer	2,500	30,000
Jane Bowes	Programmer	2,500	30,000
Mike Smith	Programmer	2,500	30,000
Jim Dean	Programmer	2,500	30,000
Pat Jackson	Programmer	2,500	30,000
Randi Jones	Programmer	2,500	30,000
Bob Nies	Programmer	2,500	30,000
Mary Kramer	Controller	2,916	35,000
Jack Bozz	Sales Mgr	3,333	40,000
Lisa Powell	Sales	1.667	20,000
Gwen Rudd	Sales	1,667	20,000
Chris Isles	Production Mgr	3,333	40,000
Marc Kramer	President	6,250	75,000
Jean Mims	Secretary	1,667	20,000
Tax/Benefits		**9,792**	**117,503**
Business Supplies		**150**	**1,800**
Copier paper		50	600
Computer Disks		50	600
File Folders		20	240
Note Pads		20	240
Pens/Pencils		10	120
Computers/software		**1,393**	**16,716**
Accounting		42	500
Design		417	5,000
Marketing		100	1200
Server		417	5,000
General		417	5,000
Electric		**500**	**6,000**
Internet Connection		**2,000**	**24,000**
McMahon Communications Office		1,500	18,000
McMahon Communications Web Hosting		500	6,000

	No. of Subscriptions	Monthly	Yearly
Magazine Subscriptions	**No. of Subscriptions**	**400**	**4800**
Business Journal	5	33	400
Business Week	2	22	260
Entrepreneur	2	22	260
Forbes	2	22	260
Fortune	3	66	792
Inc.	1	2	24
Interactive News			
(free distribution)	12	0	0
Success	5	8	72
Wall Street Journal	1	100	1,200
Web Master	15	25	300
Web Today	15	50	600
Web World	15	50	600
Travel		**5,000**	**60,000**
Health Insurance		**8,750**	**105,000**
Business Insurance		**417**	**5,000**
Legal		**1,667**	**20,000**
Accounting		**833**	**10,000**
Advertising		**2,492**	**29,904**
Business Journal		1,083	13,000
County Business Review		542	6,500
State Cable TV		867	10,400
Marketing Materials		**484**	**5,808**
Brochures		250	3,000
Business Cards		67	800
Folders		167	2,000
Mail		**667**	**8,004**
Bills		16	192
Brochures		250	3,000
Business Letters		53	640
Event Invitations		333	4,000
Mail Machine		15	180

	Monthly	Yearly
Rent	**5,000**	**60,000**
Federal Express	**500**	**7,000**
Memberships	**292**	**3,504**
Chamber of Commerce	42	500
Internet Business Alliance	83	1,000
Rotary	42	500
Technology Council	1,25	1,500
Miscellaneous	**1,000**	**12,000**
Total	**79,172**	**950,059**

Once this spreadsheet is completed, the president should give it to all of his managers to review and ask them to come back with suggestions on what can be eliminated from the budget. Then give it to the company's accountant, controller, and board members and ask them for their suggestions on areas the company can save money. This will allow everyone to have input and point out anything that management may have missed.

At the end of this exercise, management will be surprised to know how much money was saved, and employees and board members will applaud management's leadership. The added benefit of this exercise is that it builds a stronger team and gives management a stronger respect for the value of money

Chapter 8

How to Handle
Layoffs

"Have you ever told a coal miner in West Virginia or
Kentucky that what he needs is individual initiative to go out and
get a job when there isn't any?"

—ROBERT F. KENNEDY (1925–1968)
U.S. Senator and Attorney General

Few, if any, turnarounds don't involve eliminating jobs. Turnarounds by their definition mean the company is losing money, which means costs have to be reduced as management finds a way to increase sales. The biggest expense in most businesses is people.

I've worked with presidents of large companies who have had to let people go as they downsize their company. They will tell you it isn't an easy decision, but one that has to be made if the company is to survive. These executives have told me it is a little easier in a large company because they haven't had an interaction with many of the people let go. Unfortunately for those being let go, they appear to be nothing more than a number on a balance sheet when the decision is being made.

Leaders of small companies usually know and see all of their people on a regular basis. They know their children, spouses, and their personal problems. They also know that many of the people they let go are hard workers, and circumstances beyond their control are going to temporarily turn their lives upside down.

Most people start a business because they want to create fun, financially rewarding opportunities for themselves and their communities. Entrepreneurs enjoy receiving accolades for creating jobs and making the community a better place to live. Next to going bankrupt, laying people off is the most humiliating and depressing part of running a business.

> They know their children, spouses, and their personal problems.

How to Prepare Yourself

Before laying anyone off, management needs to meet and go over what will be told to employees and how people are going to be dismissed. The following is the checklist many of my client's use before letting people go.

- Identify the people who are being let go and ask their managers who can assume the additional responsibilities.
- Put together a memo to give out to the employees outlining plans for the company.

- Select a date and time for a company meeting and put together a written outline on what management plans to discuss.
- Decide what date and time the president, department managers, or the head of human resources is going to meet with the laid-off employees. Employers always look good if they can provide some type of severance and health care coverage, and can assist people with finding a new opportunity. One of my clients always asked the people being laid off if he could assist them, and then he would write and call people he knew who might look to hire them.
- Write down a list of clients who might be affected by the layoffs and plan how you will explain the company's action to them.

It is normal to feel depressed and for management to share their disappointment with those being laid off. Management will feel it is letting the individual and their family down. For the short term, management will be on an emotional roller coaster.

How to Handle Those Being Laid Off

Managers should take the time to meet with each employee individually. Managers shouldn't be surprised at the range of emotions from the people being let go. Some employees will be angry, some will be shocked and, surprisingly, some will be relieved. When a company is not doing well, there are people who can't handle the stress, but they don't want their fellow workers to think they are abandoning the ship. They are happy to leave.

Management should show concern for their employees' well-being and tell the employees how they plan to help them out. The company's offer to help people being laid off will go a long way in mending fences and building loyalty with those who are staying. Management must take responsibility for the company's current situation and not blame the employees.

> It is normal to feel depressed and for management to share their disappointment with those being laid off.

One of my clients blamed everyone on his management team except himself, which polarized his relationship with his managers and the employees. The situation was so bad that he had to hire an outsider to manage the company for fear of losing the whole company.

Management should provide each employee with a reference letter and information on how they can take advantage of Cobra if they are eligible. Cobra is a federal law that requires companies with more than twenty employees to offer medical benefits to laid-off employees. The employees have to pay for these benefits.

Don't dispute the employee's right to collect unemployment so you can save money on unemployment insurance. Remember that you may want to bring back those same people when the company returns to profitability. Also, they could be potential customers or might still be able to refer business or recommend future employees. It's not prudent to make enemies of former employees.

> It's not prudent to make enemies of former employees.

Interview with Bill Macaleer, Thirty-Year Veteran in Human Resource Consulting

Bill Macaleer, a graduate of Princeton University, is the president of Growth Management Strategies in Great Valley, PA. Mr. Macaleer works with all sizes of companies and has a very strong small business practice. He has helped many clients work through the painful process of letting good people go and then trying to keep the surviving employees focused on staying and getting the company back to being successful.

What are the main reasons business owners terminate employees and what do I need to be aware of as a business owner/leader?

There are generally four situations that can result in the termination of an employee:

- Company-wide down-sizing or reduction in force (RIF)
- Unsatisfactory job performance
- Antisocial behavior or threats

- Supervisor has an occasional reactionary dismissal that occurs without warning

While each of these situations will call for some differences in approach and handling, most of the guidelines below will apply in all these incidents. The focus of your book is around a "turnaround," which indicates that approaching the termination issue as it relates to a RIF is what you basically are seeking.

Executives who are seeking guidance in how to conduct terminations will be concerned about

- Legal issues and possible threat of lawsuits
- Treating terminated employees fairly
- Impact on the remaining employees
- Impact on the business

Addressing these concerns begins before the termination meeting takes place. There are several areas that executives should pay attention to, in order to increase the chances of avoiding problems when employees have to be terminated.

Does a small company need to have written policies and procedures?

Absolutely! Have in place sound policies, procedures, documentation that will support the termination decisions when they occur. This is where most companies fail to properly protect themselves.

- Handbook or other policy documents that clearly outline the performance and behavior that is expected and what is not satisfactory that could lead to termination.
- Performance review program that is regular, fair, consistent, and thorough.
- Means for employees to address and correct problems and criticisms before termination

> Have in place sound policies, procedures, documentation that will support the termination decisions when they occur.

- If the termination is the result of disciplinary action, insure that any progressive disciplinary steps were closely followed and documented
- Records and documentation to enable a review of past terminations, trends, issues that occurred and the impact of current terminations on age or gender discrimination or other compliance-related issues.
- Trained managers and supervisors who know how to handle a termination without putting the company at undue risk.
- Termination procedures, checklist, forms in place prior to the event, communicated and understood by those who will be implementing terminations.
- Reviewing labor, employment or other agreements to insure there aren't violations of terms of those agreements when the termination is implemented.

How do you prepare yourself and the employees when you plan to lay people off?

I would recommend the following steps:

- Develop sound business reasons for the decision to implement a RIF and develop clear communication tools to be used during the process.
- Document business goals and objectives to be accomplished as the result of the RIF.
- Review any possible alternatives to having a RIF and document in case challenged. Such alternatives might include: early retirement plans, restructuring debt, bringing inside activities that were outsourced, having a voluntary severance plan, put a freeze on hiring, reducing wages and benefits, reducing work hours, allowing unpaid leave or sabbaticals or temporary shutdowns.
- Analyze all job activities and identify jobs or job functions that can be eliminated or consolidated into other jobs and carefully document.

> Develop sound business reasons for the decision to implement a RIF and develop clear communication tools to be used during the process.

- Identify the core competencies and essential job functions that the company must have to meet its strategic goals.
- Determine what is your qualified employee pool from which to draw the core competencies needed and the criteria that is essential for future performance.
- Evaluate and rank employees in accordance with the competencies and essential job functions needed. Use sound criteria such as performance standards, productivity, variety and level of skills or potential for training, attendance, and disciplinary records.
- Have the rankings thoroughly reviewed by more than one executive to ferret out any biases or favoritism, minimize circumstantial undocumented information or unforeseen business reasons, and insure overall fairness.
- Develop and have legal review of the waiver to be used in exchange for consideration given by the company to the terminated employee.
- Develop and conduct the RIF plan so it is consistent with the company's stated goals and documented rationale.
- Review the RIF plan with appropriate managers and supervisors on a confidential, "need to know" basis and insure they are properly trained to be able to assist with the implementation of the RIF.
- Strategize carefully about the notification day and carefully prepare what you are going to communicate.
- Be prepared to treat the employee as well as possible, offering whatever economic assistance (severance, benefit continuation) as is feasible and whatever help you can in terms of the job search (possible leads, contacts, and outplacement assistance.)

What are the guidelines for an actual termination meeting?

- Conduct the notification in person in a private meeting at a place where others cannot observe what is happening.

> Strategize carefully about the notification day and carefully prepare what you are going to communicate.

- Communicate clearly with the employee. Be forthright and open while at the same time protecting the employee's dignity and privacy.
- Give defensible reasons for the termination and be sure to avoid any perception that the manner in which the employee was treated was unfair. Do not make or imply any accusations or threats even if threatened.
- Be prepared to deal with employee's feelings in a calm, understanding, but professional manner.
- Watch your attitude and body language so you do not send the wrong message.
- Maintain good eye contact.
- Ask open-ended questions that encourage the employee to talk about their concerns and feelings.
- Be a good, attentive listener and summarize what you heard the employee say from time to time.
- Be sure the employee has ample opportunity to have their say.
- Be appropriately empathetic but do not say your are sorry.
- Overlook and do not address verbal attacks, accusations, exaggerations, or sarcasm.
- Control your emotions as best as possible while appearing sympathetic and helpful.
- Maintain focus on the long-term goal to manage an effective termination that minimizes risk of violence or lawsuit.
- Focus on the termination issue and establishing goals for the individual.
- Observe behavior and points made and document after the meeting.
- Help the employee remain calm and focused on what needs to be done for the future.
- Discuss practical matters such as return of records, equipment, keys.
- Talk about the final paycheck or how severance pay will be handled.

> Maintain focus on the long-term goal to manage an effective termination that minimizes risk of violence or lawsuit.

- Discuss any benefit continuation and how that will be handled.
- Carefully direct the discussions toward what the employee needs to do for the future in those instances where the employee wants to dwell on the past. Give guidance on how the employee can take control of the situation and what is in the individual's best interests.
- At the end of the meeting summarize your understanding of what has taken place and any identified action items that you and the individual must do.
- Discuss and decide how telephone calls and correspondence to the terminated employee will be handled, when they are to vacate their work area, terms for coming back onto the premises, how references will be handled, how outplacement or other assistance will be handled.
- Discuss any waiver and other forms that will be required as part of the termination. Provide copies and give the employee time, separate from the meeting, to review and discuss with an attorney if needed.
- Make sure the employee has no further questions.
- Identify whom the employee can contact if they have questions or concerns. This is especially important if it becomes evident during the meeting that the employee is too upset to think logically about the future.

How should business leaders deal with the remaining employees?

Attention needs to be paid to the remaining employees, moving the organization forward, and insuring the objectives of the RIF are achieved and the problems that resulted in the need for the RIF are overcome. This is another area where many executives do not do an effective job because they become so involved in the problems of the business.

> Identify whom the employee can contact if they have questions or concerns.

- Meetings of the remaining employees should be held either companywide or by department. The surviving employees need to be recommitted.

- Explain the reason for the RIF and the business changes that are taking place.
- Outline the goals that you are attempting to achieve and the new direction or mission of the company.
- Establish a communications vehicle with the remaining employees so they can have concerns and questions addressed and resolved quickly.
- Delegate and empower employees to support and assist in achieving the goals. Create special team-based or quality circle programs where appropriate.
- Carefully review and implement the consolidation of jobs or departments to avoid conflicts or confusion. Effectively explain changes and allow employees the opportunity to provide feedback.
- Be reassuring. Find ways to overcome resistance to change and paralysis caused by fear of what is happening. Train your managers and supervisors to look for signs and take corrective actions.

If I need to let people go, what should and shouldn't I say to them?

See previous comments in point 3, guidelines for the termination meeting. Above all, keep it simple and as positive as possible. *Your services are no longer needed. The company appreciates your service and contribution. (If not for cause) We would be pleased to provide a reference (if not for cause). Business demands require we make some staffing reductions. This is not a reflection on you or your fine performance while employed with us. We want to make that very clear.*

Do I need a witness present?

Yes, it always a good idea to have a witness present, especially if there is the possibility that the termination meeting might not go smoothly. Have the human resources person or the executive with HR responsibility present, if not another officer or member of the Board.

> Keep it simple and as positive as possible.

Do I need to write anything?

There is no requirement to have a written document but we recommend:

- A termination letter is prepared outlining the terms of the termination and referring to benefits related requirements, final pay, any severance to be paid, return of company property, keys etc. (We use a termination checklist to develop a letter and prepare for the meeting).
- A script is prepared for what will be said, not to read from, but as a reference. It can even be bullet items to be covered during the termination interview.

Are there any types of legal forms I need to fill out?

Not really. There will be a notice you will receive from Unemployment, which will ask for some basic information about the nature of the termination, and if you are going to dispute the unemployment claim. There is a requirement to send out certain information relative to COBRA (continuation of medical benefits) and a time schedule when this must go out. Notification to any insurance or benefit providers about the termination also should be sent.

Are there any types of documents I have to have my former employee fill out?

- COBRA forms for continuation of medical benefits
- Any forms required for withdrawal from a 401(k), pension, savings, credit union, or similar plan

Am I required to give them a severance package?

No, there is no legal or statutory requirement to do so.

If I want to provide a severance package, what should be in it and how much money should I pay?

This is an economic question and will depend on what the company can afford. Many organizations will give a minimum of two

> Notification to any insurance or benefit providers about the termination also should be sent.

weeks. A rule of thumb is one to two weeks for each year of service up to a cap based on the company's economic situation and the goals for the RIF.

Do noncompetes remain intact when you let someone go?

This is a legal question. The company should emphasize with the departing employee that there is a noncompete agreement. However, conventional wisdom is that they are not very enforceable when a company lets someone go, especially if it is for poor performance.

It is a good idea to attempt to get a waiver agreement signed by the terminated employee in exchange for consideration (severance etc. but not any benefits for which they would otherwise be entitled). This waiver should reinforce the terms of the noncompete agreement as well as waiving certain rights to sue the company. Such a waiver should be knowing and voluntary. It should have legal review before presentation to the employee. The waiver can waive any existing or past rights but not any rights that may arise in the future after the termination. It should definitely include a specific waiver under ADEA (Age Discrimination Act).

Should I have a meeting of all employees after the termination and what should I say?

See point 4 above about getting remaining employee's recommitted.

If the individual is a key person, or if just one individual is terminated, it probably does not make sense to call a meeting and make the event more important than it is. If there is a general downsizing, then a meeting of the survivors is very much in order. They will want some assurances that the other shoe is not going to drop and what the future holds for them and the company.

> If there is a general downsizing, then a meeting of the survivors is very much in order.

How to Handle the Survivors

Laying people off affects more people than those being let go. The survivors are upset at seeing their colleagues go. Initially, the employees are in shock, then shock becomes anger and anger changes to mourning. They blame management and they don't want to hear excuses.

More importantly, they want to know what management is going to do for their colleagues and how management plans to fix the problems. When management addresses the remaining employees, they need to say positive things about those being let go and accept blame for the current circumstances.

Employees need to be permitted to ask questions and vent their frustration. One client made the mistake of not allowing people to voice how they felt and ask questions. It was an enormous misjudgment on her part, because people thought she was cruel and heartless. The people she wanted to keep started sending out their resumes.

Once everyone has had a chance to voice their opinions, tell them that management and the board has developed a turnaround plan. Show them a copy of the finished or draft plan. Let them know everyone will be getting a copy to review and that the next company meeting will take place within a week to discuss the contents of the plan.

Encourage people to come armed with questions and suggestions about the plan. Management's door should be open and employees should be encouraged to speak to their superiors in private if that is more comfortable for them than speaking in a public forum. Remember that layoffs are traumatic and the psychological damage takes time to heal, so management must be patient.

What to Say to Vendors and Customers

Don't think for a minute that the company's vendors and customers aren't going to find out what is going on. The old saying that "good news travels fast and bad news travels faster" is absolutely true. Management will be surprised when it receives calls from vendors and customers wanting to know if the rumors of the company's imminent demise are true, before management has even told the employees.

> Remember that layoffs are traumatic and the psychological damage takes time to heal, so management must be patient.

The vendors are going to be concerned about being paid, and customers will want to know if they need to find a new vendor. The best response is to be proactive with both groups. Let them know that the company is going through a difficult period, but that management has made changes in the business that will return it to profitability.

Management must be honest, sincere, humble, but confident. These two groups are going to listen for panic in the voices and written correspondence they hear and receive from management. Any message of doubt will send them scurrying for lawyers and calling new vendors.

Handling Negative Comments from Competitors

Management has no control over what competitors say.

There isn't a lot management can do about negative comments made by its competitors. Competitors will see this as a time to put the company out of business or at least cripple the company so it is no longer a threat. The only course of action is to focus on the current problems and focus on increasing revenue. Management has no control over what competitors say, but management does have control over its own reactions.

Chapter 9

How to Negotiate Debts

"If you think nobody cares if you're alive, try missing a couple of car payments."

—Earl Wilson (1907–1987)
American newspaper columnist

Once a company runs into trouble, management can bet there are a lot of people standing in line waiting to be paid. When money becomes scarce, leaders of troubled companies usually just pay the employees, the rent, electric, telephone, health insurance, and the banks. Notice that I didn't say they paid the taxing authorities. No matter how many stories people read about what can happen to individuals and companies that don't pay their taxes, owners of small companies feel they are either so small that no one will notice and/or by the time they do the company will be back on track.

I have consulted with two companies that owed a mound of debt to outside investors and taxing authorities and survived to tell about it. Here are stories of two companies who got into serious trouble and how they managed to pull themselves out.

Example One: Simple Turnaround

My client was a thirty-year-old charismatic visionary who was a former world-class athlete. He ran a small mall made up of 200 mom-and-pop stores that sold everything from quilts made in the Pennsylvania Dutch Amish country to leather jackets for motorcyclists, as well as antiques.

When my client had taken over the mall, it was 60 percent unoccupied and the landlord was sure he was going to have to close it down and possibly sell the land to commercial developers. There were two resort hotels within walking distance of this mall that catered to people from New York, Northern New Jersey, and the New England area who wanted to visit historic sites like Valley Forge and the Brandywine Battlefield. These out-of-town guests also liked to shop and buy unusual or hard-to-find items like homemade doll lampshades, shoofly pie, and old music records.

John, who came from New York, thought if he could populate the mall with a variety of unusual stores and colorful shop owners, his fellow New Yorkers would open up their wallets and spend money. No one could sell the dream better or spend money quicker than John. He refurbished the mall, bought himself a company car

> My client was a thirty-year-old charismatic visionary who was a former world-class athlete.

—a Jaguar—charged handmade suits to the company, and took cash out of the safe to go to the casinos.

Although the mall was filled to capacity and practically all of the tenants were paying their rent, the company was losing money and not paying its vendors. John hated the day-to-day details of running the business. He liked being the free-spending entrepreneur, so he hired someone, Mary, to manage the business.

The first day on the job, Mary was handed a stack of bills and told no vendors will deliver anything because the company owed them all money. John wasn't available for Mary to speak with because he decided to take a two-week vacation with his girlfriend in Europe. Mary asked the bookkeeper if John had spoken to these people. The bookkeeper explained that when they called John didn't return their calls, and for those who came in person he turned on the charm and told them they would receive a check by the end of the week.

The mall needed light bulbs and other maintenance products, so Mary thought she would try to develop relationships with other vendors until John got back. Apparently, John's reputation for not paying people got around town and no one would do business with the mall. People were hanging up on Mary as soon as she said where she was from.

Mary's grandfather, who owned many businesses during his lifetime, had once told her that he ran into a similar problem during the Depression. He described to Mary how he contacted all of his vendors and told them he wanted to go on a payment plan. She looked at her cash flow and realized that with a few adjustments she could pay the vendors off within three months. It just required a little belt tightening.

Mary sent a letter to all of the vendors inviting them to lunch to tell them about the changes that were taking place and how they were going to be paid back. All of the vendors called and said they would attend. At the meeting, Mary acknowledged their right to be angry and that she understood why they were unwilling to give the company any additional credit. She showed them simple financial projections of where the company was that day and where it would be by the end of the quarter.

> Apparently, John's reputation for not paying people got around town and no one would do business with the mall.

Mary was lucky in the sense that her problem was occurring just as the Christmas season was beginning, so all of the empty space would be leased and merchants would be paying additional fees because the mall would have extended hours. Before the vendors left, Mary gave each of them a one-third deposit on the balance of their bill and made sure the company paid the rest on time. Not one of the vendors elected not to continue providing the mall with supplies and service after receiving their first payment and hearing about the mall's plans.

The next hurdle was to convince the bank that the company was a good risk. In the past, if Mary couldn't afford to pay the bank the entire monthly sum she owed, she didn't send them anything. Banks will work with companies to a point because they don't want to write off a loan or take over the business. They want to see a plan for repayment and are more concerned about the company paying the interest on the loan than paying the principal because that is how they make their money. Banks will even consider recapitalizing the loan by stretching out payments to decrease the monthly payment the company has to pay. Mary worked with her bankers to recapitalize her loans, which they were glad to do rather than having to takeover Mary's business.

Finally, after having made sound payment arrangements with suppliers and creditors, the new manager was able to convince her boss to go on a financial diet and the mall continued to be a success.

Example Two: Complex Turnaround

Another client of mine was the owner of an interactive multimedia company. She tried to expand without having the necessary capital for expansion. Also, some of the projects the company had taken on were mismanaged, which lead to cost overruns. This client, who we will call Sally, hired an experienced manager named Sam. As soon as Sam stepped into his office the bookkeeper gave him a list of thirty-five vendors to whom the company owed money.

In addition to owing vendors money, the company made a critical mistake of not paying its federal employee taxes and using the

> Banks will even consider recapitalizing the loan by stretching out payments to decrease the monthly payment the company has to pay.

money as working capital. This is one of the biggest mistakes a company can make. Regardless of whether or not the company is incorporated, the government can shut the business down and sell the assets to pay off back taxes. If the assets aren't sufficient, the government can sell the owner's personal assets.

Even worse, banks become very leery of lending money to people who, in the bank's view, are trying to defraud the government. Using tax money to pay off creditors unfortunately isn't unusual. There are numerous businesses that do this and most end up being forced out of business.

Within days of Sam's arrival, he was inundated with telephone calls from irate vendors who wanted to know when they would be paid. Working with the former chief operating officer, who became chief technical officer, Sam determined that he needed to restructure the company from top to bottom. The owner of the company was only too glad to wash her hands of the matter because she didn't have the experience to know what to do with the situation she created.

Sam put together a five-step plan that he went over with the management group. The plan called for eliminating 40 percent of the workforce, closing a satellite office, selling one of their divisions, and not spending one penny on anything new. It would be painful he told them, but the company would survive and hopefully turn around within twelve months. Everyone liked the plan, except the owner. The plan would dismantle everything she had built over the last year, but her future depended on this turnaround being a success.

First Step: Meet With Employees

Sam gathered all of the employees together and gave them the brutal truth about the company's current position. He went on to tell them that the mistakes that were made were a classic example of company growth outpacing available capital, but that management had a plan to fix the company.

One employee asked if they would be getting paid, and another asked if management would have to let anyone go. Sam told him that everyone would be paid and that management was looking at options

> She didn't have the experience to know what to do with the situation she created.

in terms of restructuring the company. Sam didn't want to say, at that point, he would be laying people off because he didn't want a mass exodus.

Second Step: Letter to the Vendors

It is very important to communicate with everyone the company owes money to and let them know the company isn't going out of business. Vendors will work with management if management keeps them informed of the company's plans and progress and pays something toward the debt. It is important to communicate with vendors so they don't file lawsuits and force the company into bankruptcy.

Filing for bankruptcy is something management wants to avoid at all costs, especially if the company is small. The legal and accounting fees could put the business under. In midsize and large companies for which there are significant assets to sell and management is trying to buy time, this strategy may make sense. For small companies, filing for bankruptcy is not good under any condition because once the company files for bankruptcy it is placed under someone else's control. Even with today's enlightened attitude about bankruptcy, there is a negative stigmatism.

The letters sent to vendors should be short and simple and provide them with the opportunity to directly communicate with management if they have any questions. Below is a sample letter one of my clients used:

> For small companies, filing for bankruptcy is not good under any condition because once the company files for bankruptcy it is placed under someone else's control.

Joe Smith
President
Smith CD-ROMs
111 Smith Way
Jonesville, PA 19000

Dear Joe:

You have been a terrific vendor and I am sorry we are behind in paying you. Unfortunately, you are not the only vendor we owe money to. We made the classic entrepreneurial mistake of expanding too quickly without having the proper capital to support our growth. You may have gone through something similar during your business career.

We intend to pay you back. What we would like to do is pay you over a period of one year at a rate of 10 percent interest. Enclosed is our first payment. We will attempt to send you a check each month. If we financially can't pay you something or at all, I will personally call you to let you know.

I think it will be a waste of time for you to employ a lawyer to sue us for what is owed, because that will force us into bankruptcy and only the lawyers make money in those situations. You should also know that we owe the federal government back taxes as well and we will be working out a payment plan with them. This may affect the timing of our payments to you, but I will keep you informed.

If you would like to discuss this with me in person or have any questions, please give me a call. I also will be glad to show you our books so you are comfortable with what I am telling you. Thank you in advance for your patience and understanding. You can count on our business when we get out of this unfortunate mess.

Sincerely,
Sam Wilson
President

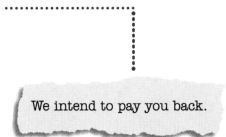

We intend to pay you back.

The key is in keeping management's promise of constant communication and returning telephone calls. Most people understand and some will even help the company try to find additional business because that will benefit them. Any vendor who has been through a similar situation will appreciate what management is going through and will applaud their sincerity and honesty.

The company owed money to over thirty-five vendors and not one took the company to court. Sam even received letters of thanks from people once they received all of their payments. The worst action a manager can take is to hide because that makes people nervous and they start dialing for their lawyers. Management should focus its energies on bringing in revenue and building lasting relationships, not taking depositions and liquidating company assets.

> Sam elected to tackle the vendors first because there were so many of them and he wanted to minimize the damage they can do by informing others.

Step Three: Working with the Government

You might have thought the first people Sam contacted would be the government, based on what they can do to a company and the individuals running the company. However, Sam elected to tackle the vendors first because there were so many of them and he wanted to minimize the damage they can do by informing others of the company's situation and dragging management into court.

Although he wasn't surprised that the company was using government money to fund itself, Sam was shocked to learn that this had been going on for six months and the owner had no plan on how she was going to pay back taxes. Sam told the owner he wouldn't be surprised if the Internal Revenue Service were preparing to shut her down as they spoke.

The government wants to be paid, but it also doesn't want to see a company go bankrupt. More importantly, the government doesn't want the negative publicity of having to force a company into bankruptcy and cause people to lose their jobs. Therefore, the government is willing to work with management, but management has to be reasonable.

As soon as Sam knew the company owed the Internal Revenue Service money, he drove to their office and met with one of their caseworkers. The IRS is very receptive and accommodating when management comes to them first. Most people hope the IRS either never catches them or, in the case of Sam's employer, they hope revenues allow them to catch up. The latter thinking is quite common, but not acceptable to the IRS.

The IRS agent Sam worked with was very experienced at handling these types of situations and asked for copies of the company's accounts receivables and payables. Then she asked if Sam had a business plan that demonstrated how management was going to turn the company around.

After she received the plan and read it, she asked Sam to go over it with her and her boss. For three hours Sam went over every detail of the plan and discussed a payment schedule. She told Sam that the owner had no credibility with her because the owner didn't come to her shortly after the problem occurred. If Sam left now, the caseworker said, they would close the company down.

Sam had the company make a good faith payment. Because the IRS agent trusted Sam, she put no liens on the assets of the business, thereby allowing management to find financing. Three months into the payment process, Sam knew he was going to be late or only able to make a partial payment. He notified the agent handling their case immediately, and she told Sam to pay what he could and make up for it next month.

Later that year, Sam had to initiate a payment plan with the state and local taxing authorities because he couldn't afford to pay these two taxing authorities in addition to the IRS and the vendors. Because Sam contacted the state and local authorities and let them know about the company's situation. They too were patient and agreed to work out a payment plan.

> Because the IRS agent trusted Sam, she put no liens on the assets of the business.

Step Four: Informing the Clients

Management doesn't want its clients to hear from someone else, especially a competitor, that the company is on shaky ground. Sam's company had blue chip clients, the kind that becomes nervous if they think a vendor can't deliver what was promised. Sam's business took deposits on work that would be done in the future for clients. Once clients found out that Sam's business was in trouble, they were concerned that their money was gone and they wouldn't receive any service for the money they prepaid.

Sam used the same process with his clients that he did with his vendors. He called all of them first and then followed up the calls with letters. He told each client that his or her money was safe and that the company just had a temporary setback. Each client received a quick briefing on the turnaround plan and the offer to review the company's financial records.

Step Five: Informing New Vendors

Sam believed in being totally honest with everyone. Because the company was well known in the industry, it had a lot of vendors calling to do business. Sam told new vendors whose product or service the company could use up front about the situation, and if they wanted to do business with the company, great. Not one vendor turned Sam down; since Sam was informing them up front, they knew they could trust him.

> Sam was informing them up front, they knew they could trust him.

Final Comments

The bottom line in negotiating debt is trust and consistency. If creditors believe management and management backs up its assurances by making payments on time or by informing creditors of difficulties, creditors will typically work with you. When dealing with debt, management should always put itself in the shoes of its creditors and act accordingly.

Preparing for the Future

Summary of Part III

This final section provides insights into:

- **Building sales through traditional and non-traditional means**
- **Attracting outside board members**
- **Attracting new capital**

Client Audit

"We view a customer who is complaining as a real blessing in disguise. He or she is someone we can resell."

—Louis Carbone (1905–)
Vice President, National Car Rental Agency

Chapter 10

10: CLIENT AUDIT

She called her two account executives in and asked them why wasn't she told about the unhappiness of these large and long-standing customers.

Joan Jones was the president of a small temporary employment agency called JJ Temporary Services. Jones's agency supplied secretaries and other types of clerical help to companies in her region. Over a period of five years she grew out of her home office to an office on Main Street. Her sales went from $50,000 her first year to $1 million in her fifth year.

Everything appeared to be going well when her bookkeeper walked in one day and told her that four of their top five clients were unhappy and were not planning to renew their contracts. These four clients represented 60 percent of the company's business and 40 percent of the company's profits.

Joan asked her bookkeeper why she hadn't heard about this before. She called her two account executives in and asked them why she wasn't told about the unhappiness of these large and long-standing customers. The two account executives said they were as surprised as Joan was. They admitted they were so busy trying to bring in new business that they hadn't spoken to their existing customers in a long time.

Joan asked them when the last time was that they spoke to the customers who were leaving them. Both account executives said it was at least eight to twelve weeks ago. Joan asked the bookkeeper if the temporary people whom they placed with the client knew about the client's displeasure. She said she didn't communicate with the assigned employees other than to collect their time sheets and process their checks.

Joan called the clients and asked them why they weren't retaining her firm's services and would they reconsider. The clients said they felt neglected and that it appeared to them that Joan was only interested in getting new clients and not keeping the old ones happy. Joan asked them what could she have done differently and the clients told her that the account executives, Joan herself, or someone in the organization should have called just to see how things were going more than once a quarter.

Anyone who has been in business for any length of time knows that it is easier to retain and grow with existing clients than it is to bring in new clients. Experienced business people know that retaining clients is essential to getting new clients because it sends a message to prospects that you provide quality service. Income from existing clients also allows you to recruit new clients.

Obviously, Joan knew what she was doing because the business kept growing, but the question is what could she have done differently to make sure she kept her hand on the pulse of her existing clients. There was no reason Joan should be in jeopardy of losing her long-standing clients since they were willing to retain her services when she had no credibility and was just getting started.

Business owners are used to having outside accountants audit their books to make sure they know what clients are paying them, how long it takes clients to pay, what the company is spending money on, and whom they are spending it with. Business owners need to "audit" their clients to make sure they are happy and will continue to buy from the company. An outside firm should perform a "client audit" so clients can see that the company is serious about wanting their input to improve their product/service. Clients are more apt to give their honest opinion to an independent party than they will directly to the company that supply their product/service for fear of offending the company.

Ten Questions to Ask Clients

Audits should be short and focus on only the most significant issues the business needs answers and guidance on. The following are ten questions and the reasons why companies need to know the answers in order to retain business.

1. What is your impression of the company?

This is important to know because the answer to this question will tell you where you stand with your customer, what kinds of projects they might use or not use you for, and if they plan to continue to use you or someone else.

> Clients are more apt to give their honest opinion to an independent party than they will directly to the company that supplies their product/service for fear of offending the company.

2. How often do you speak to your account representative?

You may be under the impression that your account representatives are speaking to their clients between once a week and once a month when the client is lucky to hear from the account representative once a quarter.

Many accounts are lost not because the quality of the product wasn't good, but because the client feels neglected. How many marriages have gone up in flames when one spouse feels they are doing a good job and then the other asks for a divorce? Perception is reality.

> Perception is reality.

3. How would you rate the quality of the product/service?

You may think the quality of product/service is top notch while your client may feel it is fair.

4. How does the company compare to your other vendors in terms of quality of service?

This is a follow-up to question three. This question gives you insight into what your client views as quality and why. A physician practice that I was advising was losing patients, not because their bedside manner was poor but because a competing practice offered Sunday hours and had a Web site that provided answers to a variety of questions that didn't require calling a doctor and waiting for an answer. Patients felt the competing practice was doing more to make their lives easier.

5. Do you feel the company goes out of its way to keep your business or just does enough to fulfill your needs?

One of my clients was surprised to hear from a long-standing client that the only reason they bought from them in the past was that they were the only game in town. Once a competitor arrived that was willing to provide a comparable product at a similar price, my client started to lose business. When the client finally spoke to his customers, the customer felt everyone in the company had an attitude that the customer was lucky to be getting service at all because they were the only company that offered this particular product.

6. Are you driven by price over quality when making purchases?

Everyone will say they want a good product at a good price, but we all know that there are organizations where price is more important than quality. I have seen companies spend millions of dollars on advertising a Web site and then spend very little on its development. You need to know so you can decide whether to adjust your price or drop the client.

I had a client who wanted a price that was lower than we could afford to give. I introduced the client to a smaller company that could do it for them at the price they wanted and would give us a finder's fee for making the introduction and helping close the sale.

7. What could the company offer or do that would be valuable to you?

Asking your clients what you could offer will tell you what their needs are, what new opportunities you can go after, and what you are currently missing in your product/service offering that will help you retain the client and possibly expand the relationship.

When Joan Jones employed an outside consultant to audit her clients, she found out that the companies wanted to eliminate some full-time positions and were looking to outsource the work to a temporary agency. Although Joan's firm didn't offer the services the company was looking for, no one else locally did either, and it afforded Joan the opportunity to expand and diversify her business.

> I had a client who wanted a price that was lower than we could afford to give.

8. What isn't the company doing now that you wish they would do?

Sometimes asking the same question in a different way can yield better, different, and new results. Although this question is similar to question seven, the client may look at the question as an opportunity to suggest an additional service they think the vendor could and should offer based on the type of work the vendor does.

One of my clients was a trade association that was looking for new profit making opportunities. The trade association's client auditor asked one of the members what service the association could offer that would be of use to them. The member said he wished the association would run their seminars and meetings since the association knew how to do it already and it would save his people a lot of time and aggravation.

> Strategic planning for the future is very important.

9. What will be your greatest needs over the next six to twelve months?

Strategic planning for the future is very important. Asking the client what they project their needs will be will help you do your planning. You may find out from a variety of clients that they are all anticipating a need that you hadn't considered, and this need could open up new opportunities. If you don't know about these future needs you could be caught flat-footed and lose your clients to someone who is prepared to meet their needs.

An independent grocer in my region noticed that there were more Hispanics moving in and shopping at his store. Over time this new group of customers was beginning to leave. The store owner asked one of his Hispanic employees to talk to people in the Hispanic community and find out why they stopped shopping at his store. The employee came back and said that they couldn't find food they were used to getting where they came from and because they were still learning English they couldn't read the signs.

10. Would you serve as a reference for this company?

If a client won't serve as a reference, then you know something is wrong and you need to jump in right away and fix it. It's funny how you can ask questions one through nine and think you are making progress, and when you ask the last question it is like getting splashed with a cold bucket of water. This should spur the owner of the business to ask for a face-to-face meeting with the client so the owner can make the client happy enough to want to endorse the owner's business to future prospects.

Conducting an Audit of Your Web Site

Companies of all sizes are embracing the promise of the Internet to bring in sales and service existing clients at a rate unheard of in any business in any time in history. According to Jupiter Communications, a firm that studies industry trends, business-to-business and consumer Web site development and growth is growing at 1,000 percent per month.

For those businesses that are developing Web sites to attract and retain customers, an audit of your Web site is a must. There are forty different points of success, outlined below, you need to analyze to ascertain whether the site is creating new sales opportunities, retaining clients, and reducing client service costs. Follow this Internet audit outline to make sure your Web site is providing value to your customers and to yourself.

Web site content checklist

How many times have you gone to a company's Web site and not been able to easily find basic information about the company? Does your Web site require the user to go on a treasure hunt to find key company information? If it does, how many clients do you think you have lost? I had a client that was one of the first companies to put up a Web site, but they did such a poor job that instead of bringing in business, it sent a negative message to clients and prospects and it lost them business. Your company's Web site should have the following information readily accessible:

- Company telephone number
- Company e-mail address
- Company mailing address
- Educational information
- Executive contacts

To attract and retain customers, an audit of your Web site is a must.

- Individual customer service contacts
- Press releases
- Testimonials
- Site map

> Compare content for substantive value.

Competition

- Site focus
- Compare content for substantive value
- Ease of site navigation
- Benchmark user extras such as calculators, video, and audio
- Timeliness of content changes
- Ease of finding corporate contacts
- Ease of using electronic commerce

Customer Interviews

- Clients image of company
- Sites that impress users
- Site usage
- Value of the site
- Ways to improve site

Internal Interviews

- Improvement suggestions from nonsales and marketing personnel
- Tracking management's sales and service goals against performance

Marketing Materials

- URL on brochures
- URL on business cards
- URL on folders
- URL in newspaper advertisements
- URL on stationary

Technical Functionality

- Customer applications
- Database search and retrieval capability
- Download time
- Ease of electronic commerce options—catalog and cash register
- Ease of use and accuracy of site calculators
- Ease of navigation
- E-mail
- Links to other sites
- Screen view on 15- and 17-inch monitors
- Use of audio
- Use of video
- Use of programming languages such as Java

Ease of electronic commerce options—catalog and cash register

Chapter 11

Inexpensive Ways to Create Sales

"You don't concentrate on risks. You concentrate on results.
No risk is too great to prevent the necessary job from getting done."

—CHARLES E. "CHUCK" YEAGER (1923–)
American test pilot

Management has cut every unnecessary expense, tried to collect all its outstanding debts, managed to keep its creditors at bay, and stopped business with all nonpaying customers. The quest for raising new capital is ongoing and may never stop based on management's objectives. The only area left to improve is the top line: sales.

Bringing in new sales is not only important from a cash flow prospective, but for employee morale as well. Everyone is rejuvenated when new business comes in the door. Employees feel needed and part of a winning team.

Conversely, nothing is more defeating than losing old reliable clients because they feel the company is substandard or does not have a future. Everyone feels as though he or she is on the Titanic.

> Bringing in new customers is more expensive than harvesting new opportunities with existing customers.

Preserving and Expanding Your List of Clients

Companies that can't keep their existing clients will not be around to bring in new ones. The cost of bringing in new clients varies from business to business. Bringing in new customers is more expensive than harvesting new opportunities with existing customers.

Existing companies have a bias toward buying from their existing supplier if the supplier provides quality at a fair price. Companies hate to interview new vendors because it takes time away from the problems they would like to focus on and requires them to teach the new vendor about their company.

Ten Best Ways to Attract and Keep Customers

Through the last fifteen years of consulting with a variety of companies, I have found ten best ways to attract and keep customers:

1. Advisory Board

Develop an advisory board made of the company's top ten or fifteen clients. Advisory boards are different from boards of directors in that they have no financial responsibility to the shareholders of the company. The sole job of advisory board members is to provide advice and feedback to management.

One trade association I worked for had various advisory boards, and each board met quarterly to give the staff direction, advice, and feedback on whatever they requested. At each meeting the executive director asked the following three questions:

- What do you think of our organization?
- What do we need to change to serve you better?
- What are we currently not offering that we should to keep your business?

Many companies are afraid to ask their customers what they think for fear the response will be negative. Only the most secure and success-driven companies care what their customers think and react to their suggestions. The ones that don't will continue to make the same mistakes until they are out of business.

The best advisory board meetings are ones that have set agendas and ask open-ended questions that allow the board members to provide input on subjects that are important to them. Management should take copious notes and provide copies to each person who attended.

It's also important that management listens with an open mind and not become defensive. Management should respond by first acknowledging the criticism and then explaining the decisions that were made, if appropriate. The board may reconsider their criticism and instead make a positive suggestion. Management should inform the advisory board whenever the board's suggestions will be considered and report back to the board regarding implementation of the suggestions.

> Many companies are afraid to ask their customers what they think for fear the response will be negative.

Example

An associate of mine ran a trade association. She hosted ten to fifteen meals a year that brought together fifteen to twenty representatives from each member company. She asked the group the three questions:

- Why did you join the organization?
- What can the organization do to serve your company better?
- What does the organization do that you don't like that we should eliminate?

My associate would receive 150 suggestions and would narrow the list down to three suggestions that her association would implement. She then would write a business plan to implement the new ideas and would send a survey out six months after the new service was implemented to see if it was effective. This worked so well that the organization's retention rate usually was around 95 percent.

The board of another trade association, whose membership was spiraling downward for three years, agreed to merge with her organization. The first step she took to re-energizing the organization was to host a series of focus groups to hear what the members had to say. Much to her surprise, this was the first time the members had been asked for their input. Once they realized the organization was not being run for the benefit of the staff but rather for the membership, they developed a renewed interest.

When former members heard about the changes in the organization, membership grew by 100 percent in one year. My associate's board was surprised to find out that she did not have to fire even one staff member. She only needed to make some minor adjustments.

> When former members heard about the changes in the organization, membership grew by 100 percent in one year.

2. Thank-You Notes

Each time the company receives a new order, send a thank-you note to the client. Clients appreciate being thanked for their business. It's similar to having dinner at someone's home and not thanking them.

Some people give gifts, which is nice and usually appreciated but not necessary, especially when you are running on a tight budget. Some companies do not allow their employees to accept gifts for fear they will be predisposed to always doing business with that vendor. A simple thank-you letter goes a long way to developing a good long-term relationship. Below is a sample letter.

Sample Thank-You Letter

Dear John:

Thank you for giving us an opportunity to service your company. We will continue to keep you abreast of the latest developments in our industry and keep our eyes open for possible business opportunities for your company as well. Please do not hesitate to call me if I can be of service in any way.

Sincerely,
Marc Kramer
President

3. Client Referrals

Understand your client's business so that your company can be in a position to steer new business to them. Nothing makes a client happier than a vendor sending them new business.

Example

A member of my friend's trade association was a financial printer. They were very supportive of her organization through buying sponsorships and tables at various events.

One day, she was meeting with the president of a company going public and she asked him if he had chosen a financial printer for his public offering. He said no, and she immediately contacted her member about the opportunity and made an introduction to the company's chief financial officer who was selecting the outside vendors.

> Nothing makes a client happier than a vendor sending them new business.

4. Clipping Service

Send articles and information regarding new developments in your industry that will save your clients money or increase business. Clients also appreciate articles about competitors in their industry or about themselves. Below is an example of what one of my clients did for one of their customers.

Example

My client had a very large manufacturing customer who had little experience with the Internet. My client sent them twenty to thirty articles a month on the subject and another five stories on their competition or industry in general. The customer contact told my client that while they didn't have time to read all the articles he sent them, they were very impressed with how well he understood their business.

Well-designed newsletter is important.

5. Newsletter

Develop a newsletter that provides information on your industry and overall business information. Inexpensive software such as Microsoft Office allows you to create the newsletter yourself. While having an attractive, well-designed newsletter is important, the content is the most critical factor. The information in the newsletter must be well thought-out and well written.

Example

My client ran a mall made up of mom-and-pop stores. Most merchants had very little formal business experience or training. If a merchant failed, it cost the mall money to collect past rent and find another renter. My client thought the best way to reduce the number of failing merchants was to constantly educate them on smart business practices. To that end, he sent a four-page monthly newsletter to each merchant that provided retail marketing sales tips such as how to stack merchandise, when to have a sale, and how to interact with customers.

6. Seminars

Run quarterly seminars for clients on your company's area of expertise. Company-run seminars provides a platform to showcase new services and products in an educational environment. Seminars make a statement to clients about the quality of service you provide.

It's not necessary to hold the seminar in a hotel. Companies that have suitable in-house facilities such as a conference room can save room rental and travel expenses and build a stronger psychological connection with their clients. Also, consider having one of your vendors host the seminar, since it could develop into new business for them as well.

Example

One of my Web site development clients partnered with one of the largest telecommunication companies in the world. This company was interested in hosting Web sites on their computers and selling access to the Internet. They offered to provide roundtrip transportation for our clients to their offices, do a seminar on Web site hosting and Internet access, and provide them with lunch. This made a strong impression with my client's customers. The fact that my client's company had such a close relationship with this highly respected company, as evidenced by that company's participation in the seminar, made a strong, positive impression with my client's customers.

7. Vendor Referrals

Vendors can be a great source of lead generation. If they believe that your company is aggressive, provides a quality product or service, and will help close more sales, then they will provide sales leads to you. Vendors who have Web sites might be willing to provide links from their Web site to their customer's Web site, and include their customers in advertisements, which can help generate sales.

> Vendors can be a great source of lead generation.

Example

The interactive client in the previous example developed an affiliation with Apple Computer. Apple was so impressed with the devotion this company had to its products that its salespeople were constantly referring new business. They even offered to provide cooperative advertising, which is free advertising provided by the vendor.

8. Newspaper Column

Small daily and weekly newspapers and monthly magazines are always looking for experts on various business topics to author articles. Publications typically do not pay anything to the writers, but the free advertising and association is very valuable to the company.

Example

A client of mine could not afford advertising in their industry publication but wanted exposure to sell their software product. Their chief programmer was an expert in a new emerging computer technology. The chief programmer offered to write a column and the magazine accepted. The magazine was so impressed with the programmer's writing skills that they asked him if he would be interested in writing monthly articles. The company, which had been teetering on the brink of failure, was flooded with telephone calls for orders and two venture capitalists inquired about investing.

9. Networking Meetings

Create a small networking group of five to ten of your customers and potential customers. Make sure that attendees are not competitors, and have open discussions on various business topics that will help everyone in the room improve their bottom line.

> Make sure that attendees are not competitors.

Example

A business associate of mine, who ran a small marketing communications company, didn't have an advertising budget. But he did have a conference room and enough money to provide pizza and beer for his customers and prospects. Every Friday, at the end of the day, he hosted an informal get-together for people to discuss whatever was on their mind. The sessions became so valuable to the attendees that they paid my friend to run similar meetings for them. Soon his sales increased over 20 percent from this simple tactic.

10. Create a New Organization

Sometimes it is very hard to get in front of your prospects. You may have a product or service that is used by many industries, but don't have the financial wherewithal or personnel to cover all of them. On the other hand, you may have a product that provides value to a specific niche, but they may be geographically dispersed. Creating an organization that provides value to your target market can cast you in a different light, attract new business, and help retain existing business.

Example

There was a small Web site marketing firm that was living hand to mouth. They had talent but were finding it difficult to get in front of companies who could use their services. The founding partners decided that the region they lived in needed an organization that helped companies get a return on their Web sites through intelligent marketing. They wrote to people in large organizations who had made a big investment in the Internet and told them about their idea.

The marketing people in these organizations embraced the idea. People who would never take the time to meet with this firm were inviting and paying for their lunches. These same people were now offering to fund the new organization and provide resources to make it a success. As the organization developed, the founding members became familiar with the partners, found them to be knowledgeable, and started to send them business. Today that firm sits on the board of the organization as a successful company.

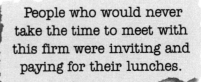

People who would never take the time to meet with this firm were inviting and paying for their lunches.

Final Comments

You do not need a lot of money to bring in and retain sales. You just need to be creative and leverage other people's resources that would benefit from your ideas and concepts. For example, one of my clients had no marketing budget, but his firm was one of the top sellers in their geographic region of a particular type of IBM computer. My client offered to put together a seminar for IBM if IBM would underwrite the cost of promotion, the facility, and refreshments. IBM liked the quality of the prospects and provided a list of additional companies to invite. The event was a success and my client added some new customers.

Using the Internet to Cut Costs and Boost Sales

"The Net is a 10.5 on the Richter scale of economic change."

—NICHOLAS NEGROPONTE
American writer and director, MIT media laboratory

Chapter 12

The acceptance of the Internet as a tool for business has saved many companies from going out of business. It's probably the best and most cost-effective medium to promote a company's products and services and generate new sales.

Egghead Software, headquartered in California, grew to a chain of over sixty retail stores selling business-to-business and business-to-consumer computer software and CD-ROMs. The cost of real estate, advertising each store location, and the personnel to man those stores, coupled with the competition of bigger competitors, was quickly driving the company out of business. Management closed all of its stores, centralized their entire business in one location, and focused their advertising budget on a direct-mail campaign to old customers and new prospects. Today, Egghead is profitable.

Many business people read that companies like Disney, Ford, and First Union Bank spend hundreds of thousands, and in some cases, millions, of dollars developing their Web site and wonder how can they afford to have a Web site. The reason large companies pay so much to create their Web sites is because they require the building and connecting of numerous and large databases, which requires armies of programmers and teams of people to coordinate content.

For most small businesses, an effective Web site can be developed for less than $25,000 if an outside firm is hired to do it. Off-the-shelf programs can be found at business and computer supply stores or by going to the Web site of our previous example, www.egghead.com.

> In some cases, millions, of dollars developing their Web site.

Hiring An Outside Developer

There are many good small Web site development firms around the country. The best way to find a good developer is to contact your local chamber of commerce, a regional advertising agency, or ask local companies who have an Internet presence for a recommendation.

There are ten key questions you want to ask a developer when you are evaluating them.

1. Who have you developed Web sites for and can you give me references to speak with?

The Internet has been around long enough that anybody who is serious about developing Web sites has either developed a client list of work they have done for themselves or as part of another organization. Ask to speak directly to clients and ask them the following:

- Was the quality of work better or worse than you expected?
- Is the firm good at returning calls?
- Are they good at explaining technical jargon in layman's terms?
- Were they able to meet an agreed-upon schedule?

2. What size monitor and what speed of modem do you develop for?

This is one of the most important questions you can ask early in the process. One of my clients asked this question, and the graphic artist responded that wasn't his concern but that of the technical staff of my client's company. Experienced developers know that you develop the graphics to fit a 15-inch monitor and a modem speed that was built into last year's computers.

Developing quality graphics that don't take a long time to show up on your screen when viewing the Web site is paramount to attracting and retaining users to your site. Unless the person works in a company that has a dedicated telephone connection that allows for graphics to download quickly onto a screen, you want to make sure that the site doesn't have an overwhelming number of graphics and pictures.

> Experienced developers know that you develop the graphics to fit a 15-inch monitor and a modem speed that was built into last year's computers.

3. Do you have your own in-house graphic artist?

It isn't essential, but it is a plus because that means the artist has a rapport with the programmers, which makes for easier, quicker, and cleaner development of a Web site.

4. Do you have your own programmers and what platforms can they develop for?

You want to know that your Web site is compatible with the hardware and software you use to run your company. This means if your company uses Microsoft's operating system, then you want programmers who understand how to design for that system. Over time, you may want to connect your corporate databases to your Web site for your clients and salespeople to access.

A good project manager will explain all of the technical issues in layman's terms.

5. Who will be managing my project and what is their experience?

You want to know who will be held accountable and working with you to develop your site. You want to make sure you like and trust this person. A good project manager will explain all of the technical issues in layman's terms, provide creative and technical suggestions, and know how to set schedules and expectations. Avoid project managers who appear disorganized or promise the world.

6. Will I be able to view the site as it is being constructed from my computer?

You don't want the developer to send you your home page design on a computer disk or in some type of form that requires you to download and open it yourself. You want to go onto the Internet and type in a Web site address (called a URL) and see what it looks like on your screen. This will allow you to make suggested changes.

7. Do you have a copywriter to create my content?

A good copywriter is as important as good graphics and technology. Web site copy writing style is short and to the point with a high usage of bullets. Ask that all copy be posted to the site to view from your computer screen. Note in writing all of your suggested changes and send it to the developers.

8. How will I make future changes to the site?

Ask the developer to program the site so that you can type in any changes in Word that will convert automatically to HTML (hypertext markup language) and fit into the designated part of the site you want changed.

9. Is the site structured to grow with my business?

A developer can take a look at your site map, which is akin to an architect's plan for a house. Through this plan, the developer can see the proposed future content and plan for access to databases and the use of new technology such as video and audio. He can also look at the current hardware and software you are using and help develop a plan that won't require building a whole new site shortly after the first one is put up.

10. Who will maintain my site?

You want to know if they will help you with future graphic and content changes if needed. Also, you want to know if they will continue to host your site, which means store the content on a computer connected to the Internet, or whether you will have to hire a separate company, an Internet Service Provider (ISP), to do it. Your third option is to put your site on a dedicated computer in your own office and buy a telephone connection that connects you to the Internet.

Finally, you want to have a hybrid contract that pays the developer by the hour but does not exceed a certain price. Sometimes during the course of developing a site, items you thought you wanted were eliminated or put off, which requires less work on the part of the developer. Having a hybrid of an hourly and fixed price protects your up- and downside.

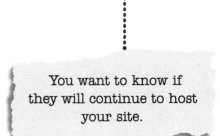

You want to know if they will continue to host your site.

Doing It Yourself

There are a few products out on the market that will allow you to create your own Web site for less than $100 and without knowing Web site authoring languages and codes such as HTML (hyper text markup language). Because you are in turnaround mode and every dollar saved is essential, developing your own Web site is the best way to participate in this new medium and create new sales and marketing momentum. Having a Web site also makes a statement that you are forward thinking and that the business plan is not going under.

When evaluating Web site development software, you need to look at the following five elements:

Ease of use. You don't have hours to teach yourself a new programming language or graphics software packages, so you need a product that requires very little technical skill. You only want to focus on the content you want on the site and want a product that will help you deliver that content quickly.

Software/hardware compatibility. The development software needs to be compatible with your computer and have the potential to integrate with your accounting and warehouse software. You don't want to spend $1,000 or more on integration to use your $50 program.

Scalability. You might be adding a lot of new products and services to your site over time, and you want to make sure that the software you purchase will meet your needs for at least two years. You don't want to waste time rebuilding the site within six months of initially building it.

Technical quality. No matter how easy it is to use, a software package that doesn't work is of no value.

Support. Because software development products are relatively inexpensive to buy, they don't provide free support. It is important to know that they have a Web site that provides answers to common questions not answered in the software itself, and that they have a pay-as-you-use help desk with a live person to answer questions.

There are a handful of do-it-yourself Web site development software packages. The ones we are recommending fit the above criteria and are easy to find in most software and business supply stores.

Interclient's Fast Catz. This product is extremely easy to use. The step-by-step instructions walk the user through each field the user needs to fill out in order to have a functioning electronic

> The development software needs to be compatible with your computer.

commerce Web site. Loading the software and seeing the finished product on the Internet will take less than thirty minutes.

There are a couple of shortcomings to this product. First, the current version only allows you to display twelve products. The company is currently upgrading the product so it can offer users 200 products. For most companies, 80 percent of their business may come from only a handful of products, therefore, offering only the company's best-selling products makes the most sense.

Second, the graphics selection is minimal, especially compared to the other product mentioned in this chapter. Don't underestimate the importance of good graphics, especially in this medium. Poor graphics can turn a user off, and they won't even attempt to use the site.

Just as important as good graphics is technical workability, and this product has no discernable technical problems. (www.fastcatz.com)

PrimeCom Interactive's QuickSite. Developing an e-commerce site using this product will take approximately two hours. There is an easy-to-use video and written tutorial. The tutorial guides you through a basic goal and objective setting for how you plan to use your Web site to develop business. It then takes you through development, hosting of the site on PrimeCom's computers, and arranging for the user to establish an Internet address. The software even provides definitions to common Internet terms that may not be so common to first-time users.

QuickSite is rich in home page templates with over 350 to choose from. The user can select a predeveloped home page for a particular industry such as accounting, antiques, and food. There are also general templates that can be customized to fit your needs. It is probably the most robust product currently out on the market. (www.primecom.com)

QuickSite is ideal for businesses that want to list *all* of their products and services and who would like to eventually convert from having an expensive brick-and-mortar presence to using inexpensive warehouse space and a computer.

> Just as important as good graphics is technical workability, and this product has no discernable technical problems.

Other Costs

Web Site Address

A Web site address is called a URL (uniform resource locator). You can obtain a domain name, the name registered for a Web site address, from Internic (http://rs.internic.net) for less than $200. You can also purchase a Web site address from an ISP.

Hosting

You need to get it on the Internet, which is called posting.

Once you have developed your Web site, you need to get it on the Internet, which is called posting. The companies mentioned previously that sell you do-it-yourself software will host your Web site on their computers and obtain a Web site address for you. The cost of hosting starts at $25 a month and goes up depending on the amount of space on the host's hard drive your site takes on a computer.

Internet Connection

You may decide to host your own Web site, and that will require a dedicated telephone or cable television connection. The cost for such a connection can range from a few hundred dollars to $1,000 a month.

Developing a Plan

Before you begin developing your site, you need to develop a plan for the site or you will waste a lot of time and effort. One of my clients refused to develop a site plan and insisted they knew exactly what they wanted. Before long, my client spent almost $70,000 with nothing of substance to show for it. A good Web site plan has the following ten components:

1. *Overview.* As an executive summary in a business plan, this gives the developer an understanding of the business goals, user focus, and types of information that will be found on the site.

2. *Internal Analysis.* No matter how small the business, people from different departments should be interviewed and asked the following types of questions:

   - What image is the business trying to project?
   - How can the Internet help us be more successful?
   - What kinds of information should be found on the site?
   - What kinds of information should we capture from the site?

3. *External Analysis.* You need to talk to your customers and ask them the following types of questions:

   - What is your image of our business?
   - What makes us unique?
   - What kinds of information would you like to find on our site?
   - What Web sites are you impressed with?

4. *Competitive Analysis.* This is important so that you don't develop a Web site that when launched is not as least as good as the competition's. You want to focus on the following:

   - What types of information they offer?
   - Do they give away anything for free?
   - How do they capture prospect information?
   - What does their site provide that is special?

5. *Marketing Recommendation.* No one knows your Web site exists without marketing. Marketing recommendations look at the following:

   - Cable television—an expensive advertisement on cable television promoting the site;
   - Direct mail—a postcard with the home page of the Web site sent to customers, prospects, and vendors;
   - E-mail—announcements of the site's existence sent by e-mail to customers, prospects, and vendors;
   - Print—small newspaper advertisement with the Web site address;

What makes us unique?

- Public relations–press releases sent to local media informing them about the new site and what makes it unique.

6. *Site Content Recommendation.* A site can't be built unless the developer knows what types of information the owner of the site wants to deliver and to capture. Capturing quality user information will improve overall company marketing and sales performance. Typical information found on a Web site should be as follows:

- Company description–background information about the company;
- Product/service description–description of the products and services offered;
- Corporate contacts–names, titles, telephone numbers, and e-mail addresses of company contacts;
- Corporate newsletter–an on-line newsletter informing users about the company's new products and services and information about changes in the industry;
- Site Map–maps of the site so users can find information without having to manually search the site.

7. *Web Site Work Schedule.* A schedule of the types of information populating the site, the programming language for each section, the person responsible for that section, and when that section should be written and posted to the site.

8. *Web Site Maintenance Schedule.* Once the content plan has been completed, a future maintenance schedule to keep the site fresh and timely has to be developed.

9. *Site Map.* A map of what is located on the site. This gives the content and technical developers an understanding of how information should be laid out.

10. *Launch Schedule.* This ties together the actual development, testing, and marketing of the site. The launch plan can be broken down by days, weeks, or months.

> Capturing quality user information will improve overall company marketing and sales performance.

Sample Web Site Plan

OVERVIEW:

The business of selling commercial insurance and personal insurance is both complex and simple. The simple part is that everyone who comes to someone like Kadoch Insurance Agency is primarily looking for the best financial deal. The complex part, which many times determines who gets invited to bid on an opportunity, is the ability to make the process as painless as possible and be viewed as an honest organization run by competent professionals.

Kadoch Insurance Agency, which has a Web site, is in the process of developing a more robust site to meet the competition—*McGregor Group*, *Star Insurance Agency*, and *Hansen Insurance Capital*—and exceed it in order to maintain their top status in the area of purchasing lottery winnings, commercial insurance, and now personal insurance.

The current Web site does not represent what employees and many brokers feel is the strongest company in the industry in terms of funding capability and level of integrity. A strategy for an improved Web site was developed based on the following:

Interviews. Employees, clients, prospects, brokers, and attorneys were asked a series of questions by telephone regarding what they saw as Kadoch Insurance Agency's strengths, weaknesses, and information that should be found on Kadoch Insurance Agency's new site. An emphasis was put on client service.

Competitive Analysis. The sites of the three main competitors as marked by the marketing department—McGregor, Star Insurance Agency, and Hansen Insurance—were analyzed.

Surveys. Kadoch Insurance Agency conducted surveys with prospects and clients to find out their interests, concerns, and needs.

Endorsement Letters. The contents of endorsement letters were reviewed to understand why clients chose Kadoch Insurance Agency and what they did with their money.

User Technology. Each client, prospect, attorney, and broker was asked about their personal computer hardware technology. The design and information recommendations in this plan were based on the users being able to access and navigate the site with ease.

Internal Technology. Reviewed the current in-house technology capability to insure that the existing technology can handle on-line requests, access to internal databases, and can scale up over time.

The strategy for the site was focused first on using it to support client service needs and, second, as a marketing tool. Kadoch Insurance Agency personnel and outside users were mostly in agreement on how the site would be used and what information should be found on it.

INTERNAL ANALYSIS:

It is clear from interviews with Kadoch Insurance Agency employees that a quality Web site is important in the overall marketing and service strategy of the company. Many of the employees were embarrassed that an organization with such strong financial backing would appear so weak and unprofessional. The employees who were interviewed were as follows:

- Raphael Kadoch, president
- Jacqueline Kadoch, vice president of marketing
- Rita Kadoch, vice president of sales

Using the Internet to project the right image

"We need for clients to see us as trustworthy and responsive. We are in a field that is comprised of two groups. One is the sleazy entrepreneurial type, and the other is a bureaucratic organization. We want people to feel like they are dealing with people who care about them."

"We are a public company and that is a major strength, and we need to capitalize on that using our Web site."

"Our competitors philosophy is 'get everything you can.' We don't do that. We have an underwriting criteria that prevents us from taking everything a potential client has and we want to convey that message and image to prospective clients."

"Letting clients know that we are a solid company."

"The most important thing the Web can do is build our legitimacy."

Improving client service through the Internet

"Attorneys who are negotiating with us would like to see (any pertinent documents.")

"A referral network of attorneys around the country."

"Information for attorneys explaining our referral process. We pay fees for referrals. We need to give them options."

"A calculator that allows them to plug in numbers to give them an understanding of what they can get for their customer."

"Our sales process needs to be improved, but we are working on that. Our funding time has lengthened since we have become more corporate."

"Transaction steps."

"Information about the salespeople."

Improving influencer and deal maker relationships

"Our biggest weakness is the broker industry. We have developed technology that we haven't shared with brokers yet."

"We won't do business with attorneys who won't sign off payoffs. We can't accommodate a lot of business on the broker end. We need to open up our loan program to brokers."

"Brokers and attorneys want to know how can they do a deal quickly and easily."

"Attorneys want to know how the attorney can be paid?"

Building credibility and client service:

"The Web site must be easy to use, friendly, and able to help them solve problems. I don't want a site that tells people how good we are."

"I want the broker to be able to do the transaction over the Internet. I want to share our technology with select brokers and attorneys. We want them to be as technologically advanced as we are."

"Background information on Kadoch Insurance Agency."

"Our discount rates on loans and he can sell it to the client. That way he can keep the distance."

"Commission schedule."

"Like attorneys, brokers need downloadable forms."

"Brokers need to see the rates we are willing to pay."

"We should password protect access to our underwriting guidelines."

"Tips for brokers on how to develop leads. The leads are developed through looking at court documents."

EXTERNAL ANALYSIS

Clients, brokers, attorneys, and past prospects were interviewed. They were asked a short series of questions that ranged from what their image of Kadoch Insurance Agency is to their experience in dealing with Kadoch to what they would like to find on Kadoch's Web site.

Clients and past prospects were most interested in knowing the following in this order:

1. Cost
2. Client service
3. Quality of the product

The attorneys and brokers felt Kadoch could provide greater value if they provided answers to the following:

1. Kadoch's process
2. The states and insurance companies that are agreeable to selling commercial and home owners insurance
3. Ability to move the process through use of the Internet

Everyone interviewed gave Kadoch high marks for integrity and deal speed. The area both groups felt Kadoch fell short was post-decision service. Post-decision service is providing the necessary information to come to closure on a deal that has been agreed upon by both parties. Both groups said Kadoch personnel are hard to get a hold of and that answers to questions are not uniformly when speaking with one Kadoch representative or another.) When asked or give a specific example interviewed individuals couldn't give one.

Kadoch managers admitted that there were problems in servicing clients and communicating the appropriate information to make a transaction run smoother. All agreed the Internet could have a positive impact on how Kadoch interacted with clients, brokers, and attorneys.

Below is the feedback received from clients, attorneys, and brokers.

Information that influences selection

("The process for how they buy your settlement.")

"I would like to hear what other customers think about them. I would like to see a chat room to speak with other lawsuit winners."

"I would like to know that the state lottery isn't the only group to sell to."

"I would like to know how they handle payment problems or issues with Kadoch Insurance Agency."

("I would like to know if you could sell a portion or have to sell the whole amount.")

"Knowing Kadoch Insurance Agency's financial stability was very important to me."

"I would promote the fact most of these brokers aren't as well capitalized."

"I would like to know what they are willing to pay on the dollar. It would be better than bargaining. It's like shopping for a car. It's a very unpleasant experience. It would make Kadoch Insurance Agency appear more honest."

Going beyond the competition

"Providing advice on how to select an investment advisor would be good. Advice on how not to squander your money."

"I would like information on how to buy stocks and bonds and then a good discount with a brokerage firm."

"Travel discounts would be valuable."

"I would like to see information for investing written for a layman. A lot of people don't know the difference between a stock, bond, or money market. That would make it an excellent site. There is no site now that is easily understood. You expect a finance company to have finance information."

"I would like to read about how to pick an attorney and someone to invest my money."

ATTORNEY AND BROKER INSIGHTS

Perception of Kadoch Insurance Agency

"They are disorganized and there is no one with leadership capabilities. We only do business with them because they give good rates or the client has already sold part of the deal."

"They are a good company, but not the swiftest. Metropolitan is probably the best around and Kadoch Insurance Agency is second. Kadoch Insurance Agency's problem is that they don't always get back to you. I like the people and the company."

"They are a company that has good financing. Tom Herman and Cindy Snider are very good people. The service is very good."

"Kadoch Insurance Agency has the quickest turnaround times for bids I have ever seen and you can quote me."

"They need more internal support in the commercial insurance side. They would like me to do a lot more than I would like to do and other insurers have more support staff. If my client requires a lot of hand-holding, that will influence my decision on whether to use Kadoch Insurance Agency."

Tools and support for brokers

"I would like to see bid turnaround time."

"Real commitments on how quickly they can close and fund a deal."

"Keep brokers up to date on what insurance companies are recalcitrant and which ones work with brokers."

"I would like to know which states are court order states and I would go to that site all of the time."

Information for clients

"Clients want to know fast they can get their money."

"How the process works."

"The Kadoch Insurance Agency should tell clients the types of documents they need to do a deal-settlement and release agreement, benefits letter, and annuity."

"How to get the documents without pissing the other insurance companies off."

"Clients need to know that they shouldn't tell the insurance company they are going to sell their payments because they try to talk them out of it."

"Education about insurance companies and what the controversy is about.

There are states that won't allow someone to (assign their winnings to for a lump-sum settlement.")

COMPETITION

When speaking with attorneys, brokers, and clients, the vast majority of firms providing lump-sum payments are considered "sleazy," "fly by night," and "scam artists." Therefore, the competition is narrowed down greatly. Kadoch Insurance executives typically look at McGregor, Star Insurance Agency, and Hanson Agency as main competitors.

Each of the three competitors currently has a Web site that is more robust and creates a better image with targeted parties. When interviewing targeted parties, especially attorneys and brokers, all three competitors were given high marks for having a Web site, but Hansen Insurance's site stood out because of their deal process information.

Competitors Web Site

Comparison Criteria	McGregor Group	Star Insurance Agency	Hansen Insurance
Level One:			
Company Contacts	X	X	X
Company Financials			
Company Address	X	X	X
E-mail Addresses	X	X	X
800 Telephone Number	X	X	X
Question and Answer		X	X
Employment Opportunities	X		X
Sales Process		X	X
On-line Application	X	X	X
Testimonials	X		X
Level Two:			
Tax Information		X	
Endorsement Letters			
Client Success Stories			
Industry News			X
Attorney Information			
Payment Calculator	X		X
Case Studies	X		
Level Three:			
Investment Advice		X	
Business Startup Advice			
Discounts			
Lottery Links			X
Freebies			X
Attorney Map			
Commercial Insurance Case History			

Analysis of McGregor's Web Site

Mission: The mission of the McGregor Web site is to provide information to anyone who is in the market to sell a portion or all of a lottery or lawsuit settlement. This encompasses both winners and lawyers who represent them. The company uses the face of the founder on the Web site to make the firm appear human and friendly.

Functionality: McGregor has been smart in its use of technology. They don't use a lot of pictures, so the pages quickly download. There are e-mail addresses to various executives for those comfortable using e-mail. They also provide an easy-to-use on-line application.

User Reward: The only apparent reward for the user is the examples of how people have sold their payment streams to McGregor. A section of their site is called "The National Funding Chronicle." Unfortunately, using the word chronicle is misleading. It is just another on-line brochure promoting the company. There is no valuable information the reader takes away that they can apply to their situation.

Owner Benefit: The only benefit, albeit a good one, is that anyone who fills out the on-line application for review of their situation and anyone interested in receiving their newsletter on-line is captured in their database.

Analysis of Star's Web Site

Mission: As soon as you hit the home page for Star Insurance Agency's Web site, you clearly understand their message, which is that they are strong and sound and have money and they understand middle America. This is accomplished by showing an imposing building that looks like the capitol or bank found in a small town, and the color scheme is green for money.

Functionality: The site is easy to use and obviously developed for home users, whose modem speed is slow compared to a corporate connection. There are few pictures, graphics, and charts, so downloading pages takes no time and users don't leave the site frustrated. The application component is easy to use.

User Reward: The information is concise and easy to understand. Their target markets—lottery, commercial insurance, and workman's compensation—know exactly where to go to sell all or part of their payments. Professionals such as brokers and attorneys learn from the site superficially how their program works. There is a quarterly newsletter called the "Winners Circle" for lottery award winners.

Owner Benefit: There is an on-line application for interested parties to fill out, which allows them to develop a database of prospects.

Analysis of Hansen's Web Site

Mission: Hansen Agency wants to convey to prospects, attorneys, and brokers that the company can be trusted and is the best, and accomplishes this with a symbol on the home page that states "Code of Ethics" and the slogan "America's Largest Lottery Purchaser."

Functionality: The site is easy to use but doesn't download quickly because of the fancy animation and graphics.

User Reward: Users are encouraged to come back through a special section listing all of the insurance companies in each state. Prospective clients are also given a forty-five-minute prepaid telephone calling card for just contacting Hansen Insurance.

They also will send a free videotape explaining how the company buys various types of settlements. Hansen Insurance is the only site that spells out approximately what someone trading in a certain payment stream would receive in exchange for a lump sum. There are articles and legislative updates for prospective sellers, attorneys, and brokers.

Owner Benefit: The benefit to Hansen Agency having a site is capturing names from people who apply for information on selling their payments.

MARKETING SITE

Marketing Kadoch services is a difficult task because of the different types of clients and influencers. This section focuses on the most cost-effective ways to market the Kadoch Web site. The focus of the marketing needs to be broken down by group.

Homeowners: Homeowners come from every walk of life. Some are professionals with college degrees who read *Psychology Today*, and others are manual laborers who read *Muscle* magazine.

Direct Mail. A postcard with the Web site address should be sent to all homeowners. The postcards should encourage them to look at the Web site and receive a free gift. The gift could be the book *Retiring Right* or a list of books and audiotapes to choose from on investing, starting a business, and travel.

Internet. There are two sites Kadoch should consider buying banner advertising on. The first is Yahoo, an Internet site portal/search engine, and second, America Online, an Internet portal/destination site. For each site, Kadoch should buy banner space on the search page that lists various lottery sites and link the Kadoch advertisement to the Kadoch Web site.

Kadoch Letter and Marketing Materials. Everything Kadoch sends out should have the Internet address on it.

Regional Cable Television. Kadoch should run advertisements focused on this market. Each advertisement should display the Internet address in the beginning and end of the advertisement.

Commercial Insurance: Most of the commercial insurance winners are people from modest backgrounds, and the size of their settlements is small in comparison to homeowners. The influencers, attorneys, and brokers are the easiest group to target because of the common industry publications they read.

Direct Mail. A postcard with the Web site address should be sent to all attorneys and brokers in Kadoch database.

Internet. There are two sites Kadoch should consider buying banner advertising on. The first is Yahoo, an Internet site portal/search engine, and second, America Online, an Internet portal/destination site. For each site, Kadoch should buy banner space on the search page that lists companies that handle commercial insurance and link to Kadoch's Web site. More importantly, Kadoch should purchase the first meta tag, which is the computer code that puts sites in a certain order when doing a search, when a user types in "Commercial Insurance."

Publications. The vast majority of leads for commercial insurance deals come through attorneys and brokers. The publications they read and Kadoch should advertise in are *American Bar Journal, Federal Bar Journal, Commercial Law Legal Bulletin* and *Business Law Today.* The advertisements should show a picture of the home page with the site's Internet address.

Personal Insurance: This is a new group for Kadoch. The people who generally buy life insurance policies of $500,000 or more, according to the American Insurance Association, are people with college degrees and earn in excess of $50,000 a year.

Direct Mail. A letter should be sent to nursing home chains and nurses who specialize in handling terminally ill patients. The letter should be one page with an attached flyer showing the section of the Web site that deals with personal insurance.

Internet Sites. This group is typically interested in health-oriented sites. Kadoch should consider sponsoring a section on a Web site called "InteliHealth."

Marketing To All Groups: The following are suggestions for marketing to all three groups.

Booklet. Develop a booklet that helps Kadoch convey to clients and prospects their understanding and methodology for helping clients sell their insurance payment streams. Providing a book will create a certain image with each group. The book would provide the following insights:

- Selection of a firm to sell payments streams to and how the process works
- Selection of brokers and legal counsel and how that industry works
- Advice and personal rights when working with insurance companies

- Managing your money
- Starting a business

At the end of each chapter could be the Internet address to drive readers to the site for updated information. Each chapter would feature experts and Kadoch Insurance Agency clients who have gone through various experiences related to the target market.

CONTENT RECOMMENDATIONS

The strategy for the content that will be found on the Kadoch Insurance Agency site was based on interviews with past clients, prospects, attorneys, brokers, internal personnel, and through analyzing and studying competitor Web sites.

Universal Themes

There were four recurring themes all potential users identified as important to developing a quality Web site:

1. Ability to service small to medium-size companies
2. Honesty and integrity
3. Kadoch's process from the client's interest in selling all or part of their payments to closure
4. Internal contacts and where they fit into the process

Client-Specific Interests

Clients and prospects said an effective Web site would have to give a sense of personal interaction and assistance in making a decision on how much of their payment streams they needed to sell to meet their needs.

1. Kadoch personnel contact information
2. Payment ranges
3. Tax consequences

Attorney/Broker Interests

The ability to have legal information on how each state is dealing with individuals selling their payment streams to companies and the ability to follow a client's paper work on-line was at the top of this group's wish list.

1. Legal issues and how to overcome them by state
2. Ability to follow payment process through the Internet
3. Downloadable forms

MENU BUTTONS

Based on the information derived through interviews and competitive analysis, the following is the recommendation for menu buttons for the Kadoch site:

1. Company Background
2 Homeowners
3 Commercial Insurance
4 Personal Insurance
5 Attorneys/Brokers
6 Client Services
7 Site Map

Company Background

Company. An open letter from the president about the history of the company, its mission, and her thoughts on its future.

Company Contacts. Names, pictures, telephone numbers, addresses, and e-mail addresses of the key figures in legal, accounting, sales, and client service.

Company Financials. Description of company's financial backing and capabilities.

Transaction Information. Number of transactions completed, time transactions took to complete, and average size of transactions.

Endorsements. Quotes with pictures from happy clients listed by client type, attorneys, and brokers.

Homeowners

Process. A flow chart with written descriptions of the process individuals go through when selling all or part of their payments to Kadoch. This section would also list which states do not allow winners to sell their winnings.

Questions & Answers. The ten most asked questions and corresponding answers. This section would also have the president's e-mail.

Payment Range. A table giving a range of settlement figures and how those calculations were developed in layman's terms.

Taxes. Explanation of the tax clients must pay. This section will have a chart estimating the various taxes (federal, state, county, and municipal) and a calculator.

Post Services. Description of the password-protected part of the site that is only for Kadoch clients.

Professional Advisors. A list of attorneys and brokers (name, address, telephone number, fax number, e-mail, Web site address, and experience) across the country who have dealt with Kadoch.

Application. An on-line application for prospective clients to request information to sell their annuity stream.

Commercial Insurance

Process. A flow chart with written descriptions of the process individuals go through when selling all or part of their payments to Kadoch.

Dealing with Insurers. A description of the dispute between insurance companies and buyers of commercial insurance. Advice on how to get around the insurance company that is pressuring the prospect not to sell their annuity stream. A list of insurance companies that are amenable to not fighting settlement winners on selling their payment streams. A list of reasons insurance companies will tell sellers they can't or shouldn't sell and answers to counteract those statements. Also a checklist with scanned-in copies of forms to ask insurance companies for.

Questions & Answers. The ten most asked questions and corresponding answers. This section would also have the president's e-mail.

Taxes. Explanation of the tax clients must pay. This section will have a chart estimating the various taxes (federal, state, county, and municipal) and a calculator.

Post Services. Description of the password-protected part of the site that is only for Kadoch clients.

Professional Advisors. A list of attorneys and brokers (name, address, telephone number, fax number, e-mail, Web site address, and experience) across the country who have dealt with Kadoch.

Application. An on-line application for prospective clients to request information to sell their annuity stream.

Personal Insurance

Process. A flow chart with written descriptions of the process individuals go through when selling all or part of their payments to Kadoch.

Questions & Answers. The ten most asked questions and corresponding answers. This section would also have the president's e-mail.

Taxes. Explanation of the tax clients must pay. This section will have a chart estimating the various taxes (federal, state, county, and municipal) and a calculator.

Post Services. Description of the password-protected part of the site that is only for Kadoch clients.

Professional Advisors. A list of attorneys and brokers (name, address, telephone number, fax number, e-mail, Web site address, and experience) across the country who have dealt with Kadoch.

Application. An on-line application for prospective clients to request information to sell their annuity stream.

Attorneys/Brokers

Process. The process attorneys would go through when dealing with Kadoch.

Sales Tips. This section would provide a step-by-step process for finding new clients, and each month a different experienced broker would be interviewed about their sales and service techniques.

Downloadable Forms. All transaction forms Kadoch requires to consummate a deal. These forms can also be filled out on-line and a number assigned by Kadoch once they are e-mailed back to Kadoch.

Legal Updates. Outcomes of any cases related to state homeowner insurance and commercial insurance fraud.

Client Services

This part of the site is password protected and is only for clients.

Investment Information. This section would explain in layman's terms different investment vehicles. A certified financial planner would write a monthly column. Clients would be able to e-mail questions and a financial planner would answer select questions.

Alumni. Information on what different alumni are doing with the winnings and settlements.

Starting a Business. This section will discuss how to start a business, and each month a different successful businessperson from a variety of industries will be interviewed about what it takes to run a business. The interviews will be archived. There will be links to franchising, the Small Business Administration, and other business sites.

Bookstore. Each client can receive up to $100 in free books each year on such topics as investing, starting a business, and travel.

Discounts. There would be hotel, car, long-distance, book, and other discounts offered.

Referral Awards. Clients who refer new clients will receive a choice of gifts including airline tickets, vacations, or free use of a credit card. The size of the gift will be commensurate with the size of the deal.

Tax Information. This information can be sponsored and populated by Kadoch's accounting firm.

Investment Information. A financial planning firm can sponsor this section, and a different investment tip can be provided each month.

Entrepreneurship. Deloitte & Touche or a university's small business development center can sponsor and populate this part of the site.

Development Checklist for Kadoch Insurance Agency Web Site

COMPANY BACKGROUND	PAGES	TYPE OF INFORMATION	INFO LOCATION	MONTH	INFORMATION DEVELOPER
Company	1	Word/HTML	Marketing	1	Writer
Company Contacts	1	Word/HTML and e-mail links	Marketing	1	Writer
Company Financials	1	Word/HTML	Marketing/legal	1	Writer
Transaction Information	1	Word/HTML	Marketing	1	Writer
Endorsements	2	Scanned-in letters	Marketing	1	Web developer
Homeowners					
Process	1	Flow charts, pictures, word	Marketing	1	Web developer/writer
Questions & Answers	2	Word/HTML	Marketing/legal	1	Writer
Payment Range	1	Spreadsheet	Marketing/legal	1	Writer
Taxes	1	Database or spreadsheet	Marketing	1	Web developer
Post Services	1	Word/HTML	New	2	Writer
Professional Advisors	1	Database or spreadsheet	Marketing	2	Web developer
Application	1	Word with e-mail link	Marketing	1	Web developer
Commercial Insurance					
Process	1	Flow charts, pictures, word	Marketing	1	Web developer/writer
Dealing with Insurers	2	Word/HTML	Marketing	1	Writer
Questions & Answers	2	Spreadsheet	Marketing/legal	1	Writer
Taxes	1	Database or spreadsheet	Marketing	1	Web developer
Post Services	1	Word/HTML	New	2	Writer
Professional Advisors	1	Database or spreadsheet	Marketing	2	Web developer
Application	1	Word with e-mail link	Marketing	1	Web developer

COMPANY BACKGROUND	PAGES	TYPE OF INFORMATION	INFO LOCATION	MONTH	INFORMATION DEVELOPER
Personal Insurance					
Process	1	Flow charts, pictures, word	Marketing	1	Web developer/writer
Questions & Answers	2	Word/HTML	Marketing/legal	1	Writer
Taxes	2	Spreadsheet	Marketing	1	Writer
Post Services	1	Word/HTML	New	2	Web developer
Professional Advisors	1	Database or spreadsheet	Marketing	2	Writer
Application	1	Word with e-mail link	Marketing	1	Web developer
Attorneys/Brokers					
Process	1	Flow charts, pictures, word	Marketing	1	Web developer/writer
Sales Tips	1	Word/HTML	New	2	Writer
Downloadable Forms	3	Word/HTML	Marketing/legal	2	Web developer
Legal Updates	2	Word/HTML	Marketing/legal	2	Kadoch Insurance Agency legal/writer
Client Services					
Investment Information	10	Word/HTML	New	2	Writer
Alumni	10	Word/HTML, pictures	Marketing	2	Web developer/writer
Starting a Business	10	Word/HTML	New	2	Writer
Book Store	2	Word/HTML, e-mail	New	2	Web developer/writer
Discounts	1	Word/HTML	New	2	Writer
Referral Awards	1	Word/HTML, e-mail	Marketing	2	Writer
Total	**71**				

Maintenance Checklist for Kadoch Insurance Agency Web Site

COMPANY BACKGROUND	PAGES	TYPE OF INFORMATION	INFO LOCATION	WK FREQ.	MAINTAINER
Company	1	Word/HTML	Marketing	26	Web master
Company Contacts	1	Word/HTML and e-mail links	Marketing	4	Web master
Company Financials	1	Word/HTML	Marketing/legal	4	Web master
Transaction Information	1	Word/HTML	Marketing	4	Web master
Endorsements	2	Scanned-in letters	Marketing	26	Web developer
Homeowners					
Process	1	Flow charts, pictures, word	Marketing	26	Web developer/WM
Questions & Answers	2	Word/HTML	Marketing/legal	12	Web master
Payment Range	1	Spreadsheet	Marketing/legal	26	Web master
Taxes	1	Database or spreadsheet	Marketing	52	Web developer
Post Services	1	Word/HTML	New	26	Web master
Professional Advisors	1	Database or spreadsheet	Marketing	4	Web developer
Application	1	Word with e-mail link	Marketing	52	Web developer
Commercial Insurance					
Process	1	Flow charts, pictures, word	Marketing	26	Web developer/WM
Dealing with Insurers	2	Word/HTML	Marketing	12	Web master
Questions & Answers	2	Spreadsheet	Marketing/legal	12	Web master
Taxes	1	Database or spreadsheet	Marketing	52	Web developer
Post Services	1	Word/HTML	New	26	Web master
Professional Advisors	1	Database or spreadsheet	Marketing	4	Web developer
Application	1	Word with e-mail link	Marketing	52	Web developer

Company Background	Pages	Type of Information	Info Location	Wk Freq.	Maintainer
Personal Insurance					
Process	1	Flow charts, pictures, word	Marketing	26	Web developer/WM
Questions & Answers	2	Word/HTML	Marketing/legal	12	Web master
Taxes	2	Spreadsheet	Marketing	52	Web master
Post Services	1	Word/HTML	New	26	Web master
Professional Advisors	1	Database or spreadsheet	Marketing	4	Web master
Application	1	Word with e-mail link	Marketing	52	Web developer/WM
Attorneys/Brokers					
Process	1	Flow charts, pictures, word	Marketing	26	Web developer/writer
Sales Tips	1	Word/HTML	New	4	Writer
Downloadable Forms	3	Word/HTML	Marketing/legal	12	Web developer
Legal Updates	2	Word/HTML	Marketing/legal	4	Web master
Client Services					
Investment Information	10	Word/HTML	New	4	Web master
Alumni	10	Word/HTML, pictures	Marketing	4	Web developer/WB
Starting a Business	10	Word/HTML	New	4	Web master
Book Store	1	Word/HTML, e-mail	New	26	Web developer/WB
Discounts	1	Word/HTML	New	26	Web master
Referral Awards	1	Word/HTML, e-mail	Marketing	4	Web master

Launch Plan

Month	Action Item
1.	Develop site plan
2.	Show site plan to developers and get quotes
3.	Decide whether to develop the site in-house or use an outside developer
4.	Develop first phase of the site
5.	Test site
6.	Market site
7.	Get customer feedback on the site

Glossary of Internet Terms

Ad Banner: The most common form of advertising on the Internet's World Wide Web; usually a horizontal rectangle at the top or bottom of a page that contains text, graphics, and interactive elements and which is hyperlinked to the advertiser's own Web site.

Brick-and-mortar: An informal term for physical retail stores, as opposed to on-line, direct-mail or telephone-order sales channels.

Browser: A program which allows computer users to read text-and-graphic pages on the Internet's World Wide Web; the two most popular browsers are Netscape's Navigator and Microsoft's Internet Explorer.

Click-through: A measure of the number of Web surfers who viewed a given banner advertisement, clicked on it and verifiably viewed the linked page. The number and/or rate of click-through is a much more valid measurement of on-line advertising effectiveness than other measures such as hits.

E-commerce: The practice of conducting sales transactions via the Internet. E-commerce payments are usually made via credit cards and the process of handling.

Hosting/hosting Facility: The process in which a file server holds the contents of a Web site in its memory and "serves" or delivers the necessary information to individual computer users as they request it. A hosting facility is a for-hire bank of computers which hosts a number of Web sites. These facilities are equipped with high-end computers and redundant systems to provide high traffic capacity, fast service, and protection against outages.

Internet: A worldwide network of computers originally designed to support government and scientific communications. In 1994, a protocol called the World Wide Web and a new type of computer program,

> The number and/or rate click-through is a much more valid measurement of on-line advertising effectiveness than other measures such as hits.

the browser, made using the Internet much more user-friendly, and worldwide usage began to grow exponentially. Currently some 67 million people use the Internet worldwide and more than 142 million are projected to use it by the year 2002.

Links: A connection from a word or image on a Web page to another page, often on a different Web site. By clicking on the link, the viewer commands her browser to jump to the linked page almost instantaneously. Links can be very valuable sources of traffic referral on the Web.

Login: The process of requiring a Web site visitor to log in, or enter their name and other information; this information is typically collected in a database.

Promotions: A class of marketing tactics designed to incentivize a customer to make a purchase. Promotions generally fall into categories: sales, coupons, premiums, contests, and rebates.

Server: A computer that contains the files and programs that make up a Web site. The server receives requests from consumers' computers via the Internet and sends out the requested information. Also called a "file server."

Verticals: A shorthand term for vertically integrated market segments; the segment consists of all parties involved in the industry, from manufacturer through retailers and their marketing suppliers. (e.g., in the consumer electronics Vertical, Sony is a manufacturer, Best Buy is a retailer, Crutchfield's is a catalog/on-line retailer.)

Web Site: A location on the Internet's World Wide Web consisting of one or more pages of text and graphics connected to each other and other Web sites by links.

> Many business owners and operators underestimate the Internet as a business tool.

Chapter 13

Finding Financing

"If it isn't the sheriff, it's the finance company. I've got more attachments on me than a vacuum cleaner."

—JOHN BARRYMORE (1882–1942)
American actor

The business plan has been written, a payment schedule with your vendors and the taxing authorities has successfully been put in place, all unnecessary expenses have been eliminated, and the new sales plan is in place. Unfortunately, the company's cash flow isn't strong enough to meet its obligations and move the business forward to be competitive. The company needs to find additional sources of funding.

Twelve Sources of Financing

> Bank financing is the least expensive form of financing.

There are basically fourteen different sources of financing. They each have their advantages and disadvantages. Below is a description of the various sources and how to prepare for the financial expectations.

Bank Financing

Everyone is familiar with bank financing because everyone in business has bought a car or a house, or taken a loan to put themselves or their children through college. Bank financing is the least expensive form of financing.

How It Works. Banks require collateral in the form of cash, property, or business contracts. Many people are not aware that you can borrow money against a business contract. If you have a government contract or a contract with a major corporation that guarantees payment, banks will provide funding to fulfill those contracts. The amount a company can borrow against a contract or property is usually 80 percent of the value of the contract or property.

Preparation Expectations. Banks require forms to be filled out. These forms ask questions about the company's sales, future projections of sales, and available corporate and personal assets to be used as collateral for a loan. If the company or management is putting up property as collateral, banks need to see a title or deed. They will then send out an independent appraiser to evaluate the property. Most commercial lenders who finance troubled companies want to see a business plan. The bank won't make a loan if they don't think the company is capable of running the business properly, and, therefore, able to pay back the loan. In addition, they don't want to loan money to a company in a dying industry.

Large commercial banks also have work out departments. Work out departments specialize in working with distressed companies. They have bankers and consultants trained to handle troubled companies. These professionals mostly focus on how to cut expenses and reorganize existing loans.

Advantages. When interest rates are low, bank financing is very economical. Banks usually don't require equity in a company. Occasionally, banks will loan money and require warrants in the company. A *warrant* allows the bank to buy stock in the company at a specified or discounted price. If the company runs into additional trouble and can't make its payments, banks will sometimes restructure the loan or allow the company to pay only the interest.

Disadvantages. If the company isn't able to repay its loans, the guarantors of the loan can lose their homes and equity in the business.

How to Keep Them Happy. Besides keeping monthly payments current, send the company's loan officer monthly financial statements and written reports on how the company is doing. Let the bank know what accounts you are targeting, because they may be able to make introductions or say something positive that will help open up new opportunities or close sales.

Internet Address. The American Business Funding Directory, which provides individuals with commercial bank contacts, can be reached at abfd.netcom.com.

> Guarantors of the loan can lose their homes and equity in the business.

Investor Angels

Investor angels are wealthy individuals who like to invest in new and troubled companies that appear to have a lot of upside potential.

How It Works. You provide your potential investors with a business plan and review it with them. Normally, you state in your plan how much capital you plan to raise and the minimum amount you need to raise before you can touch any new money that has been invested. Private placements can range from $50,000 to millions of dollars.

Investors receive common or preferred stock, or combinations of both, and in some cases warrants for additional shares as well. Preferred stock usually involves some rate of guaranteed interest paid on the invested funds. Warrants allow earlier buyers of the stock a chance to buy additional shares at the same amount should the value of the shares rise.

Before raising private capital, speak to a securities attorney to make sure you are following the laws of the state in which you are located. In addition, there are federal regulations that need to be followed.

Raising private capital can take as little as thirty days or as long as a year. Usually, if companies can't raise capital within six months, they either don't need it or they are out of business.

Preparation Expectations. Write a full business plan that shows past financial statements, current cash flow, and projected profit and loss for up to five years. Invite investors to the company's offices to meet your management team and the employees.

Advantages. Companies don't have to put up any collateral and can sometimes leverage the money raised in a private offering to get state grants.

Disadvantages. Management can lose a lot of sleep taking other people's money, since most managers feel a personal sense of obligation. Sometimes private investors want a certain amount of control before they invest. They feel the need to protect themselves in case you make bad decisions. This control can come in the form of having board seats and voting control of the company. Conceivably, the owner can be removed without cause.

Make sure you know what the person's business savvy, experience, and mental make up is before you take his or her money. If the person can't afford to lose their investment or doesn't understand the business, they could be a major thorn in management's side.

How to Keep Them Happy. Make them feel that they are part of the company's extended family. For instance, send them the same reports the company would send to its banker. Find out what contact investors may have that can lead to additional sales. Investors will

> Raising private capital can take as little as thirty days or as long as a year.

put in more capital if they see management is making the right decisions, even if the decisions aren't panning out immediately.

Internet Addresses. The American Business Funding Directory (abfd.netcom.com), along with bank contacts, provides a listing of investor angel groups. Sbaonline.sba.gov/hotlists provides links to investor angel networks in Massachusetts, New Hampshire, Pennsylvania, and Texas. [In the appendix is a sample offering memorandum. An offering memorandum is used when raising money from individuals. Please contact the state securities office to obtain the appropriate rules and regulations for the state in which you are raising money.]

Venture Capital

Some entrepreneurs call this vulture capital because they view venture capitalists in the same light as loan sharks. Venture capitalists invest money like private investors, except they usually represent groups of individuals, pension funds, and corporations.

How It Works. Venture capitalists review a company's business plan and then decide if they want to visit the company and interview the management team. If they believe management's plan, and see the potential to go public or sell the company at some point, then they may invest. It can take from ninety days—if they love the company—to six months to get venture capital.

Once the venture capitalist decides to invest, they will provide a legal document to sign. This document typically provides them with controls to protect their investment. An example may be the ability to remove the president for poor performance. Venture capitalists want warrants to buy additional shares at the current price and a non-dilution clause if the owner needs to raise additional capital.

Preparation Expectations. Management needs to provide venture capitalists with a business plan containing past and present financial information, as well as future financial projections. Before meeting with the venture capitalists, ask them for references and make sure you will be comfortable with them.

Advantages. Management doesn't have to provide collateral, although most venture capitalists will expect that management have

> Venture capitalists review a company's business plan and then decide if they want to visit the company and interview the management team.

its personal cash invested. Venture capitalists have a lot of business experience and contacts.

Disadvantages. If management isn't meeting the sales plan of the company or doesn't appear to be the right group to take the company to the next level, then management risks being removed as head of the company. The president may also be forced to sell the company before he or she is ready.

How to Keep Them Happy. Have lunch with your venture capitalists once a month and provide them with a written report and financial statements. Don't treat them as if the only value they have is the money they're able to invest. Leverage their contacts and experience.

Internet Addresses. nvst.com and sbaonline.sba.gov/hotlist

Public Funding

There are two types of government funding. The first are loans guaranteed by the Small Business Administration (SBA), and the second are loans and grants provided by states.

How It Works. There are two types of funding programs; one is federal and the other is state. The federal funding program is through the SBA. The SBA, working through commercial banks, guarantees loans that banks may not want to make on their own. The company must have collateral and must fill out various forms.

There are states, such as Pennsylvania and Ohio, that offer loan and grant programs. Funding requests over $25,000 usually requires collateral or some amount of matching capital.

Preparation Expectations. Both state and federal programs want to see the same type of business plans that venture capitalists and investor angels require.

Advantages. Management doesn't have to give up equity.

Disadvantages. Management can lose its collateral with an SBA loan. Some state programs require capital, but most don't.

How to Keep Them Happy. Keep in touch with the company loan officer or granting organization by telephone or invite them to the company offices. They will require some type of monthly or quarterly report, so make sure they receive it. Let them know if things

Have lunch with your venture capitalists once a month and provide them with a written report and financial statements.

aren't going well, so they can try to help and won't be shocked if the company can't pay back the loan.

Internet Addresses. sbaonline.sba.gov and benfranklin.org. On the Ben Franklin site is a link to a national network of private investors called the Angel Capital Electronic Network.

Vendor Funding

Vendors will, on occasion, accept stock in lieu of payments if they believe the business is synergistic with their business or has a lot of upside potential to buy products/services in the future.

How It Works. If the company cannot afford to make payments to its vendors and the vendor's products are crucial to the company's business, ask them if they will exchange debt for stock in the company. However, be prepared—most vendors will probably say no. GE Investments, the money management arm of General Electric, was started during the depression because GE saw the advantage of taking stock in lieu of payment to businesses and industries they believed had growth potential. GE and other large companies are still open to funding customers whom they believe have a lot of upside potential for buying their product.

Preparation Expectations. Like everyone else, vendors will want to see a business plan, but they will also want to know how much management expects to buy from them over a five-year period.

Advantages. It is a great way to reduce debt, and vendors can often provide prospect leads.

Disadvantages. Another shareholder to answer to.

How to Keep Them Happy. Provide them with monthly reports and sales leads.

Internet Address. Not applicable.

> Large companies are still open to funding customers whom they believe have a lot of upside potential for buying their product.

Factoring

Factors loan money using a company's accounts receivables as collateral.

How It Works. A factor has the owner fill out forms that personally guarantee repayment of the loan. The factor has the owner sign a paper that allows them to run financial checks on the company's clients. If the clients are good payers, the factor will loan between 70 to 80 percent of the value of the account receivables at a rate of 3 percent per month. This translates into an effective borrowing rate of 36 percent per year

The owner must provide the factor with copies of all accounts receivable invoices, regardless of whether they are factored or not. The invoices must also contain the address of the factor, which will receive all future payments until the relationship is over. When the factor receives the balance of the receivable, they repay the company the remaining 17 percent of the invoice. Typically, if payment by the customer is received after thirty days, the factor takes an additional 2 percent; subtract another 1 percent if the payment isn't made for ninety days.

Preparation Expectations. Factors want to receive a business plan and past and current accounts receivables. They want a list of the current account receivable contacts along with their addresses.

Advantages. This is a great source for short-term capital. Once the relationship is set up, a company can receive money within twenty-four hours of every invoice sent out once accepted by the factor. Outside of the clothing industry, most factors will tell their clients that if the client is using factoring for more than a year, there is something wrong with the business. They also may come across potential clients for their customers.

A client of mine wouldn't have survived without the ability to factor receivables. The firm she used was run by experienced business professionals, and they provided both money and business advice. Good factors provide more than money, because most factors have run or worked with a variety of businesses.

Disadvantages. The annual interest rate is 36 percent on a compounded basis.

How to Keep Them Happy. Make sure the address of the factor is on the invoice and let them know immediately if any mistakes in billing have been made or if the ability to collect will be a problem. Most factors are former bankers and business people; therefore, use their knowledge and experience when tackling problems.

Internet Address. amer-rec.com.

> Most factors will tell their clients that if the client is using factoring for more than a year, there is something wrong with the business.

Interview with a Professional Factor

Jay Starr, a graduate of the University of Pennsylvania, has helped finance troubled companies for over thirty years. He is a managing director at Philadelphia Factors in Bryn Mawr, Pennsylvania.

When should a business owner go to a factor?

Factorings core concept is that every business enterprise must operate with immediately available working capital in order to (i) maintain continuity and stability and (ii) respond to opportunities and crises. In the current business environment, accounts receivable generally are not paid on terms, may age significantly, and, therefore, may not be collected within a reliable time frame. Factoring provides critical working capital immediately based on the creditworthiness of the customer (the account debtor) rather than the provider of the goods or services.

If a business is new or has had previous difficulties, its balance sheet may not be strong enough to support a bank loan or other traditional financing, particularly in today's highly regulated and carefully monitored institutional lending environment. Because factoring principally relies on the strength of the account debtor, start-up and turnaround companies can obtain critical working capital without relying on balance sheet analysis.

How do factors screen potential clients and what information do you require from the prospective client?

Each factor has specific requirements for possible new clients. Generally, however, factors will request an application with current information, details of existing financing arrangements, tax returns, and historical financial statements. All factors will ask for a current aging of accounts receivable with account debtor names, contacts, addresses, and telephone numbers.

The factor may request the potential clients' credit files. Factors usually will analyze and research the credit of potential account debtors as part of the decision-making process.

Finally, many factors will request a pro forma cash flow from a potential client to assess the relationship between cash flow

> Factoring principally relies on the strength of the account debtor.

from operations and expenditures. The screening process often is incorporated into the process of obtaining and analyzing potential client information.

What is the smallest and largest amount of money factors will provide?

Factors range in size from small firms specializing in small business factoring to multibillion dollar firms factoring multinational companies. Consequently, the range of lending capability cannot be measured. Some factors will purchase single small invoices; most will do so only accompanied by other invoices representing a minimum amount. Many factors require monthly minimums of factored invoices; the level of those minimums may have an impact on pricing. The higher the monthly volume of factored invoices, the more advantage to the client in pricing.

> The higher the monthly volume of factored invoices, the more advantage to the client in pricing.

For how long should a factor be used?

Certain industries, such a garment and textiles, rely heavily on factoring without regard to business cycles or longevity. Generally, however, a business enterprise may use factoring until it builds its cash flow and earnings to the point where factoring can be replaced by bank or asset-based finance alternatives that will be less expensive. On the other hand, bank and asset-based financing tend to be less flexible, will require balance-sheet-oriented covenants, and may have credit limits which limit the clients capability if business growth is more dramatic than anticipated.

Are there factors that specialize in working with certain industries?

Yes. Certain industries traditionally have relied heavily on factoring—garment, textiles, furniture, and lumber, for example. Over the past decade, many factors have been acquired by banks and have expanded the scope of factoring into new industries. Equally, as new business sectors have emerged, particularly technology-based industries, factoring has become an important financing resource. Again, since factoring does not rely principally on the clients' business fundamentals, emerging and growth companies can turn to it rather, say, than venture capital without concern for weak balance sheets. Also, factoring presents an alternative to equity dilution, particularly where a business is pressed for working capital.

What is your biggest concern in dealing with a troubled company?

The first concern is whether the volume of accounts receivables eligible for factoring is sufficient to finance operations in the ordinary course. In other words, is there enough business for the enterprise to survive? Second, are the client's internal controls sufficient to permit regular and accurate reporting, at least weekly? Are those controls reliably organized to prevent tampering? In other words, can the factor rely on the accuracy of management's information in order to verify invoices, understand working capital needs, and be assured that the company has the ability to operate as a going concern?

Why do companies have to pay such a high rate of interest?

Companies like Philadelphia Factors do not charge interest, but rather charge a discount fee based on the amount of the invoice. Some factors—old-line factors—charge an interest rate on funds in service in addition to discount fees, processing fees, and other charges. As a general proposition, pricing is related to risk: the higher the risk based on the clients fundamental strength *and* the creditworthiness and general business history of the account debtors, the higher the price.

Why would a factor turn a company down?

See paragraph 6.

Do you have to put up personal guarantees?

Each factor has varying underwriting requirements. At a minimum, a client's principals should expect to sign an anti-fraud guaranty. Generally, personal guarantees by principals are required by most factors. Again, this may vary depending on the factor and on the strength of the client and its account debtors.

> Pricing is related to risk.

Is there a national association of factors to check on the credentials of a factor?

There are no licensing or credential requirements for a factor. The Commercial Finance Association is a long-established national association of banks, asset-based lenders, and factors. The CFA requires certain minimum requirements for membership, and, therefore, a member company generally will have the fundamental credentials for its business activities. Philadelphia Factors is a CFA member in good standing and I represent my company on the CFA Board of Directors. [In the appendix is a sample form that Philadelphia Factors uses with their clients. Factors usually use similar forms that are governed by state and federal laws. Please remember to have an attorney that is familiar with factoring review your documents before you sign them.]

Joint Ventures

Joint ventures involve partnering between companies where all sides add value.

How It Works. Management seeks out a company that could use its service or product to enhance their business. My client, who ran a Web site development company, looked for companies who developed computer databases and who needed a partner company to develop the interface and content for the databases. She approached companies whose skills complemented, not competed with, her company's.

Preparation Expectations. Joint venture partners want to know that their partners are knowledgeable and dependable. They want examples of work that the company has done previously, and contact names for those. Give them a thorough written and verbal presentation describing what the company can do and how management sees the partner benefiting through this relationship.

One of the firms my Web site development client partnered with was a computer hardware company. This hardware company supplied my client with both hardware and software. My client developed a Web site that provided a critical outlet for the hardware company's

> They want examples of work that the company has done previously, and contact names for those.

products. Both parties realized that working together would enhance their chances for acquiring and retaining clients.

Advantages. Being able to leverage each partner's capabilities without having to buy or create that capability. Joint venture partners can open up doors to new opportunities and, in some cases may lead to a partner's offer to become a strategic investor. Microsoft is famous for doing this, as they have demonstrated by buying stakes in such companies as Apple Computer and Comcast, one of the largest cable television operators in the world.

Disadvantages. Management has to be wary of companies who are more excited about putting a partnership together than actually making them work. Management also has to be aware of potential partners whose real intention might be to learn someone else's business so they can move into that market. Therefore, management should never share their product development process or service methodology. This is difficult to do with international corporate partners.

Partnerships are easier to put together than sharing information. The reason is that marketing people love to develop partnerships in the hope that those partnerships will produce business or keep a competitor away from a potentially good source of sales leads. Research and development people are concerned with guarding company secrets and worry that a partner will take what they learn from the partnership and compete against the company.

How to Keep Them Happy. Management only needs to do three things to keep partners happy: do quality work, stay ahead of the learning curve, and bring them new business.

Internet Address. Not applicable.

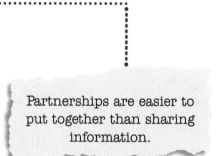

Partnerships are easier to put together than sharing information.

Venture Leasing

Venture leasing companies will provide the capital to lease equipment and software in exchange for equity or stock options and warrants for future equity. This type of leasing is for companies who can't obtain normal leases because of their credit situation.

How It Works. Venture leasing companies work the same as regular leasing companies, except they are willing to take greater risks and usually don't require a person to personally sign for a lease. Venture leasing companies are interested in reviewing the same business plan and financial statements as banks, venture capitalists, and investment bankers.

Preparation Expectations. The same information the company provided to an equity venture capitalist needs to be supplied to a venture leasing company.

Advantages. Venture leasing provides another source of capital to keep the business moving forward. They also see other opportunities and may be able to make introductions that can lead to new business.

Disadvantages. It is very expensive money. You will be paying a high interest rate because of the increased risk, and you will be giving up valuable equity that management may be able to use to bring in another investor down the road.

How to Keep Them Happy. Keep them informed as you would other investors by providing monthly financial statements and reports on the company's overall progress.

Internet Address. See cfol.com/lists.htm, which also includes a link to a Web site that has a database listing venture leasing companies throughout the United States.

Conventional Public Offering

The management offers shares of stock in the company to the public. This may seem unusual for a company in trouble, but there are companies in the technology field who can put a new spin on the direction of the company to tap into the public markets. For example, one of my business associates was running a CD-ROM game company, but the company had a difficult time selling its games because of the large amount of marketing dollars required to buy retail store shelf space.

My associate refocused the company to allow users to play the games for free on the Internet. He then sold sponsorships to underwrite each game and took a percentage of new sales that companies who sponsored the games made off of the users of his Web site. He

> It is very expensive money.

used the money to market the site to Fortune 1000 companies and hired a top-flight public relations firm to promote the new site.

How It Works. Contact an investment bank, a legal firm, or an accounting firm that specializes in taking companies public. An investment banker, accountant, and securities lawyer can walk you through the process of developing a prospectus, which covers the company's vision, strengths, weaknesses, and risks. You can find approved investment banking firms by contacting the Securities and Exchange Commission in Washington, D.C. and the National Association of Broker Dealers in New York City.

Following is a summary of the minimal financial requirements for a public listing initial listing:

- $4 million in total assets
- $2 million in total stockholders' equity
- A public float of 100,000 shares
- $1 million market value for the public float plus 300 share-holders
- $3 minimum bid price
- At least two market makers

Although the following may seem too technical, this will give management an idea of what a company needs to do to remain a public company.

- $2 million in total assets
- $1 million in total stockholders' equity
- A public float of 100,000 shares
- $200,000 market value for the public float
- 300 shareholders
- $1 minimum bid price
- At least two market makers
- Registration under Section 12(g) of the Securities Exchange Act of 1934 or equivalent

> You can find approved investment banking firms by contacting the Securities and Exchange Commission in Washington, D.C. and the National Association of Broker Dealers in New York City.

If the $1 minimum bid price requirement is not met, the issuer can still continue to qualify if the value of the public float is at least $1 million and capital and surplus is at least $2 million.

Preparation Expectations. Previously, we mentioned that there are three main types of professionals you contact when interested in going public: accountants, lawyers, and investment bankers. In addition, management needs the services of a financial printer, as well as a public relations firm that handles or specializes in public companies. Below are descriptions of what each group does in the process.

Certified Public Accountant. Depending upon the type of offering, the company's books will need to be audited for the prior two to five years.

Law Firm. To guide management through the maze of state laws and federal (SEC) regulations, an experienced securities lawyer will be required.

Public Relations Firm. To promote your IPO (initial public offering), management will need a public relations firm.

Financial Printer. Launching an IPO requires communication with shareholders, and the most widely used media is paper. While a public relations firm may be able to help in writing this material, it will have to be printed and then distributed.

Management could decide to launch the company's IPO through the World Wide Web (described in the next subsection), in which case some of the expenses associated with printing might be reduced. In addition, management could use the Internet for communicating with company advisors and as a public relations vehicle.

Of course, once the company has gone public, there are a variety of ongoing expenses, such as:

- Hosting quarterly stockholders' meetings;
- Producing quarterly and annual reports;
- Hiring accountants to review the financial records and offer an opinion on the accuracy of the records and the financial health of the business;
- Providing information to the media and stockholders.

> Launching an IPO requires communication with shareholders, and the most widely used media is paper.

If an IPO is cancelled because of adverse market conditions, those costs associated with becoming public cannot be recouped. One cost the company would not have to bear is the underwriting. Traditionally, the underwriter of an IPO takes a percentage (say 10 percent) of the offering. This percentage is the underwriter's payoff for providing their service. If there is no offering, then the underwriter receives nothing.

Advantages. A lot of money can be raised at one time. Also, people like to do business with companies that are public because they perceive them to be successful.

Disadvantages. There are a lot of financial and legal reporting requirements to various government agencies. Unhappy shareholders can sue the company, its officers, and directors if they disagree with the way the company is being run. The cost of going public is minimally $100,000. There is constant pressure to increase revenues and profits each quarter.

How to Keep Them Happy. Stay focused on increasing revenue and profits, and keep your shareholders informed of the company's mission and goals. Shareholders can be a great advocate for a company.

Internet Addresses. Go to www.sec.com, www.nasd.com, and www.nasdaq.com These three sites provide information on what the legal requirements are to go public, for a company to maintain its public status, and what broker/dealers are being investigated or disciplined. They also provide information on new ways to raise money through the public market.

> Stay focused on increasing revenue and profits.

Internet Public Offering

The Internet now provides a medium to cut out much of the function of the intermediaries in public offerings. Offerings can be brought to the public's attention at very little cost. Offering memoranda and prospectuses can be transmitted at a fraction of the cost of paper, and stock can be traded without the help of stockbrokers. The Internet can also be used to conduct stockholder public relations.

How It Works. A company puts up a Web site or works with a company like Whit Capital, which took Spring Street Beer public on the Internet, to develop a Web site soliciting potential investors.

The same information found in a prospectus is found on the Web prospectus. The money is sent to a bank, which works as the transfer agent.

Preparation Expectations. The following list of necessary information is provided by the Merger Exchange Network (4189 Bellaire Boulevard Suite 262, Houston, Texas 77025 USA, 713-667-2868, 713-661-7369, e-mail: mergers@w5.com).

> Decide on management's strategy for the company's public offering.

1. Decide on the company's business objectives and how much capital you will require to get there.
2. Prepare a thorough business plan. There is still no substitute for your company's good story.
3. Research and decide on the best route for the company to go public.
4. Decide which part of the work can be done internally and which part will require outside professionals. Interview and engage the required professionals. There are a growing number of consultants, stockbrokers, lawyers, and accountants specializing in offerings by small and medium companies. Be sure to assign specific tasks and agree to specific fees.
5. Decide on management's strategy for the company's public offering. How will the company publicize the offering and distribute the offering document? How will the stock trade after the offering? How will management increase the value of the stock over time? Management will need clear answers to guide your own actions, to answer the questions of the regulators, and to be part of the story management tells potential investors.
6. Perform due diligence if necessary (for example, if the company is acquiring a public shell company).
7. File the appropriate documents and obtain the appropriate approvals.
8. Take the offering to the public. A Web page can tell the company's story through an on-line prospectus. For some offerings, management might be able to sell the stock directly to customers, while in other cases management may need or want to work with a stockbroker. Management's strategy may

have determined that it will require promotion in other media as well.

9. Once the stock is sold, management must make sure there is an after-market for the shares. Liquidity creates value. Most companies with assets less than $4 million will start out trading on the OTC bulletin board or small exchanges like the Pacific Stock Exchange. These stocks are not listed in the newspaper and usually do not trade very often unless they have good public relations and active market makers (stockbrokers). The Internet is an excellent medium for public relations. Management must be sure the public learns of every piece of good news about the company.

10. Obtaining a NASDAQ listing is the best way to increase the value of the company's stock. Everyone is looking through the listings in the *Wall Street Journal* for the next Microsoft. Jumping from the OTC bulletin board to the NASDAQ requires $4 million in assets, $2 million in net assets, and 300 shareholders. Management may be able to get to that level more quickly by acquiring other businesses. Since the company is now public, management can often use company stock instead of cash to acquire other assets.

Advantages. The same benefits as going public conventionally, except the cost is significantly less.

Disadvantages. Many of the same problems as going public conventionally.

How to Keep Them Happy. Many investors are already familiar with the Internet, so develop a Web site and keep investors informed through daily or weekly updates, plus post quarterly financial news.

Internet Address. www.prestigeipo.com tells you how to raise money through a public offering on the Internet.

> Company stock instead of cash to acquire other assets.

Small Companies Offering Registration (SCOR)

SCOR is a public state registration through which companies can raise up to $1 million per year. It is a financial vehicle setup for small companies to raise money through individual private investors.

The investors do not have to be accredited, which means they don't have to have a minimum net worth of $2 million or $250,000 in disposable income. Most states now have provisions for SCOR offerings. The requirements for the legal and accounting work are minimal and the approval process is streamlined.

How It Works. Filling out a SCOR is similar to developing a prospectus to go public. Every state has certain requirements, so the best way to make sure the company is in compliance is to contact a securities attorney in the state where the company is headquartered. Also speak with the state's securities office, which can be found by contacting the state's department of commerce. SCOR is controlled by each individual state.

Advantages. It is not as cumbersome or as expensive as doing a public offering. There is no downside.

To use SCOR to raise capital, contact a securities attorney and have them give you the proper forms for an offering.

> It is not as cumbersome or as expensive as doing a public offering.

Public Shell

A private firm can purchase controlling shares in a public shell (a publicly listed company that has negligible assets and liabilities) and merge its assets into the shell, thus becoming a public company.

How It Works. There are companies whose controlling shareholders have sold off the assets of the company for cash and are looking for another business to invest in. The best way to find people who control public shells is to contact partners in Big Five accounting firms who work with these types of companies. Management can also contact the securities departments of large law firms to see if they are working with anyone who owns a public shell.

Some public shells have restrictions on what the money can be invested in. For example, in the 1970s there were a lot of public shells dedicated to investing in oil-related companies. They were restricted by their shareholders from investing in anything but oil-related businesses.

Preparation Expectations. Individuals who own a public shell look for the same information as venture capitalists.

Advantages. Public shells usually have sizable amounts of money at their disposal, ranging from $500,000 to millions of dollars.

Disadvantages. Management is no longer running a private company and is now under the scrutiny of the investors who have brought management into the shell, as well as individual investors who will buy future shares in the new public company. There are many legal and accounting reporting costs to bear.

How to Keep Them Happy. Stay focused on building sales and keeping costs to a minimum. Only spend money on things that will enhance the value of the company. This could mean putting off buying a building or upgrading offices.

Internet Address. Currently there is no site focused on public shells.

Venture Consultants

These are professionals who raise money for companies for a living.

How They Work: They receive an upfront fee and a percentage of the money they raise. They usually receive 5 percent of the first $1 million, then the percentage decreases based on the amount of money raised. Their upfront fees are usually subtracted from the money raised, and, in many cases, they will take part of the fee in company stock. This usually makes both investors and the owner of the business happy because it conserves cash and shows true commitment on behalf of the money raiser.

They usually receive 5 percent of the first $1 million.

Management should have only one person responsible for raising new capital: the chairman/CEO or possibly a board member, if the company has board members. Often, too many members of management become involved in raising capital, distracting them from sales and business operations.

Finally, remember that giving away equity can be more expensive than borrowing money in the long run, so be careful whom management allows to invest and how much stock the company sells.

Chapter 14

How to Pick Quality Service Providers

"My greatest strength as a consultant is to be ignorant and ask a few questions."

—PETER DRUCKER (1909–)
American business philosopher and author

Attracting star performers and empowering them is 80 percent of the success equation. The other 20 percent is getting quality outside professionals who bring the same level of value as the internal stars. Selecting good outside professionals can be a time-consuming job, but it's well worth the investment.

> Will they work with us financially if we can't afford their full fees in the beginning?

Hiring Outside Professionals

There are ten questions to ask when hiring outside professionals:

1. Do they understand our business?
2. How many years have they been in the business?
3. Have they ever worked with a distressed company?
4. Are their fees reasonable?
5. Will they work with us financially if we can't afford their full fees in the beginning?
6. What do their clients say about them?
7. When clients have left them, what were the reasons?
8. Can they grow with our business?
9. Will a seasoned executive be assigned to us or will we be used to allow a junior executive to get some experience?
10. Will they introduce us to their other clients who can potentially bring us business?

Most people just take a friend's referral, call someone in an advertisement, or hire someone they met at an event. Selecting someone that management met through a referral or event is a good way to get started, but it should not be the full extent of a service provider search. Selecting the wrong type of outside professionals can cost the company just as much money as underestimating the cost of a project or hiring the wrong key internal executive. Management needs to be selective and thorough in its evaluation and choice of key outside professionals. Most companies need four types of professionals: an accountant, a banker, an insurance broker, and a lawyer. Let's discuss each of the above ten questions and how they relate to hiring outside professionals.

Do they understand my business?

All too often business people hire outside professionals based on personality or a friend's recommendation. They hire an accountant because they hear she is meticulous and got a friend tax money back. A friend said this lawyer was terrific at helping them incorporate. The insurance broker got them a lower premium on their car insurance. The banker was helpful in getting a friend an increase on their line of credit.

Those kinds of references are a good start, but what management really needs to know is do they handle other businesses similar to ours.

Accountant. The company needs an accountant who is familiar with the tax issues and costs related to its business.

Example. If the company is a magazine, the accountant should be aware of special tax deductions for publications and have ideas on how to save money based on her experience working with other publications. The accountants for a publication a client of mine ran weren't aware that the weight of paper determined the price of the overall magazine. If they understood the business, they would have suggested going to a lower weight paper to save money. My client found out about the savings potential of going to a lower weight paper from her vendor.

Banker. Management wants a banker who has loaned money to its type of business, setup lines of credit, and is an advocate with the bank on the company's behalf with the loan committee.

Example. My client who ran a publication was in desperate need of bank financing. Her board members had a good relationship with a big regional bank, and she met with two of their top loan officers. They were smart, experienced men, but knew nothing about her business.

The loan officers were shocked to find out that it typically took us ninety days to collect advertising revenue. Ironically, one of the publication's biggest clients, and one that took more than ninety days to pay its bills, was the loan officers' bank. They didn't know that the publication billed the advertising agency that represents their bank. The advertising agency bills the bank, and then the bank pays the advertising agency and, finally, the advertising agency pays the publication.

> The company needs an accountant who is familiar with the tax issues and costs related to its business.

> Good banks and bankers are usually successful because they would have established a reputation of being consistent, fair, honest, knowledgeable, and willing to work with you in good times and bad times.

Bankers Advice

Nido Paras, who has a B.S. in Finance and an M.B.A. from the University of California at Berkeley, has twenty-five years of experience in banking, including stints in credit administration, branch management, regional sales management, asset-based lending, and loan workouts, and is a senior vice president at Silicon Valley Bank. Ash Lilani, who has a B.S. in Accounting and Finance from Bangalore University and an M.B.A. from the Philadelphia College of Textiles and Science, is vice president at Silicon Valley Bank.

How do you find a good bank and banker?

I think the best way to find a good banker is through a referral from someone you trust, such as your accountant, your lawyer, and from other entrepreneurs. Good banks and bankers are usually successful because they would have established a reputation of being consistent, fair, honest, knowledgeable, and willing to work with you in good times and bad times. When introduced through a referral, you at least have someone vouching for some or all of the above qualities that are very important to you as an entrepreneur. Once you decide to work with someone, honesty, competency, and professionalism on the entrepreneur's part will enhance your relationship further with your bank and banker over time.

What criteria should I use when deciding which bank to work with?

The most important thing in my mind is that entrepreneurs should clearly understand that the focus of the lender is based on geographical territory, size of businesses they work with, and their knowledge of your industry. An early determination of these facts will ensure that you are targeting the right bank rather than wasting precious time.

In making the decision as to which bank to go within a competitive situation, do not focus exclusively on the interest rate and fees. Look at the overall package. Ask the questions: Does this bank understand my industry? Can this bank bring added value in terms of making introductions for equity raising, strategic alliances, industry contacts, etc? Do they have

other clients in my industry? Does this bank have the reputation of supporting its clients when they go through a rough phase? Is the bank willing
to provide references? Do they have the products I will need over time? Is
the decision-making process simple? Are they responsive? Have they deliv-
ered in the term sheet what they promised us during their sales calls?

Remember, you want a bank that will be a partner in your business, one that will support you and do it in a manner that's responsive and fair.

Is a small business better with a small bank that gives more service or a bigger bank with larger cash reserves?

By and large, the service needs of a small business could probably be met adequately by both small and large banks. The issue often
relates more to the size of the loan relationship. There are instances
when being the largest borrower in a small bank is more problematic
than being the smallest borrower in a large bank. A large problem
loan in a small bank will have a more significant potential adverse
impact on the financial well-being of the bank and that fact could
result in a workout strategy less favorable to the borrower. On the
other hand, being a small borrower in a large bank may not command the level of attention forthcoming to a more significant lending relationship, and opportunities for working out of a problem
situation may thus be diminished.

If my company is in trouble and I call my banker will he cut off my loans?

One thing bankers have little tolerance for is to be surprised
about troubles in a borrower's business. Ideally, the banker should
be kept apprised of trends in the business to allow the bank as much
time as possible to evaluate the situation and negotiate a restructure
of the terms of the loan if the trends are adverse. Bankers prefer borrowers who work closely with them in good times and bad times. In
most cases, having this type of relationship is the best way to insure
that both bank and borrower resolve problems in a mutually beneficial manner.

> A large problem loan in a small bank will have a more significant potential adverse impact on the financial well being of the bank.

What kind of help can I expect from my banker when I am in trouble?

Bankers operate under the terms of the loan and are subject to internal and regulatory credit policies. It is very important for a borrower to understand these operating guidelines and to factor them in when managing the relationship with the banker. This requires that the borrower comply with all the terms and conditions of the loan and that the banker is alerted as early as possible about an impending event of default or negative developments that could cause a default. Bankers generally would like to find a way to work with these types of issues in order to preserve and maintain the relationship. This is best achieved if the banker is not surprised by problems in the business and is made aware very early on of developing problems.

> The banking relationship should be managed to avoid surprising the banker with bad news.

If my bank is panicked by my problems and wants to pull my loans, what should I do?

The banking relationship should be managed to avoid surprising the banker with bad news. If the bank is panicked despite these efforts, the alternative is to offer additional support for the loan that may induce the bank to restructure the loan or to modify the terms to allow the business to find an alternative-lending source. Many different types of lenders are available for every level of lending risk, but the most critical aspect of being in a problem situation is to have sufficient time to find that alternative. The trick is to keep the bank fully informed of the company's financial condition since that will generally insure the best outcome for working out of a troubled relationship.

Do banks have special departments that work with troubled companies?

Large banks, including regional banks, typically have in-house loan workout departments that do nothing but manage problem loans. Small independent banks generally engage outside consultants for this function to avoid the expense of having a full-time workout unit.

What do bank workout department's do?

Banks typically utilize a loan grading system for their loans to determine which loans are problem loans. The terms *criticized loans* and *classified loans* are also commonly used for problem loans. In most banks, a loan is automatically transferred to the workout department once it becomes a problem loan. Loan officers skilled in workouts whose primary goal is to restructure the loan to improve the risk or, if that fails, to manage the exit of the relationship staff these units.

Do banks recommend other professionals that can help me figure out my problems?

It would not be unusual for a bank to provide a list of consultants, CPAs, or other service providers when asked by a borrower. Banks, however, generally have a policy precluding them from recommending a particular service provider.

What are the biggest mistakes business owners of troubled companies make when dealing with their bank?

The importance of keeping the bank informed of adverse trends in the borrower's business very early on has been discussed and cannot be overemphasized. This is particularly true if the adverse trends are likely to impact the terms of the loan, causing an event of default. Borrowers should not underestimate or ignore the importance of the terms and conditions of a loan to the bank. A bank will be more inclined to work with a borrower if it is apparent that the borrower understands and recognizes the bank's concerns and shows a willingness to provide additional support to shore up a deteriorating loan. Nothing is more counterproductive than a borrower who is unwilling to acknowledge the gravity of the problems that give rise to events of default and the impact they have on the bank's perception of risk. The borrower should be prepared to provide the additional support needed to buy time and restructure the debt so that the business will have the space to implement a turnaround strategy. Without this support, which could be additional collateral or a personal guaranty, the bank may be forced to decide that an exercise of its rights and remedies is a lower risk alternative to working with the borrower.

> A bank will be more inclined to work with a borrower if it is apparent that the borrower understands and recognizes the bank's concerns and shows a willingness to provide additional support to shore up a deteriorating loan.

How many years have they been in the business?

Experience is very important to any business, but it could mean the difference between success and failure in a turnaround. Management wants professionals who have been around long enough to have personally experienced the unavoidable ups and downs of business. Management should look at professionals with ten to fifteen years of experience because these people have gone through ups and downs and have learned most of the tricks of their trade.

Accountant. An experienced accountant will know what hidden expenses to look for that can be eliminated or provide additional deductions. Someone who has been around for a while lends credibility when raising capital or selling the business.

Banker. Experienced loan officers know how to fight for their customer to get an extension or additional capital. They know how to best structure debt for it to be acceptable to the bank and not put their customer out of business.

Lawyer. Be careful about using inexperienced lawyers. Lawyers fresh out of school often take up defensive postures that are meant to protect the company. They aren't problem solvers and they don't necessarily know how to put business deals together. Inexperienced lawyers can be deal killers. Management needs attorneys experienced in turnarounds to deal with creditors, investors, and governmental agencies.

Example. A friend was involved with a spinoff of a new company from an existing company and was trying to raise outside funds. He knew many lawyers who could do an adequate job to keep him out of trouble, but he only knew a couple of attorneys who knew how to structure and quickly close a deal. He selected a lawyer that had twenty years of venture, private, and corporate capital deal-making experience. The lawyer's acumen in this area saved my friend a lot of time and money.

> They know how to best structure debt for it to be acceptable to the bank and not put their customer out of business.

Legal Insights Interview

Sam Fredericks, who has a law degree from Yale, is a founding partner at General Counsel Group in King of Prussia, Pennsylvania. He has been practicing law for over twenty-five years. Mr. Fredericks's focus has been on small companies in all stages.

If your company is in financial trouble, when should you call your attorney?

Before hand. The two elements of being able to do this are:

Element 1: Have a good accountant who's not just a bookkeeper, but gives you a little critical value-added financial management consulting, especially by putting some good tripwires in place. Specifically, he creates a few simple flash reports for you that your company financial accounting software will spit out, ideally, each week, but at least monthly ASAP after your monthly accounting close, which will show you how your business is doing in measurements that are critical to your financial health. Formulas for these reports vary widely depending on your industry, but critical measures will include where you are on cash, current ratio, overtime, hours billed for services to your customers, bank covenant compliance, etc. A good accountant will look at your business and recommend these tailored to you. Your best value in such an accountant is a small regional firm whose principals and/or staff are ex-Big Five professionals who have quality experience and know what they're doing, not a little outfit that started in a walkup over the local dry cleaners and is still there.

Element 2: The lawyer. When you see trouble coming in those flash reports or for other reasons, call the lawyer for ten minutes. Convey the key facts and ask for HIGH-LEVEL thoughts, not a library dissertation. Ask about if/what to tell the bank about covenants, potential contract disputes, your ideas to stretch the trade, etc., and factor the lawyer's reaction into your thinking. Ask for referrals to bridge loan investors, commercial finance, and others. Lawyers have contacts. Ask for ideas about defenses to problem suppliers or customers, etc.

> Have a good accountant who's not just a bookkeeper, but gives you a little critical value-added financial management consulting, especially by putting some good tripwires in place.

Is it important that your attorney have experience in dealing with troubled companies?

Yes! Otherwise he will tend to be too nice and cautious and won't know the repertoire of moves to make and what the doomsday scenario means (i.e., bankruptcy, and the first thing to know is that it is not doomsday; most companies reorganize, not liquidate, when it comes to the crunch). This is not to say that your attorney should not be nice or cautious, but your attorney needs to have the judgment from experience to know when you, and s/he, should *not* be nice or cautious and the confidence to go out there and be nasty and fast when appropriate.

Should I expect to have to pay a big retainer to my attorney?

No! A reasonable attorney is likely to charge a retainer and will first explain the projected stages of work. He will charge a reasonable retainer for each stage in sequence, so s/he doesn't get too far ahead of you and you don't get too far ahead of him/her.

> A reasonable attorney is likely to charge a retainer and will first explain the projected stages of work.

How much should I expect to pay?

The more important question is what you're going to get for what you pay. If you want to engage Big, Bigger, and Biggest, Attorneys-at-Law, go talk to Mr. Biggest and agree in advance who will actually do your work. Mr. Biggest may be the greatest experienced workout lawyer since sliced bread, and though he may charge $300 an hour he could be worth it. The problem most businesses have is that they engage Big, Bigger, and Biggest by starting in with Mr. Biggest, and then they discover that their legal work is being done by Mr. Small who charges $200 an hour and has negligible experience and is of very little value.

Your best value at a big firm is the person who just made partner (pretty good experience and quality and not too outrageous a price) and who would LOVE to acquire an account of his/her own— that means you—instead of taking handouts from a senior partner. That young partner is likely to really give his/her all for you. But if you need Mr. Biggest, make sure he'll do the work personally. If you don't need him and cost is an issue (naturally), your best value is a lean, mean, smaller law firm whose people are spinoffs from the big firms. At that kind of small firm, you should expect to pay at least one-third less than at the big firms and get pretty close to as good experience.

How important is it to get an attorney from a big name law firm?

Depends. If the other side is being represented by a small or flaky firm, the big name can scare them into settling earlier than they otherwise would, but it doesn't work most of the time. Sometimes it just inflames their egos. (They think they're big shots because you got Big, Bigger, & Biggest to oppose them. Also, they figure it will make for a big case and they'll run the clock. That's bad.) The most important factor is a good lawyer, one who has good experience, doesn't b.s. the other side (destroys trust and credibility) but is sweetly but brutally frank and will be reasonable about the facts and the various options and whose negotiating positions are therefore hard to resist.

What are the advantages and disadvantages of using a big and small firm?

Several, as follows:

Big Firm
Advantages
- Big name makes you look like you made the "safe" choice to your boss à la "We bought IBM."
- Can scare the other side more (but definitely not always).
- They've got depth in personnel and variety of talent if you need it, plus usually they have top quality if you need it. (Doesn't mean every one of their lawyers delivers value, though; their younger lawyers have good educations but today usually get very little supervision or guidance from the big shots and so often deliver mediocre results at a high price.)
- They can handle multi-location and document-intensive cases more easily then small firms.

> The most important factor is a good lawyer, one who has good experience, doesn't b.s. the other side (destroys trust and credibility).

Disadvantages

- Cost up the ying-yang. You'll often be amazed at how big the bills get, and how fast. At worst, that means you can have a good case but lose the ability to win it because you run out of cash.
- Poor value for money. You can find that expensive people who are relatively inexperienced and know zip about your business (or any business) are doing your work and outputting stuff that is very articulate and accurate but has a high irrelevance quotient.
- You're not as relatively important to them as you would be to a small firm. Big firms like to represent big guys who will be repeat business. If you're not one, they will find ways to be unenthusiastic about your cause.
- Musical chairs. Your lawyers are constantly getting reassigned.
- Poor attention. If they've got bigger fish to fry, forget getting your calls returned promptly with any regularity.

Small Firm

Advantages

- They are by definition more entrepreneurial, and they're more likely to be a "management style" fit with you.
- Cheaper; sometimes you can even negotiate a fixed fee or low-cost retainer.
- Nimbler.
- They tend to have a higher percentage of experienced people.
- You're relatively important to them, so they give you more attention.
- Fewer musical chairs.

Disadvantages

- May not impress the other side, so it is important that the lawyers' individual backgrounds are good enough to impress the other side if you need them to.

> You can find that expensive people who are relatively inexperienced and know zip about your business (or any business) are doing your work and outputting stuff that is very articulate and accurate but has a high irrelevance quotient.

- Smaller resource base, so it can't handle massive document or research projects well and don't have specialties you may need.
- Harder for them to devote huge blocks of time to your project if your project needs that.

What kind of input and advice would a good attorney provide someone whose company is in trouble?"

As follows:

1. Good attorneys start by asking questions. "What are your goals here—what do you want to achieve, and what do you want to avoid?" "What's the history of your company's troubled relationships with [whomever is making life difficult]?" "What are your company's strengths and weaknesses, especially your 'friends of the company' who may have resources—cash, knowledge, relationships—you can draw on to survive?" "What additional or different business could you do, or OTHER BUSINESS VALUE could you convey/receive, in a restructured relationship with your opponent that your opponent might go for?" (Most lawyers never think to ask that one.) Companies surveyed by Altman Weil Pensa, world's leading law firm management consultants and who are based right here in Pennsylvania, say the biggest fault of their outside counsel is: "THEY DON'T ASK ENOUGH QUESTIONS."
2. Good attorneys give certain kinds of advice: "Act like you own it." "Tell the truth, but if nothing (assets) is there, tell the other side that, and that they have to play ball if they want to get paid."
3. Good attorneys have "EQ"—emotional intelligence quotient—they get the client to ask him/herself the difficult questions, to "discover" the causes of past problems and to "discover" the solutions.
4. Good attorneys have a good client-helping process; e.g., they never say no. Instead, they give three answers (alternatives)

> **"THEY DON'T ASK ENOUGH QUESTIONS."**

to every question; and they give you credit for the wins because you made the pick and you took the risk.

What should you expect from your attorney?

A *helping person* with *references* to prove it, who *does not scare or browbeat* you. A person that gives *answers that you can understand* and that shows an *understanding of your business, creativity and flexibility*. You want a lawyer who provides *alternatives* with *pros and cons* but that are all *practical*, that come at an *agreed and predicted (in the ballpark) cost* and that leave *you in charge of the decisions*—NOT giving you orders or taking outcome determination away from you.

Are there any good general guidelines for outside counsel performance of services?

This what we have developed and give to our clients:

Outside Counsel Requirements

General: The "Company" means _____ Inc. including any and all direct or indirect subsidiaries from time to time. The "Contact Officer" means the officer titled as the "_____" of _____ Inc. from time to time regardless of what other titles, if any, such person may have. "Work" means any and all items giving rise, or which may reasonably be expected to give rise, directly or indirectly, to charges or claimed charges to the Company, whether for hourly or fixed or other professional services fees, for disbursements, or otherwise.

Specific: Unless previously approved in writing by the Contact Officer:

1. Only the Contact Officer may engage, assign matters to, or terminate outside counsel, with all matters assigned to outside counsel being under the exclusive authority, within the Company, of the Contact Officer in all respects and no other person having any authority to instruct outside counsel in relation thereto; unless in any such case the Chairman or President of _____ Inc. communicates specifically otherwise to outside counsel in writing.

> You want a lawyer who provides alternatives with pros and cons but that are all practical.

2. No work is authorized without a prior written engagement letter and budget, with written amendments from time to time, each accepted by the Company in writing. Each such engagement letter and budget, automatically upon such acceptance, is deemed to include these Requirements. The Company may prospectively change these Requirements and any budget from time to time on notice. Any aggregate amount stated in any such budget is deemed to include all fees, disbursements and other charges whatsoever relative to the matter budgeted unless a separate amount for any fee, disbursement or other charge is stated in such budget. In the event of any inconsistencies between any such engagement letter or budget and these Requirements, these Requirements control unless the Contact Officer agrees otherwise in writing.

3. No work nor billing for work outside the terms and conditions, including without limitation the hourly rates, stated in an existing engagement letter, nor billing for work not actually performed within such terms and conditions, is authorized.

4. No work nor billing for work is authorized to the extent such work exceeds budget by $[1,000] ([one thousand] dollars) or [10]% of budget, whichever is greater; provided that without regard thereto, outside counsel will promptly notify the Contact Officer when any matter is or should reasonably be foreseen likely to exceed budget.

5. All bills will be in writing and separately identify the date, description, amount, and performing individual for each element of work.

6. No legal or factual research is authorized.

7. No correspondence, memorandum or other document of more than one printed page equivalent, whether in paper, electronic, optical, or other form is authorized. No longer correspondence, memoranda, other documents authorized will be prepared until an oral precis has been received by and discussed with the Contact Officer. This requirement is not for the purpose of interfering with outside counsel's

> No billing for work not actually performed within such terms and conditions, is authorized.

independence, but, by way of example, for the verification of assumed facts, the confirmation of issues to be addressed, and the agreement of method or methods of address, in each case in the interest of effective understanding and use by the Company. In particular, no memorandum or opinion will be prepared in writing without the prior submission in writing to and clearance by the Contact Officer of its statement of facts and issues presented. Outside counsel will deliver to the Company a copy of each work product prepared or recorded in tangible form by outside counsel promptly upon completion or, if earlier, when billed or the matter or engagement is terminated for any reason.

8. No communication with third parties, including without limitation Company stockholders, directors, officers, employees, agents, vendors or customers, media, adverse parties and their respective counsel, or government or arbitrate officials, who are not outside counsel employees is authorized, other than with governmental or arbitrate officials and adverse party counsel in the normal course of previously authorized work.

9. No individual in or out of outside counsel's organization may be assigned to work on any Company matter.

10. No settlement of any Company dispute, nor commitment of the Company to any contract, arrangement, representation, warranty, or other undertaking of any kind, present or contingent, is authorized.

11. No disbursements may be paid or incurred except for budgeted ordinary, necessary and customary charges for goods and services actually furnished to, or demonstrated furnished for the exclusive benefit of, the Company. No travel, lodging, meal, entertainment or other away-from-office expenses are authorized. All air travel authorized will be economy class. All lodging authorized will be arranged and paid for by the Company. Where ground transportation charges are authorized, no rental vehicle nor private livery charges other than governmentally regulated taxi charges including fares and tips, not to exceed 25% of fares, for reasonable distances are authorized.

No communication with third parties.

Have they ever worked with a distressed company?

Any manager who has been involved in a distressed company knows the psychological and financial issues management has to deal with. Management needs professionals who are calm and experienced at advising and servicing troubled companies.

Accountant. A good accountant will be able to examine the books and advise management on what areas the company can cut back. She can also help management prepare a strong case for the company banker on why the bank should continue to loan the company money.

Banker. Management doesn't want a banker who immediately pulls the company's line of credit because the company is having difficulty paying loan payments. You should seek out a banker who tries to think of creative ways to refinance loans so payments are smaller. Also, management needs a banker who can involve other professionals from the bank to assist in developing a strategy on ways to improve the company's cash flow situation.

Legal. An inexperienced lawyer might suggest that management file for bankruptcy or for reorganization. Management may think that is a good idea because they have read of other people who have done that and emerged as a successful company once all of the problems were overcome.

Good, experienced attorneys try to save the company from spending money unnecessarily. The good attorney will inform management that filing for bankruptcy can ruin management's credit and reputation. They would tell management that filing to reorganize the company under bankruptcy laws will cost a lot of money in terms of legal and accounting fees, and that a judge and outside trustee have to approve all future expenditures. Given these conditions, it's obvious that bankruptcy should be the final option when all others have been exhausted. Instead, the experienced attorney will be aware of other options, such as sending a letter to all creditors letting them know of the current situation and encouraging them to speak with management first before employing an attorney.

Example. One of my clients who ran a Web site development company had to deal with a vendor who hired a lawyer to collect an

> Management needs a banker who can involve other professionals from the bank to assist in developing a strategy on ways to improve the company's cash flow situation.

outstanding debt the company owed them. The lawyer could have filed suit, but instead asked to meet with my client and to review his books. After a two-hour discussion with my client, the lawyer called his client and suggested they work out a payment schedule, since suing my client would only waste the vendor's money in legal fees.

Are their fees reasonable?

Management shouldn't be shy about asking for a service provider's fees up front. Make sure the charges are comparable to what others charge in the company's geographic area.

Accountants. Not every company needs one of the national accounting firms. When companies pick a national accounting firm, they are paying for the name in many cases. Unless management is looking to raise capital from venture capitalists or is trying to sell the business to a medium-size or large company, where having a big accounting firm is like getting the Good Housekeeping seal of approval, then management is spending money unnecessarily.

With the amount a company will pay for a senior associate or manager at a large accounting firm, which is a step below partner, management can engage a partner at a smaller firm. Very often, a partner at a small firm is a former manager at a big firm.

Ask the accountants if they are going to charge the company every time they pick up the telephone or whether they will provide a set price for certain services. Management is often shocked when they receive a bill that includes charges for each phone call to their accountant.

Lawyers. As with accountants, if management isn't trying to raise capital or sell the company to medium or large company, then buying the services of a lawyer from a big regional or national firm is overkill. Most corporate attorneys at small regional firms were either with large regional or national firms or with medium and large companies. Their fees, in most cases, are half that of a large firm.

Management must make sure it understands how its lawyer charges and let him know about management's expectations. Read every bill and don't hesitate to ask questions. There are times management is charged with services that they didn't ask for because the

> Make sure the charges are comparable to what others charge in the company's geographic area.

lawyer handling the company thought it was necessary. Require sign-off on everything the lawyer is working on so that you maintain financial control.

Example. A friend of mine was selling his company to another private company. My friend insisted on getting one of the big law firms to represent him. I said his transaction was too small to warrant getting one of the big firms and that the acquiring company would insist that whatever legal fees were generated would come out of the final check. My friend elected to use the large law firm and then was shocked when $20,000 was taken out of his check.

One of his investors asked if the acquiring company had used a large firm, and he stared at his feet and said no. They used a small regional firm whose fees were half what he had to pay, yet they were just as competent.

Bankers. Large banks charge a multitude of fees, from processing loan papers to the actual loan itself, for checking, and so on. A good banker will see the long-term value in the relationship if management does a good job of selling itself and will try to have fees removed or reduced. Small banks are usually more suited to small- and medium-size companies and realize that too many fees will drive away business.

Will they work with us financially if we can't afford their full fees in the beginning?

If management does a good job of selling itself, the company, and the industry, most professionals will work out suitable payment arrangements.

Accountants. Accounting firms have flexibility because they charge for their time. These professionals always budget for a certain amount of low or no-fee time for companies they believe have potential.

Example. A friend of mine started a high-end boot manufacturing company and was trying to raise capital. He went to a big accounting firm and made a presentation to a couple of the partners. They were so impressed with his experience, attention to detail, and plan for developing the company that they agreed to provide $10,000 worth of free services until he raised the money. They even offered

> A good banker will see the long-term value in the relationship if management does a good job of selling itself and will try to have fees removed or reduced.

to introduce him to some private investors. The firm also agreed to not charge him anything if any money was raised.

Lawyers. Like accounting firms, lawyers can provide flexible payment terms. There are firms that have taken stock and warrants in lieu of their fees or to make up the difference in their fees.

Example. A friend of mine used a big law firm to close a deal with a venture fund. The lawyer involved had worked many years with the venture community and entrepreneurial companies. He liked the deal and agreed to wave his upfront fees; he assigned a junior lawyer to handle the uncomplicated parts of the transaction. My friend received top-flight, big-name support for the cost of a lesser-known attorney and firm.

Bankers. Bankers can do very little, if anything, regarding loans and mortgages. They must follow state and national regulations, plus their own internal rules. The best a banker can do is allow the company to accumulate the principal and just pay the interest.

> The best a banker can do is allow the company to accumulate the principal and just pay the interest.

What do their clients say about them?

Ask service providers for references and contact those references to make sure the service provider lives up to their billing. Ask other service providers to recommend professionals outside of their field. Ask an accountant to recommend a lawyer and vice versa. Professional service providers have experience working with each other and they don't want to make a bad recommendation.

When clients have left them, what were the reasons?

Always try to find and speak with the clients who have left service providers that you are considering. There are many reasons clients leave, and a lot of them don't have anything to do with performance. Personalities and the ways of doing business may not have matched.

Can they grow with our business?

If management is trying to grow a business larger than a couple of million in sales and possibly go international, the company will need a firm that has experience in larger businesses and has an international department or affiliations with other firms around the world. The company doesn't have to be a large company to consider selling abroad. One of my clients was a mom-and-pop doll maker, and they sold their products in forty countries.

Accountants. Most companies who are considering going national and international need to hire a national accounting firm. These firms have the depth and geographic coverage to assist companies with high aspirations. Many large regional accounting firms have affiliations with other accounting firms around the country and around the world. This allows them to handle growing clients and compete with the big international firms.

Example. A friend of mine was brought in to turnaround a small $2 million electronics company. One of the first things he did was hire one of the large international accounting firms. He realized that one of his main markets was in Europe and he needed to deal with accounting and trade issues with four different countries.

Lawyers. Most large law firms have great experience in working with turnaround and growing companies and the problems they will encounter. They have lawyers schooled in the legal requirements of different countries and tax practitioners who understand different federal, state, and international tax implications. Many law firms have affiliations with law firms in other countries where they assist each other's clients.

Bankers. Ask the bank's management what their lending limit is. The answer will give you an idea for the size of companies they can handle. Most small regional banks have lending limits under $5 million. If that is a consideration, you need to develop a relationship with a large regional bank.

> Most large law firms have great experience in working with turnaround and growing companies and the problems they will encounter.

Will a seasoned executive be assigned to us or will we be used to allow a junior executive to get some experience?

Most firms of any size will assign a partner to handle complex issues and an associate to handle the smaller issues. Many times the associates will have developed an area of expertise that the partner doesn't have and can be more valuable. It is important to know that an experienced executive who has handled problems such as the ones management is facing will be available. If management wants an idea on the level of service, look at the provider's business card and see if they list their home telephone, pager and car phone number on their card. If they list their pager, and car phone number, you know they provide superior service.

Accountants. Partners of accounting firms will assign junior people to audits, but they will work with the client on personal and corporate tax strategies that determine the company's corporate structure.

Example. There is an accountant in Philadelphia who works for one of the large international firms. He is at the top of every turn-around and start-up company's list because he is known to be available to his clients twenty-four hours a day, seven days a week, and has a wealth of experience. Presidents of companies like to brag how they had a problem and this person was willing to discuss it on a Saturday night and how this person was able to provide solutions to complex problems based on experiences he had with other clients.

> Look for attorneys who don't charge every time a question is asked.

Lawyers. Look for attorneys who don't charge every time a question is asked and who know when and where to use an associate to save the client money.

Example. A business associate of mine was trying to turn around an electronics company and was having trouble with a board member. The board member so frustrated him that he thought of quitting. His attorney gave him his home number and said for him to call if he needed someone just to listen to him think out loud.

One day he called the attorney and told him about the board member and sought his advice. The attorney told him of a provision in the company board rules that allowed the president to remove one board member at his discretion without cause.

The attorney suggested his client ask to meet with the board member privately and try to work out their differences. The client followed his advice, but their differences couldn't be worked out. The attorney assisted him in scripting what he planned to tell the board regarding his removal of the board member. This attorney now has a client for life.

Banker. The larger the amount of the loan, the more senior the bank official handling the loan should be. If the company is borrowing a small amount, the banker that management is dealing with may be junior, but he probably answers to someone senior. Most banks assign senior people to work with troubled companies to provide counsel and to protect the bank's interests.

Experienced bankers usually have a deep database of contacts. Use these contacts to help your company.

Example. A banker I had known for years went out of her way to get to know every private, public, and corporate funding source. When her clients were in need of capital and the bank refused to loan more, she introduced her clients to people who would consider investing. This same banker would review their business plan, provide a critique, and review their presentation in person. This banker now has her own consulting practice and makes as much as many CEOs of midsize companies.

Will they introduce us to their other clients who can potentially bring us business?

All good service professionals should have a diverse and large database of contacts. Such a contact source is an extra value that they can use to get new business. If all else between professionals under consideration is equal, management chooses the one who can open doors for new business as well as provide advice and capital.

There are banks, accounting, and law firms that hold seminars for their clients on a wide range of topics and bring in other service providers who are expert in fields they know little about. These seminars usually attract potential new business.

> All good service professionals should have a diverse and large database of contacts.

Summary

Accountants. Contact the local chamber of commerce or local business organizations and ask your attorney and banker. Ask other business owners who they use and what they like about them.

Lawyers. Contact the local bar association and ask the company's accountant and banker.

Banker. Because accountants deal with finances, they are a good source for recommending banks and bankers. Also, contact the regional office of the Small Business Administration and any entrepreneurial or business organizations in the region.

Other. Insurance and real estate have become such commodity businesses, and companies use them so infrequently, there is little need to comment on them at length. In the case of insurance, try using the Internet to find a vendor. There are insurance companies who provide price quotes via the Web and who will allow you to buy directly without needing an insurance agent. In real estate, it is just a matter of finding the right location and negotiating an acceptable price.

In the case of insurance, try using the Internet to find a vendor.

Chapter 15

The Value and Selection of Board of Directors or Advisors

"When you look at it, anybody who runs a company, it's kind of like their own fiefdom. The other management people serve at the pleasure of the chairman, and the board of directors pretty well serves at the pleasure of the chairman. So who really watches the chairman?"

—T. Boone Pickens (1928–)
President, Mesa Petroleum Company

Having quality, experienced board members can be invaluable, especially in a turnaround. So many entrepreneurs and executives are afraid of having or using a board. Their concern ranges from worrying if the board will try to oust them, to being embarrassed over unpopular ideas, to having their authority challenged.

There are two types of boards. The one most people are familiar with is a board of directors. A board of directors has fiduciary responsibility to the shareholders of the corporation. The second type of board is a board of advisors. They have no fiduciary responsibility and serve at the pleasure of the owner of the business.

Every corporation must have a board of directors, but that board can be one person. That one person has both a fiduciary responsibility and the liabilities that go with it. When outsiders are added to the board of directors, the company needs to buy officers' and directors' liability insurance. Board members don't want to be financially responsible for anything that may go wrong that they don't have control over.

For a small company that is in turnaround mode, it is best to create an advisory board. Advisory boards serve at the pleasure of the owner/president. The company can and should grant these people stock options and/or pay them a consulting fee for their time. If the company is providing options and/or paying them a consulting fee, they will give the company their best effort. Also, paying them a consulting fee will cause management to take their suggestions seriously.

Selecting the right board members is the second most important personnel decision management will make. All to often, presidents of companies like to load their board of directors with cronies and sycophants. Naturally, management wants people it likes on the board. Management also wants people who will support them through bad times as well as good, but management shouldn't want the board to put management's needs before the business.

Unfortunately, many presidents would prefer to keep their positions of power rather than do what is best for the business. They forget they have an obligation to their investors, employees, clients, and vendors. A good board can be invaluable for the success of the company.

> Board members don't want to be financially responsible for anything that may go wrong that they don't have control over.

Executives being asked by a board of directors to turn around a company should make sure they are comfortable with the board and that the new leader has the ability to remove board members they don't think are adding value.

Selecting and Evaluating Board Members

When selecting or evaluating board members, use the same approach as you would when hiring new employees. There are ten questions management needs to ask itself when selecting and evaluating board members:

1. What types of skills, contacts, and experiences are missing among the management group that the board can fill?
2. How can these people help management grow the business?
3. What is the right mix of people?
4. How does management find quality board members?
5. How big of a board do we need?
6. Do they understand our business?
7. Can they invest or help us raise money if we need it?
8. Can they help bring in new business?
9. Should all board members be good strategic thinkers?
10. Will board members support well-thought-out, risky ideas, or will they abandon and turn on management if our ideas fail?

Below is insight into the answers for each of the above questions based on the experiences of a variety of my clients.

> When selecting or evaluating board members, use the same approach as you would when hiring new employees.

1. What types of skills, contacts, and experiences are missing among the management group that the board can fill?

Boards should be thought of as an extension of the management team. The company might need someone who has been through a turnaround. A board member should also be someone management can confide in when it doesn't know or isn't sure what to do.

Management may be looking to raise additional capital and will need the experience of a seasoned banker, investment banker, or chief financial officer to provide guidance. If management is pursuing government contracts or is focusing on a niche market, management probably wants a board member or two who has experience and contacts in that area.

At the end of the day, management needs to look at the board as a group that can fill holes in the management group and understands the company's industry.

> Have they been through the ups and downs and know what it takes to be successful?

2. How can these people help management grow the business?

Look at the company's board members and determine if they have the experience and knowledge to help the business grow over a five- to ten-year period. Have they been through the ups and downs and know what it takes to be successful? Are they people with whom management feels comfortable discussing problems and who give honest answers? The last thing management needs when running a troubled company are people who don't want to rock the boat for fear of being thrown off because management doesn't like their answers.

3. What is the right mix of people?

Try to get a mix of young and older people on the board. The younger people may be more knowledgeable about technology and what motivates younger employees. Many of my clients share the opinion that younger executives embrace ideas and change more than older executives do. The reason, according to one of my clients, is because younger executives want to make their mark.

Not everyone has to have thirty years of business experience to provide value. Many established companies would like to have had Bill Gates, chairman/CEO of Microsoft, on their board when he was in his early thirties because of his vision and understanding of the computer field and business in general. We all have met some very insightful thirty-year-olds that have more and better experiences than some fifty-year-olds.

On the other hand, receiving sage advice is reassuring. The experienced executive will teach management that the road to success is long, to have patience, and that no one is immune to going through difficult times.

Many companies are just starting to add very successful women on their boards. Unfortunately, many of these companies are doing it for the wrong reason—to show they have diversity. There are many great women business leaders, and they bring a management philosophy and approach that is ideal for small companies. Women tend to be more nurturing, better listeners, and more practical. They are used to juggling more. They are good problem solvers, especially in crisis situations that require a velvet touch over an iron fist.

4. How does management find quality board members?

Talk to the company's accounts, lawyers, and bankers; they are people who generally have a wide network. They want to see the company succeed so they are going to recommend good people. Contact professional venture capitalists and ask them for names.

Look in the business section of the local newspaper and talk to people in the trade associations and chambers of commerce the company belongs to. As management comes across good people, develop a database and add them to it.

Practically all of my clients' board members have come from the above mentioned sources. In fact, my clients tell me that some of their closest business associates and mentors were people they got to know through having them on their board.

5. How big of a board does the company need?

Small companies don't need more than seven board members. Too large of a board is unwieldy and management might not have the time to develop relationships with everyone. It's different if management is running a regional or national nonprofit because those organizations typically serve a large, diverse constituency.

> Contact professional venture capitalists and ask them for names.

6. Do they understand our business?

Would you open a bank and hire auto mechanics to run it? It is very important in a turnaround that all of the board members understand the dynamics of the industry in which the company is involved. That doesn't mean that each board member has to have a deep understanding of the business, but they need to know enough that their area of expertise can have a positive impact.

7. Can they invest or help us raise money if we need it?

Not every board member has to be wealthy enough to invest, but having a few board members who can is very valuable. When banks and venture capitalists see that some of the board members are also investors, it gives them comfort and a willingness to put their money in. If board members who can afford to put money in won't, that sends a negative message.

All of my clients tell me they personally like to see every board member have some financial stake in the company, regardless of the size of their investment. It can't be trivial, but it doesn't have to be great. This heightens the board's interest in the company and sends the signal to institutional investors that the board members have confidence in the company.

> If board members who can afford to put money in won't, that sends a negative message.

8. Can they help bring in new business?

This goes back to the value of having board members who understand and have worked in the company's industry. Board members can bring valuable contacts that can lead to sales. All of my clients believe that every board member should be thought of as another member of the sales force.

One of my clients, who ran a publication company, came up with an idea that could leverage her board's contacts. At one of her board meetings, she explained her concept and four of the board members said they knew heads of companies who would jump on this idea. Through the board's help, her concept brought in $60,000.

9. Should all board members be good strategic thinkers?

Not every board member can be a good strategic thinker, just as not every board member can be good at sales or raising money. Having board members who know how to think strategically can be invaluable. Most people are myopic and don't see how the rest of the world connects with their business. Strategic thinkers see opportunities and partnerships that will create sales relationships and new product opportunities. When speaking with strategic thinkers about marketing a product or service, their minds begin to process who would buy or use such a product or service for themselves and who could leverage this product or service for their own sales.

One of my clients who ran a Web site development company had a board member who could see where partnering with a firm that only hosted Web sites would be beneficial to both parties. A Web hosting company needs Web sites, and if they could identify people who needed them built, then both parties would benefit. The board member introduced the vice president of sales to a major Web site hosting company and a strong partnership was born.

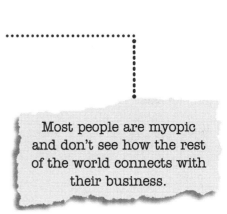

Most people are myopic and don't see how the rest of the world connects with their business.

10. Will board members support well-thought-out, risky ideas, or will they abandon and turn on management if our ideas fail?

The last problem management needs is to encounter board members second-guessing whatever new ideas management wants to implement. This can be very destructive. The best way to avoid such problems is to brief each board member in writing and then discuss it with the board as a group. Invite discussion, build consensus, and move forward.

Board Member Case Studies

Here are two case studies of how having the wrong types and mix of board members can cripple a company, and how not having a board almost killed a company.

Example One: Founder who didn't use a board

One of my clients, the founder of a multimedia company, refused to put together a board of directors or advisory board for fear that they would ask her to step down. She didn't think of how the board could help her strategize on how to fix and improve the company. Her sole concern was in her professional survival.

The first five years of my client's company's existence, the business had gross sales of $400,000 per year and six employees. When CD-ROMs became more popular and the Internet hit the market place, the company's sales more than tripled. My client had no prior experience in building a business and no mentor to help her think through the critical issues. Even worse, she was afraid to confide in her employees that she wasn't sure what to do.

Although my client read magazines like *Inc.*, which often emphasized the importance of a board, she refused to put one together. Instead she deluded herself into thinking that the company's current success was because of her brilliant salesmanship and not the use and acceptance of CD-ROM and Internet technology. In her mind, she was an empire builder.

My client began hiring people without thought as to where they would fit in and who would manage them. An office in New York was opened because surely she would capture business there as well. She launched a CD-ROM magazine without writing any type of business, marketing, or operating plan to see if she could afford to start such a business and what it would take to make it a success.

She didn't ask herself why Microsoft cofounder Paul Allen started a similar magazine and closed it down within a year because of its high cost and low return on investment.

My client's company was in such disarray that she had to hire a chief operating officer, who had to close the New York office and sell the CD-ROM magazine for a fraction of the money that was invested. If my client had put a quality board in place, they would have questioned every move and forced her to think everything through on paper before moving forward. They would have helped her develop a strategic plan and assisted her in the hiring process.

> She deluded herself into thinking that the company's current success was because of her brilliant salesmanship.

As I worked with this owner, I realized one of the main reasons she didn't look to develop a board was because she thought she would lose control of her company. She was afraid they would tell her she didn't have the experience or ability to run a business. She may have been right, but at the end of the day their advice may have made her richer and happier.

Example Two: Boards need to understand the business

One of my clients was a publications company. The board of directors of this company was blue chip. There were seven people on this board, which was made up of former chairmen and presidents of major regional advertising agencies, banks, direct marketing, and investment banking firms.

The board was well connected. Several of the board members served on the boards of regional public companies and had access to great financial resources. The board's professional connections could open the door to any advertiser. The board knew, appreciated, and expected written business, operating, and sales/marketing plans.

However, none of the board members, with the exception of the chairman, had any prior experience in publications of any kind. As seasoned as this board was, it didn't appreciate the difficulty of build-ing a publication company. Worse, the board underestimated how competitive the market place was for publications and the pool of potential advertising for magazines and newspapers.

The board, along with twenty-five other individuals, invested between $12,500 to $100,000 in the initial round of financing, which totaled $500,000. This investment initially funded one of the two publications, a magazine targeted at the antique buying community. In a short period of time, management failed to make its numbers and the money was eaten up in less than six months.

The principal owners of the two publications underestimated the time it would take to be profitable. They previously told the lead investors of the group that they probably needed twice as much money as was invested to make their numbers.

> The board's professional connections could open the door to any advertiser.

While the first magazine was having its problems, the second magazine, a business publication, also needed a cash injection. The lead investors put in additional money without actually studying the inner workings of the business publication. Within three months, that cash was spent with no improvement in the fortunes of the second publication.

The investors brought in a person with newspaper publishing experience and broad business contacts, which would hopefully translate into increased advertising revenue. Admittedly, the new president was just as naive as the board in terms of how quickly one could have an impact on sales and cost savings.

When the new president arrived, except for the two publishers, the employees had never met or seen the board at the company offices. Board members didn't know that monthly magazines book their advertising two months in advance and that the final layout of each issue was done a month in advance of the day it came out. They didn't know the various ways a magazine could reduce its cost, such as by changing the weight of the paper used to print the magazine.

There were no strategic planning sessions to talk about whether the editorial content encouraged readership and advertising. No simple face-to-face surveys were done with advertisers or readers to get their feedback. Board members didn't review competing publications to see what they were doing right or visit successful publications outside the region.

The worst part was that none of the board members had ever financed or spoken to anyone who had financed a magazine before. Once the new president took over he began to devour industry publications and sent articles to the board members. If the board had bothered to read industry publications before investing, or at least once they invested, they would have realized less than one percent of new magazines survive, and the ones that do usually lose a lot of money for two to three years.

This board of experienced investors believed management when it said it could turn a profit in six months. Any seasoned investor knows that few ventures ever make half the revenue they project, and the business usually needs twice as much money as management thinks it needs. Because the board really didn't understand the busi-

> When the new president arrived, except for the two publishers, the employees had never met or seen the board at the company offices.

ness, every time management said it needed a cash infusion, the investors said they needed to think about it.

While the investors thought about it, management's activities ground to a halt. The president, chairman, and the other managers would gather in the president's office and discuss their options. In retrospect, the president should have done two things.

First, she should have sheltered her management team from this problem. They had no control over whether the investors would continue to fund the business, but they did have control over their daily activities. The appropriate course of action would have been to tell them to pretend the company was flush with cash and focus on making the company more successful.

Second, the investors should have been put on notice that if they didn't have the stomach to keep funding the company they should close it down and everyone would find new positions. The president told me she was sure the management group wouldn't want to hear such a suggestion, but the pain of not knowing each week whether funding was available was like playing Russian roulette.

Finally, one of the two major investors came down to the company's offices, reviewed the accounts payable and receivable situation, and discussed management's next step. He realized that the company would need funding for a long period of time before it would turn around. The president told the chairman and the two key investors they needed a more experienced magazine president and that she had found that person and was stepping down. They met this individual, who also happened to have worked with the chairman in another publishing venture, and made him president of the company.

> The investors should have been put on notice that if they didn't have the stomach to keep funding the company they should close it down and everyone would find new positions.

Chapter 16

Completing Turnaround

"Treat Employees like partners, and they act like partners."

—Fred Allen (1916–)
Chairman, Pitney-Bowes Company

Finally, the management team has successfully turned around the company and it is now prosperous again. Employees are happy because their jobs are safe, and management has learned that turning a company around is similar to losing weight—it is a tough, arduous, and emotionally draining process.

Management has learned that the real reason the company got into a jam wasn't because they miscalculated the market, the company's employees were lazy, or the gods were against the company. It was because management lost focus. Management stopped doing the little things that helped make it a success.

Look at competitors and other companies that have been successful over a long period of time. Successful companies pay a lot of attention to execution and surrounding themselves with smart, hard-driving professionals, not Yes men.

Managers can never forget that they are representing the shareholders, employees, clients, and vendors. All of those groups are counting on management to make the right decisions.

> Managers can never forget that they are representing the shareholders, employees, clients, and vendors.

Developing Safeguards to Avoid Another Crisis

In keeping with the diet analogy, management has to continue to do the same things going forward as management did in turning the company around. Below is a list of action items and processes the company needs to continue to follow to avoid falling back into bad habits.

1. *Never skip the weekly staff meeting.* Time and again I have seen companies miss a weekly meeting and make some excuse for not conducting it. The next week rolls around and it happens again, and before you know it the lines of communication break down and you are back to square one.
2. *Hold semiannual strategic planning sessions.* Every six months, the management team and board of directors should meet outside of the company and re-evaluate the company strategy against the current business plan.

3. *Update the company business plan.* Nothing stands still in life or in business, so management needs to constantly alter its plans. Review and rewrite sections of the business plan. The president of the company needs to ask the board and the management team to look it over and give their thoughts. Share the highlights of the plan with the employees and ask them for their feedback.

4. *Hold monthly company meetings.* Management should constantly communicate with the employees and ask for their input. Management should never allow the employees to feel they have no control over their destiny.

5. *Evaluate management.* The president of every company hopes that their management team will grow as professionals and guide the company to the next level. Unfortunately, that doesn't always happen. Some people thrive on turnarounds and have a difficult time staying motivated when the pressure is off. Others may not be able to manage growth. Managers should be evaluated quarterly, and company leaders shouldn't hesitate to remove or add new people if the current team isn't getting the job done.

6. *Keep a close eye on the cash.* Just because the company is out of danger doesn't mean management should stop asking accounting how much money is in the bank and how the company is doing at collecting its receivables. Management should continue to review and approve expenses. The accounting people should be constantly re-evaluating expense items like telephone, insurance, and maintenance.

7. *Stay in contact with customers.* During a six- to eight-week cycle, call customers to make sure they are happy.

8. *Hold semimonthly board meetings.* Management and the board should meet every other month. Also, have the board visit the company to ask questions of the employees. They might uncover some problem or hear an idea that management wasn't aware of that will improve the company.

9. *Continuously educate.* Don't stop educating yourself and the employees. Circulate articles and bring in speakers that

> Some people thrive on turnarounds and have a difficult time staying motivated when the pressure is off.

discuss what is happening in the industry and new techniques that will help everyone grow as professionals.

10. *Hand out awards.* Remember to single out people who are making a contribution. Management needs to show employees on a daily basis that they appreciate their effort.

Self Evaluation

It's difficult for leaders to evaluate themselves. It requires a high degree of introspection and honesty about a manager's ability to lead the company. Most people have a gut feeling about whether what they are doing is right or wrong. They know if they are doing a good job or not.

In every organization I consult with I ask the leaders the following questions to determine what areas they need to improve on and whether they believe they should continue to be the leader of their company.

Are you excited to get to the office every day?

When leaders would rather watch reruns of Barney with their children, then they know they have a problem.

Are you getting to the office before the employees and staying after they leave?

Leaders don't necessarily have to be the first in or the last to leave; however, question whether you are leading by example. If you are coming in late and leaving early, employees won't feel you are pulling your weight and they won't care that you are the president. People will become disgruntled quickly.

Are you able to come up with new visions for the future and communicate them effectively?

If you are still motivated by the business, you will think about it all the time and come up with powerful ideas. When most of your

> It's difficult for leaders to evaluate themselves.

thinking revolves around your golf game or a hobby, you know you either need a long vacation–or a permanent one.

Do I have the management skills to grow the business?

The chairman of the multimedia company for whom I consulted recognized she didn't have the people skills to run the business. Today, she is a very happy employee of the company who acquired her organization.

Can I still motivate the employees?

Leaders of small companies have to lead by example, intelligence, or personality. If you notice good employees aren't performing to a certain level, you may need a new leader. That doesn't mean you have to leave the company, but bring someone in to run the day-to-day operations.

Leaders who continue to ask themselves questions, constantly strive to improve the business, avoid letting their ego get in the way, and do the little things well will succeed.

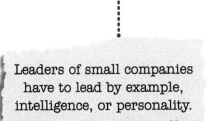

Leaders of small companies have to lead by example, intelligence, or personality.

Appendix A

Bankruptcy Court Form

(Official Form 1) (9/97)

FORM B1	**United States Bankruptcy Court** **Eastern District of Pennsylvania**	**Voluntary Petition**

Name of Debtor (if individual, enter Last, First, Middle): Blank	Name of Joint Debtor (Spouse) (Last, First, Middle):
All Other Names used by the Debtor in the last 6 years (include married, maiden, and trade names):	All Other Names used by the Joint Debtor in the last 6 years (include married, maiden, and trade names):
Soc. Sec./Tax I.D. No. (if more than one, state all):	Soc. Sec./Tax I.D. No. (if more than one, state all):
Street Address of Debtor (No. & Street, City, State & Zip Code):	Street Address of Joint Debtor (No. & Street, City, State & Zip Code):
County of Residence or of the Principal Place of Business:	County of Residence or of the Principal Place of Business:
Mailing Address of Debtor (if different from street address):	Mailing Address of Joint Debtor (if different from street address):

Location of Principal Assets of Business Debtor
(if different from street address above):

Information Regarding the Debtor (Check the Applicable Boxes)

Venue (Check any applicable box)
- ☐ Debtor has been domiciled or has had a residence, principal place of business, or principal assets in this District for 180 days immediately preceding the date of this petition or for a longer part of such 180 days than in any other District.
- ☐ There is a bankruptcy case concerning debtor's affiliate, general partner, or partnership pending in this District.

Type of Debtor (Check all boxes that apply)
- ☐ Individual(s)
- ■ Corporation
- ☐ Partnership
- ☐ Other_____
- ☐ Railroad
- ☐ Stockbroker
- ☐ Commodity Broker

Chapter or Section of Bankruptcy Code Under Which the Petition is Filed (Check one box)
- ☐ Chapter 7
- ☐ Chapter 9
- ■ Chapter 11
- ☐ Chapter 12
- ☐ Chapter 13
- ☐ Sec. 304 - Case ancillary to foreign proceeding

Nature of Debts (Check one box)
- ☐ Consumer/Non-Business
- ☐ Business

Filing Fee (Check one box)
- ■ Full Filing Fee attached
- ☐ Filing Fee to be paid in installments (Applicable to individuals only.) Must attach signed application for the court's consideration certifying that the debtor is unable to pay fee except in installments. Rule 1006(b). See Official Form No. 3.

Chapter 11 Small Business (Check all boxes that apply)
- ☐ Debtor is a small business as defined in 11 U.S.C. § 101
- ☐ Debtor is and elects to be considered a small business under 11 U.S.C. § 1121(e) (Optional)

Statistical/Administrative Information (Estimates only)
- ☐ Debtor estimates that funds will be available for distribution to unsecured creditors.
- ☐ Debtor estimates that, after any exempt property is excluded and administrative expenses paid, there will be no funds available for distribution to unsecured creditors.

THIS SPACE IS FOR COURT USE ONLY

Estimated Number of Creditors	1-15	16-49	50-99	100-199	200-999	1000-over
	☐	☐	☐	☐	☐	☐

Estimated Assets	$0 to $50,000	$50,001 to $100,000	$100,001 to $500,000	$500,001 to $1 million	$1,000,001 to $10 million	$10,000,001 to $50 million	$50,000,001 to $100 million	More than $100 million
	☐	☐	☐	☐	☐	☐	☐	☐

EstimatedDebts	$0 to $50,000	$50,001 to $100,000	$100,001 to $500,000	$500,001 to $1 million	$1,000,001 to $10 million	$10,000,001 to $50 million	$50,000,001 to $100 million	More than $100 million
	☐	☐	☐	☐	☐	☐	☐	☐

(Official Form 1) (9/97)

Voluntary Petition *(This page must be completed and filed in every case)*	Name of Debtor(s): Blank	FORM B1, Page 2

Prior Bankruptcy Case Filed Within Last 6 Years (If more than one, attach additional sheet)		
Location Where Filed: – None –	Case Number:	Date Filed:

Pending Bankruptcy Case Filed by any Spouse, Partner, or Affiliate of this Debtor (If more than one, attach additional sheet)		
Name of Debtor: – None –	Case Number:	Date Filed:
District:	Relationship:	Judge:

Signatures

Signature(s) of Debtor(s) (Individual/Joint)

I declare under penalty of perjury that the information provided in this petition is true and correct.
[If petitioner is an individual whose debts are primarily consumer debts and has chosen to file under chapter 7] I am aware that I may proceed under chapter 7, 11, 12, or 13 of title 11, United States Code, understand the relief available under each such chapter, and choose to proceed under chapter 7.
I request relief in accordance with the chapter of title 11, United States Code, specified in this petition.

X_____
Signature of Debtor

X_____
Signature of Joint Debtor

_____
Telephone Number (If not represented by attorney)

_____
Date

Signature of Debtor (Corporation/Partnership)

I declare under penalty of perjury that the information provided in this petition is true and correct, and that I have been authorized to file this petition on behalf of the debtor.

The debtor requests relief in accordance with the chapter of title 11, United States Code, specified in this petition.

X_____
Signature of Authorized Individual

_____
Printed Name of Authorized Individual

_____
Title of Authorized Individual

_____
Date

Signature of Attorney

X_____
Signature of Attorney for Debtor(s)

_____
Printed Name of Attorney for Debtor(s)

Middleman & Matour, P.C.
Firm Name
Two Penn Center Plaza
Suite 710
Philadelphia, PA 19102
Address

(215) 564-5900
Telephone Number

_____
Date

Exhibit A

(To be completed if debtor is required to file periodic reports (e.g., forms 10K and 10Q) with the Securities and Exchange Commission pursuant to Section 13 or 15(d) of the Securities Exchange Act of 1934 and is requesting relief under chapter 11)
☐ Exhibit A is attached and made a part of this petition.

Exhibit B

(To be completed if debtor is an individual whose debts are primarily consumer debts)
I, the attorney for the petitioner named in the foregoing petition, declare that I have informed the petitioner that [he or she] may proceed under chapter 7, 11, 12, or 13 of title 11, United States Code, and have explained the relief available under each such chapter.

X_____
Signature of Attorney for Debtor(s)   Date

Signature of Non-Attorney Petition Preparer

I certify that I am a bankruptcy petition preparer as defined in 11 U.S.C. § 110, that I prepared this document for compensation, and that I have provided the debtor with a copy of this document.

_____
Printed Name of Bankruptcy Petition Preparer

_____
Social Security Number

_____
Address

Names and Social Security numbers of all other individuals who prepared or assisted in preparing this document:

If more than one person prepared this document, attach additional sheets conforming to the appropriate official form for each person.

X_____
Signature of Bankruptcy Petition Preparer

_____
Date

A bankruptcy petition preparer's failure to comply with the provisions of title 11 and the Federal Rules of Bankruptcy Procedure may result in fines or imprisonment or both. 11 U.S.C. § 110; 18 U.S.C. § 156.

Form 4. LIST OF CREDITORS HOLDING 20 LARGEST UNSECURED CLAIMS

United States Bankruptcy Court
Eastern District of Pennsylvania

In re   Blank _____,   Case No._____

                                      Debtor

                                                        Chapter_____ 11 _____

LIST OF CREDITORS HOLDING 20 LARGEST UNSECURED CLAIMS

Following is the list of the debtor's creditors holding the 20 largest unsecured claims. The list is prepared in accordance with Fed. R. Bankr. P. 1007(d) for filing in this chapter 11 [or chapter 9] case. The list does not include (1) persons who come within the definition of "insider" set forth in 11 U.S.C. § 101, or (2) secured creditors unless the value of the collateral is such that the unsecured deficiency places the creditor among the holders of the 20 largest unsecured claims.

Name of creditor and complete mailing address, including zip code	Name, telephone number and complete mailing address, including zip code, of employee, agent, or department of creditor familiar with claim who may be contacted	Nature of claim (trade debt, bank loan, government contract, etc.)	Indicate if claim is contingent, unliquidated, disputed, or subject to setoff	Amount of claim [if secured, also state value of security]

In re ___Blank_____,   Case No._____
                              Debtor

LIST OF CREDITORS HOLDING 20 LARGEST UNSECURED CLAIMS
(Continuation Sheet)

Name of creditor and complete mailing address, including zip code	Name, telephone number and complete mailing address, including zip code, of employee, agent, or department of creditor familiar with claim who may be contacted	Nature of claim (trade debt, bank loan, government contract, etc.)	Indicate if claim is contingent, unliquidated, disputed, or subject to setoff	Amount of claim [if secured, also state value of security]

In re   Blank _____,   Case No._____
                              Debtor

LIST OF CREDITORS HOLDING 20 LARGEST UNSECURED CLAIMS
(Continuation Sheet)

Name of creditor and complete mailing address, including zip code	Name, telephone number and complete mailing address, including zip code, of employee, agent, or department of creditor familiar with claim who may be contacted	Nature of claim (trade debt, bank loan, government contract, etc.)	Indicate if claim is contingent, unliquidated, disputed, or subject to setoff	Amount of claim [if secured, also state value of security]

In re ___Blank___   _____   Case No._____

                                        Debtor

LIST OF CREDITORS HOLDING 20 LARGEST UNSECURED CLAIMS
(Continuation Sheet)

Name of creditor and complete mailing address, including zip code	Name, telephone number and complete mailing address, including zip code, of employee, agent, or department of creditor familiar with claim who may be contacted	Nature of claim (trade debt, bank loan, government contract, etc.)	Indicate if claim is contingent, unliquidated, disputed, or subject to setoff	Amount of claim [if secured, also state value of security]

DECLARATION UNDER PENALTY OF PERJURY ON BEHALF OF CORPORATION OR PARTNERSHIP

I, the of the corporation named as the debtor in this case, declare under penalty of perjury that I have read the foregoing List of Creditors Holding 20 Largest Unsecured Claims and that it is true and correct to the best of my information and belief.

Date_____   Signature_____

Penalty for making a false statement or concealing property: Fine of up to $500,000 or imprisonment for up to 5 years or both.
18 U.S.C §§ 152 and 3571.

APPENDICES

United States Bankruptcy Court
Eastern District of Pennsylvania

In re   Blank

_____
Debtor

Case No. _____

Chapter _____ 11 _____

SUMMARY OF SCHEDULES

Indicate as to each schedule whether that schedule is attached and state the number of pages in each. Report the totals from Schedules A, B, D, E, F, I, and J in the boxes provided. Add the amounts from Schedules A and B to determine the total amount of the debtor's assets. Add the amounts from Schedules D, E, and F to determine the total amount of the debtor's liabilities.

NAME OF SCHEDULE	ATTACHED (YES/NO)	NO. OF SHEETS	ASSETS	LIABILITIES	OTHER
A - Real Property	Yes	1	0.00		
B - Personal Property	Yes	3	0.00		
C - Property Claimed as Exempt	No	0			
D - Creditors Holding Secured Claims	Yes	1		0.00	
E - Creditors Holding Unsecured Priority Claims	Yes	1		0.00	
F - Creditors Holding Unsecured Nonpriority Claims	Yes	1		0.00	
G - Executory Contracts and Unexpired Leases	Yes	1			
H - Codebtors	Yes	1			
I - Current Income of Individual Debtor(s)	No	0			N/A
J - Current Expenditures of Individual Debtor(s)	No	0			N/A
Total Number of Sheets of ALL Schedules		9			
Total Assets			0.00		
Total Liabilities				0.00	

Copyright (c) 1993-1998 - Best Case Solutions, Inc. - Evanston, IL - (800) 492-8037   Best Case Bankruptcy

In re   Blank   Case No._____
                                    ,
                          Debtor

SCHEDULE A - REAL PROPERTY

Except as directed below, list all real property in which the debtor has any legal, equitable, or future interest, including all property owned as a cotenant, community property, or in which the debtor has a life estate. Include any property in which the debtor holds rights and powers exercisable for the debtor's own benefit. If the debtor is married, state whether husband, wife, or both own the property by placing an "H," "W," "J," or "C" in the column labeled "Husband, Wife, Joint, or Community." If the debtor holds no interest in real property, write "None" under "Description and Location of Property."

Do not include interests in executory contracts and unexpired leases on this schedule. List them in Schedule G - Executory Contracts and Unexpired Leases.

If an entity claims to have a lien or hold a secured interest in any property, state the amount of the secured claim. (See Schedule D.) If no entity claims to hold a secured interest in the property, write "None" in the column labeled "Amount of Secured Claim."

If the debtor is an individual or if a joint petition is filed, state the amount of any exemption claimed in the property only in Schedule C - Property Claimed as Exempt.

Description and Location of Property	Nature of Debtor's Interest in Property	Husband, Wife, Joint, or Community	Current Market Value of Debtor's Interest in Property, without Deducting any Secured Claim or Exemption	Amount of Secured Claim
None				

Total >   0.00

_0_ continuation sheets attached to the Schedule of Real Property

(Report also on Summary of Schedules)

In re   Blank _____ ,   Case No._____

                              Debtor

SCHEDULE B - PERSONAL PROPERTY
(Continuation Sheet)

Type of Property	N O N E	Description and Location of Property	Husband, Wife, Joint, or Community	Current Market Value of Debtor's Interest in Property, without Deducting any Secured Claim or Exemption
10. Annuities. Itemize and name each issuer.	X			
11. Interests in IRA, ERISA, Keogh, or other pension or profit sharing plans. Itemize.	X			
12. Stock and interests in incorporated and unincorporated businesses. Itemize.	X			
13. Interests in partnerships or joint ventures. Itemize.	X			
14. Government and corporate bonds and other negotiable and nonnegotiable instruments.	X			
15. Accounts receivable.	X			
16. Alimony, maintenance, support, and property settlements to which the debtor is or may be entitled. Give particulars.	X			
17. Other liquidated debts owing debtor including tax refunds. Give particulars.	X			
18. Equitable or future interests, life estates, and rights or powers exercisable for the benefit of the debtor other than those listed in Schedule of Real Property.	X			
19. Contingent and noncontingent interests in estate of a decedent, death benefit plan, life insurance policy, or trust.	X			

Sub-Total >   0.00
(Total of this page)

Sheet _1_ of _2_ continuation sheets attached
to the Schedule of Personal Property

In re   Blank _____,   Case No._____
                                    Debtor

SCHEDULE B - PERSONAL PROPERTY
(Continuation Sheet)

Type of Property	N O N E	Description and Location of Property	Husband, Wife, Joint, or Community	Current Market Value of Debtor's Interest in Property, without Deducting any Secured Claim or Exemption
20. Other contingent and unliquidated claims of every nature, including tax refunds, counterclaims of the debtor, and rights to setoff claims. Give estimated value of each.	X			
21. Patents, copyrights, and other intellectual property. Give particulars.	X			
22. Licenses, franchises, and other general intangibles. Give particulars.	X			
23. Automobiles, trucks, trailers, and other vehicles and accessories.	X			
24. Boats, motors, and accessories.	X			
25. Aircraft and accessories.	X			
26. Office equipment, furnishings, and supplies.	X			
27. Machinery, fixtures, equipment, and supplies used in business.	X			
28. Inventory.	X			
29. Animals.	X			
30. Crops - growing or harvested. Give particulars.	X			
31. Farming equipment and implements.	X			
32. Farm supplies, chemicals, and feed.	X			
33. Other personal property of any kind not already listed.	X			

Sub-Total >   0.00
(Total of this page)
Total >   0.00

Sheet __2__ of __2__ continuation sheets attached
to the Schedule of Personal Property

(Report also on Summary of Schedules)

In re Blank   Case No._____

                        Debtor

SCHEDULE B - PERSONAL PROPERTY

Except as directed below, list all personal property of the debtor of whatever kind. If the debtor has no property in one or more of the categories, place an "x" in the appropriate position in the column labeled "None." If additional space is needed in any category, attach a separate sheet properly identified with the case name, case number, and the number of the category. If the debtor is married, state whether husband, wife, or both own the property by placing an "H," "W," "J," or "C" in the column labeled "Husband, Wife, Joint, or Community." If the debtor is an individual or a joint petition is filed, state the amount of any exemptions claimed only in Schedule C - Property Claimed as Exempt.

Do not list interests in executory contracts and unexpired leases on this schedule. List them in Schedule G - Executory Contracts and Unexpired Leases.

If the property is being held for the debtor by someone else, state that person's name and address under "Description and Location of Property."

Type of Property	N O N E	Description and Location of Property	Husband, Wife, Joint, or Community	Current Market Value of Debtor's Interest in Property, without Deducting any Secured Claim or Exemption
1. Cash on hand	X			
2. Checking, savings or other financial accounts, certificates of deposit, or shares in banks, savings and loan, thrift, building and loan, and homestead associations, or credit unions, brokerage houses, or cooperatives.	X			
3. Security deposits with public utilities, telephone companies, landlords, and others.	X			
4. Household goods and furnishings, including audio, video, and computer equipment.	X			
5. Books, pictures and other art objects, antiques, stamp, coin, record, tape, compact disc, and other collections or collectibles.	X			
6. Wearing apparel.	X			
7. Furs and jewelry.	X			
8. Firearms and sports, photographic, and other hobby equipment.	X			
9. Interests in insurance policies. Name insurance company of each policy and itemize surrender or refund value of each.	X			

Sub-Total >   0.00
(Total of this page)

  2   continuation sheets attached to the Schedule of Personal Property

In re   Blank _____,   Case No. _____
                        Debtor

SCHEDULE D - CREDITORS HOLDING SECURED CLAIMS

State the name, mailing address, including zip code, and account number, if any, of all entities holding claims secured by property of the debtor as of the date of filing of the petition. List creditors holding all types of secured interests such as judgment liens, garnishments, statutory liens, mortgages, deeds of trust, and other security interests. List creditors in alphabetical order to the extent practicable. If all secured creditors will not fit on this page, use the continuation sheet provided.

If any entity other than a spouse in a joint case may be jointly liable on a claim, place an "X" in the column labeled "Codebtor," include the entity on the appropriate schedule of creditors, and complete Schedule H - Codebtors. If a joint petition is filed, state whether husband, wife, both of them, or the marital community may be liable on each claim by placing an "H," "W," "J," or "C" in the column labeled "Husband, Wife, Joint, or Community."

If the claim is contingent, place an "X" in the column labeled "Contingent." If the claim is unliquidated, place an "X" in the column labeled "Unliquidated." If the claim is disputed, place an "X" in the column labeled "Disputed." (You may need to place an "X" in more than one of these three columns.)

Report the total of all claims listed on this schedule in the box labeled "Total" on the last sheet of the completed schedule. Report this total also on the Summary of Schedules.

■ Check this box if debtor has no creditors holding secured claims to report on this Schedule D.

CREDITOR'S NAME AND MAILING ADDRESS, INCLUDING ZIP CODE	CODEBTOR	Husband, Wife, Joint, or Community	DATE CLAIM WAS INCURRED, NATURE OF LIEN, AND DESCRIPTION AND MARKET VALUE OF PROPERTY SUBJECT TO LIEN	CONTINGENT	UNLIQUIDATED	DISPUTED	AMOUNT OF CLAIM WITHOUT DEDUCTING VALUE OF COLLATERAL	UNSECURED PORTION IF ANY
		H W J C						
Account No.								
			Value $					
Account No.								
			Value $					
Account No.								
			Value $					
Account No.								
			Value $					
0 continuation sheets attached			Subtotal (Total of this page)					
			Total (Report on Summary of Schedules)				0.00	

In re   Blank _____,   Case No. _____

Debtor

SCHEDULE E - CREDITORS HOLDING UNSECURED PRIORITY CLAIMS

A complete list of claims entitled to priority, listed separately by type of priority, is to be set forth on the sheets provided. Only holders of unsecured claims entitled to priority should be listed in this schedule. In the boxes provided on the attached sheets, state the name and mailing address, including zip code, and account number, if any, of all entities holding priority claims against the debtor or the property of the debtor, as of the date of the filing of this petition.

If any entity other than a spouse in a joint case may be jointly liable on a claim, place an "X" in the column labeled "Codebtor," include the entity on the appropriate schedule of creditors, and complete Schedule H - Codebtors. If a joint petition is filed, state whether husband, wife, both of them, or the marital community may be liable on each claim by placing an "H," "W," "J," or "C" in the column labeled "Husband, Wife, Joint, or Community."

If the claim is contingent, place an "X" in the column labeled "Contingent." If the claim is unliquidated, place an "X" in the column labeled "Unliquidated." If the claim is disputed, place an "X" in the column labeled "Disputed." (You may need to place an "X" in more than one of these three columns.)

Report the total of claims listed on each sheet in the box labeled "Subtotal" on each sheet. Report the total of all claims listed on this Schedule E in the box labeled "Total" on the last sheet of the completed schedule. Repeat this total also on the Summary of Schedules.

■ Check this box if debtor has no creditors holding unsecured priority claims to report on this Schedule E.

TYPES OF PRIORITY CLAIMS (Check the appropriate box(es) below if claims in that category are listed on the attached sheets.)

☐ **Extensions of credit in an involuntary case**

Claims arising in the ordinary course of the debtor's business or financial affairs after the commencement of the case but before the earlier of the appointment of a trustee or the order for relief. 11 U.S.C. § 507(a)(2).

☐ **Wages, salaries, and commissions**

Wages, salaries, and commissions, including vacation, severance, and sick leave pay owing to employees and commisions owing to qualifying independent sales representatives up to $4000* per person earned within 90 days immediately preceding the filing of the original petition, or the cessation of business, which ever occurred first, to the extent provided in 11 U.S.C. § 507 (a)(3).

☐ **Contributions to employee benefit plans**

Money owed to employee benefit plans for services rendered within 180 days immediately preceding the filing of the original petition, or the cessation of business, whichever occurred first, to the extent provided in 11 U.S.C. § 507(a)(4).

☐ **Certain farmers and fishermen**

Claims of certain farmers and fishermen, up to $4000* per farmer or fisherman, against the debtor, as provided in 11 U.S.C. § 507(a)(5).

☐ **Deposits by individuals**

Claims of individuals up to $1,800* for deposits for the purchase, lease, or rental of property or services for personal, family, or household use, that were not delivered or provided. 11 U.S.C. § 507(a)(6).

☐ **Alimony, Maintenance, or Support**

Claims of a spouse, former spouse, or child of the debtor for alimony, maintenance, or support, to the extent provided in 11 U.S.C. § 507(a)(7).

☐ **Taxes and Certain Other Debts Owed to Governmental Units**

Taxes, customs duties, and penalties owing to federal, state, and local governmental units as set forth in 11 U.S.C § 507(a)(8).

☐ **Commitments to Maintain the Capital of an Insured Depository Institution**

Claims based on commitments to the FDIC, RTC, Director of the Office of Thrift Supervision, Comptroller of the Currency, or Board of Governors of the Federal Reserve System, or their predecessors or successors, to maintain the captial of an insured depository institution. 11 U.S.C. § 507(a)(9).

*Amounts are subject to adjustment on April 1, 1998, and every three years thereafter with respect to cases commenced on or after the date of adjustment.

_____0_____ continuation sheets attached

In re   Blank   Case No._____

_____
                        Debtor

SCHEDULE F - CREDITORS HOLDING UNSECURED NONPRIORITY CLAIMS

State the name, mailing address, including zip code, and account number, if any, of all entities holding unsecured claims without priority against the debtor or the property of the debtor, as of the date of filing of the petition. Do not include claims listed in Schedules D and E. If all creditors will not fit on this page, use the continuation sheet provided.

If any entity other than a spouse in a joint case may be jointly liable on a claim, place an "X" in the column labeled "Codebtor," include the entity on the appropriate schedule of creditors, and complete Schedule H - Codebtors. If a joint petition is filed, state whether husband, wife, both of them, or the marital community may be liable on each claim by placing an "H," "W," "J," or "C" in the column labeled "Husband, Wife, Joint, or Community."

If the claim is contingent, place an "X" in the column labeled "Contingent." If the claim is unliquidated, place an "X" in the column labeled "Unliquidated." If the claim is disputed, place an "X" in the column labeled "Disputed." (You may need to place an "X" in more than one of these three columns.)

Report total of all claims listed on this schedule in the box labeled "Total" on the last sheet of the completed schedule. Report this total also on the Summary of Schedules.

■ Check this box if debtor has no creditors holding unsecured nonpriority claims to report on this Schedule F.

CREDITOR'S NAME AND MAILING ADDRESS INCLUDING ZIP CODE	CODEBTOR	Husband, Wife, Joint, or Community H W J C	DATE CLAIM WAS INCURRED AND CONSIDERATION FOR CLAIM. IF CLAIM IS SUBJECT TO SETOFF, SO STATE.	CONTINGENT	UNLIQUIDATED	DISPUTED	AMOUNT OF CLAIM
Account No.							
Account No.							
Account No.							
Account No.							
<u> 0 </u> continuation sheets attached				Subtotal (Total of this page)			
				Total (Report on Summary of Schedules)			0.00

In re Blank _____, Case No._____
                          Debtor

SCHEDULE G - EXECUTORY CONTRACTS AND UNEXPIRED LEASES

Describe all executory contracts of any nature and all unexpired leases of real or personal property. Include any timeshare interests.
State nature of debtor's interest in contract, i.e., "Purchaser," "Agent," etc. State whether debtor is the lessor or lessee of a lease.
Provide the names and complete mailing addresses of all other parties to each lease or contract described.

NOTE: A party listed on this schedule will not receive notice of the filing of this case unless the party is also scheduled in the appropriate
       schedule of creditors.

■Check this box if debtor has no executory contracts or unexpired leases.

Name and Mailing Address, Including Zip Code, of Other Parties to Lease or Contract	Description of Contract or Lease and Nature of Debtor's Interest. State whether lease is for nonresidential real property. State contract number of any government contract.

  0   continuation sheets attached to Schedule of Executory Contracts and Unexpired Leases

In re   Blank _____,   Case No. _____
                        Debtor

SCHEDULE H - CODEBTORS

Provide the information requested concerning any person or entity, other than a spouse in a joint case, that is also liable on any debts listed by debtor in the schedules of creditors. Include all guarantors and co-signers. In community property states, a married debtor not filing a joint case should report the name and address of the nondebtor spouse on this schedule. Include all names used by the nondebtor spouse during the six years immediately preceding the commencement of this case.

■ Check this box if debtor has no codebtors.

NAME AND ADDRESS OF CODEBTOR	NAME AND ADDRESS OF CREDITOR

__0__ continuation sheets attached to Schedule of Codebtors

United States Bankruptcy Court
Eastern District of Pennsylvania

In re   Blank _____

                                Debtor

Case No. _____

Chapter _____ 11 _____

DECLARATION CONCERNING DEBTOR'S SCHEDULES

DECLARATION UNDER PENALTY OF PERJURY ON BEHALF OF CORPORATION OR PARTNERSHIP

         I, the of the corporation named as the debtor in this case, declare under penalty of perjury that I have read the foregoing summary and schedules, consisting of __10__ sheets *[total shown on summary page plus 1]*, and that they are true and correct to the best of my knowledge, information, and belief.

Date_____   Signature_____

Penalty for making a false statement or concealing property: Fine of up to $500,000 or imprisonment for up to 5 years or both.
18 U.S.C §§ 152 and 3571.

United States Bankruptcy Court
Eastern District of Pennsylvania

In re   Blank _____ ,   Case No. _____

                                               Debtor

                                               Chapter _____ 11 _____

STATEMENT OF FINANCIAL AFFAIRS

      This statement is to be completed by every debtor. Spouses filing a joint petition may file a single statement on which the information for both spouses is combined. If the case is filed under chapter 12 or chapter 13, a married debtor must furnish information for both spouses whether or not a joint petition is filed, unless the spouses are separated and a joint petition is not filed. An individual debtor engaged in business as a sole proprietor, partner, family farmer, or self-employed professional, should provide the information requested on this statement concerning all such activities as well as the individual's personal affairs.

      Questions 1 - 15 are to be completed by all debtors. Debtors that are or have been in business, as defined below, also must complete Questions 16 - 21. **If the answer to any question is "None," or the question is not applicable, mark the box labeled "None".** If additional space is needed for the answer to any question, use and attach a separate sheet properly identified with the case name, case number (if known), and the number of the question.

DEFINITIONS

"In business." A debtor is "in business" for the purpose of this form if the debtor is a corporation or partnership. An individual debtor is "in business" for the purpose of this form if the debtor is or has been, within the two years immediately preceding the filing of the this bankruptcy case, any of the following: an officer, director, managing executive, or person in control of a corporation; a partner, other than a limited partner, of a partnership; a sole proprietor or self-employed.

"Insider." The term "insider" includes but is not limited to: relatives of the debtor; general partners of the debtor and their relatives; corporations of which the debtor is an officer, director, or person in control; officers, directors, and any person in control of a corporate debtor and their relatives; affiliates of the debtor and insiders of such affiliates; any managing agent of the debtor. 11 U.S.C. § 101.

1. Income from employment or operation of business

None State the gross amount of income the debtor has received from employment, trade, or profession, or from operation of the debtor's business from
■   the beginning of this calendar year to the date this case was commenced. State also the gross amounts received during the **two years** immediately preceding this calendar year. (A debtor that maintains, or has maintained, financial records on the basis of a fiscal rather than a calendar year may report fiscal year income. Identify the beginning and ending dates of the debtor's fiscal year.) If a joint petition is filed, state income for each spouse separately. (Married debtors filing under chapter 12 or chapter 13 must state income of both spouses whether or not a joint petition is filed, unless the spouses are separated and a joint petition is not filed.)

              AMOUNT   SOURCE (if more than one)

2. Income other than from employment or operation of business

None State the amount of income received by the debtor other than from employment, trade, profession, or operation of the debtor's business during
■   the **two years** immediately preceding the commencement of this case. Give particulars. If a joint petition is filed, state income for each spouse separately. (Married debtors filing under chapter 12 or chapter 13 must state income for each spouse whether or not a joint petition is filed, unless the spouses are separated and a joint petition is not filed.)

              AMOUNT   SOURCE (if more than one)

3. Payments to creditors

None a. List all payments on loans, installment purchases of goods or services, and other debts, aggregating more than $600 to any creditor, made
■   within **90 days** immediately preceding the commencement of this case. (Married debtors filing under chapter 12 or chapter 13 must include payments by either or both spouses whether or not a joint petition is filed, unless the spouses are separated and a joint petition is not filed.)

NAME AND ADDRESS OF CREDITOR	DATES OF PAYMENTS	AMOUNT PAID	AMOUNT STILL OWING

None b. List all payments made within **one year** immediately preceding the commencement of this case to or for the benefit of creditors who are or
■   were insiders. (Married debtors filing under chapter 12 or chapter 13 must include payments by either or both spouses whether or not a joint petition is filed, unless the spouses are separated and a joint petition is not filed.)

NAME AND ADDRESS OF CREDITOR AND RELATIONSHIP TO DEBTOR	DATE OF PAYMENT	AMOUNT PAID	AMOUNT STILL OWING

4. Suits, executions, garnishments and attachments

None ■ a. List all suits and administrative proceedings to which the debtor is or was a party within **one year** immediately preceding the filing of this bankruptcy case. (Married debtors filing under chapter 12 or chapter 13 must include information concerning either or both spouses whether or not a joint petition is filed, unless the spouses are separated and a joint petition is not filed.)

CAPTION OF SUIT AND CASE NUMBER	NATURE OF PROCEEDING	COURT OR AGENCY AND LOCATION	STATUS OR DISPOSITION

None ■ b. Describe all property that has been attached, garnished or seized under any legal or equitable process within **one year** immediately preceding the commencement of this case. (Married debtors filing under chapter 12 or chapter 13 must include information concerning property of either or both spouses whether or not a joint petition is filed, unless the spouses are separated and a joint petition is not filed.)

NAME AND ADDRESS OF PERSON FOR WHOSE BENEFIT PROPERTY WAS SEIZED	DATE OF SEIZURE	DESCRIPTION AND VALUE OF PROPERTY

5. Repossessions, foreclosures and returns

None ■ List all property that has been repossessed by a creditor, sold at a foreclosure sale, transferred through a deed in lieu of foreclosure or returned to the seller, within **one year** immediately preceding the commencement of this case. (Married debtors filing under chapter 12 or chapter 13 must include information concerning property of either or both spouses whether or not a joint petition is filed, unless the spouses are separated and a joint petition is not filed.)

NAME AND ADDRESS OF CREDITOR OR SELLER	DATE OF REPOSSESSION, FORECLOSURE SALE, TRANSFER OR RETURN	DESCRIPTION AND VALUE OF PROPERTY

6. Assignments and receiverships

None ■ a. Describe any assignment of property for the benefit of creditors made within **120 days** immediately preceding the commencement of this case. (Married debtors filing under chapter 12 or chapter 13 must include any assignment by either or both spouses whether or not a joint petition is filed, unless the spouses are separated and a joint petition is not filed.)

NAME AND ADDRESS OF ASSIGNEE	DATE OF ASSIGNMENT	TERMS OF ASSIGNMENT OR SETTLEMENT

None ■ b. List all property which has been in the hands of a custodian, receiver, or court-appointed official within **one year** immediately preceding the commencement of this case. (Married debtors filing under chapter 12 or chapter 13 must include information concerning property of either or both spouses whether or not a joint petition is filed, unless the spouses are separated and a joint petition is not filed.)

NAME AND ADDRESS OF CUSTODIAN	NAME AND LOCATION OF COURT, CASE TITLE & NUMBER	DATE OF ORDER	DESCRIPTION AND VALUE OF PROPERTY

7. Gifts

None ■ List all gifts or charitable contributions made within **one year** immediately preceding the commencement of this case except ordinary and usual gifts to family members aggregating less than $200 in value per individual family member and charitable contributions aggregating less than $100 per recipient. (Married debtors filing under chapter 12 or chapter 13 must include gifts or contributions by either or both spouses whether or not a joint petition is filed, unless the spouses are separated and a joint petition is not filed.)

NAME AND ADDRESS OF PERSON OR ORGANIZATION	RELATIONSHIP TO DEBTOR, IF ANY	DATE OF GIFT	DESCRIPTION AND VALUE OF GIFT

8. Losses

None ■ List all losses from fire, theft, other casualty or gambling within **one year** immediately preceding the commencement of this case **or since the commencement of this case.** (Married debtors filing under chapter 12 or chapter 13 must include losses by either or both spouses whether or not a joint petition is filed, unless the spouses are separated and a joint petition is not filed.)

DESCRIPTION AND VALUE OF PROPERTY	DESCRIPTION OF CIRCUMSTANCES AND, IF LOSS WAS COVERED IN WHOLE OR IN PART BY INSURANCE, GIVE PARTICULARS	DATE OF LOSS

9. Payments related to debt counseling or bankruptcy

None ■ List all payments made or property transferred by or on behalf of the debtor to any persons, including attorneys, for consultation concerning debt consolidation, relief under the bankruptcy law or preparation of the petition in bankruptcy within **one year** immediately preceding the commencement of this case.

NAME AND ADDRESS OF PAYEE	DATE OF PAYMENT, NAME OF PAYOR IF OTHER THAN DEBTOR	AMOUNT OF MONEY OR DESCRIPTION AND VALUE OF PROPERTY

10. Other transfers

None ■ a. List all other property, other than property transferred in the ordinary course of the business or financial affairs of the debtor, transferred either absolutely or as security within **one year** immediately preceding the commencement of this case. (Married debtors filing under chapter 12 or chapter 13 must include transfers by either or both spouses whether or not a joint petition is filed, unless the spouses are separated and a joint petition is not filed.)

NAME AND ADDRESS OF TRANSFEREE, RELATIONSHIP TO DEBTOR	DATE	DESCRIBE PROPERTY TRANSFERRED AND VALUE RECEIVED

11. Closed financial accounts

None ■ List all financial accounts and instruments held in the name of the debtor or for the benefit of the debtor which were closed, sold, or otherwise transferred within **one year** immediately preceding the commencement of this case. Include checking, savings, or other financial accounts, certificates of deposit, or other instruments; shares and share accounts held in banks, credit unions, pension funds, cooperatives, associations, brokerage houses and other financial institutions. (Married debtors filing under chapter 12 or chapter 13 must include information concerning accounts or instruments held by or for either or both spouses whether or not a joint petition is filed, unless the spouses are separated and a joint petition is not filed.)

NAME AND ADDRESS OF INSTITUTION	TYPE AND NUMBER OF ACCOUNT AND AMOUNT OF FINAL BALANCE	AMOUNT AND DATE OF SALE OR CLOSING

12. Safe deposit boxes

None ■ List each safe deposit or other box or depository in which the debtor has or had securities, cash, or other valuables within **one year** immediately preceding the commencement of this case. (Married debtors filing under chapter 12 or chapter 13 must include boxes or depositories of either or both spouses whether or not a joint petition is filed, unless the spouses are separated and a joint petition is not filed.)

NAME AND ADDRESS OF BANK OR OTHER DEPOSITORY	NAMES AND ADDRESSES OF THOSE WITH ACCESS TO BOX OR DEPOSITORY	DESCRIPTION OF CONTENTS	DATE OF TRANSFER OR SURRENDER, IF ANY

13. Setoffs

None ■ List all setoffs made by any creditor, including a bank, against a debt or deposit of the debtor within **90 days** preceding the commencement of this case. (Married debtors filing under chapter 12 or chapter 13 must include information concerning either or both spouses whether or not a joint petition is filed, unless the spouses are separated and a joint petition is not filed.)

NAME AND ADDRESS OF CREDITOR	DATE OF SETOFF	AMOUNT OF SETOFF

14. Property held for another person

None ■ List all property owned by another person that the debtor holds or controls.

NAME AND ADDRESS OF OWNER	DESCRIPTION AND VALUE OF PROPERTY	LOCATION OF PROPERTY

15. Prior address of debtor

None ■ If the debtor has moved within the **two years** immediately preceding the commencement of this case, list all premises which the debtor occupied during that period and vacated prior to the commencement of this case. If a joint petition is filed, report also any separate address of either spouse.

ADDRESS	NAME USED	DATES OF OCCUPANCY

DECLARATION UNDER PENALTY OF PERJURY ON BEHALF OF CORPORATION OR PARTNERSHIP

I declare under penalty of perjury that I have read the answers contained in the foregoing statement of financial affairs and any attachments thereto and that they are true and correct to the best of my knowledge, information and belief.

Date_____   Signature_____

Penalty for making a false statement or concealing property: Fine of up to $500,000 or imprisonment for up to 5 years or both. 18 U.S.C §§ 152 and 3571.

In re   Blank _____,   Case No._____

                                     Debtor

                                                       Chapter_____11_____

COMPENSATION STATEMENT OF ATTORNEY FOR THE DEBTOR(S)

1. The undersigned is the attorney for the debtor(s) in this case.

2. The total compensation promised the undersigned by the debtor(s) for the services rendered or to be rendered in connection with this case is $_____0.00__; the only compensation which has been received from the debtor(s) or any other person on said account is $_____0.00__; the balance due thereon is $_____0.00__; and the source of compensation paid or promised, if a source other than the debtor(s), is:

3. The undersigned further states that no understanding or agreement exists for a division of fees or compensation between the undersigned and any other person or entity, except any agreement he may have for the sharing of his compensation with a member or members or regular associate of his law firm and except:

4. $_____0.00__ of the filing fee has been paid.

_____   _____

Date   *Attorney for Debtor(s):*

                                                Middleman & Matour, P.C.
                                                Two Penn Center Plaza
                                                Suite 710
                                                Philadelphia, PA 19102
                                                (215) 564-5900

[Required by Rule 2016(b) to be filed and transmitted to the United States Trustee within 15 days after the order for relief. (Not to be filed in lieu of an Application for Compensation which may be filed pursuant to Bankruptcy Rule 2016.)]

COMPENSATION STATEMENT OF ATTORNEY FOR THE DEBTOR(S)

United States Bankruptcy Court
Eastern District of Pennsylvania

In re   Blank _____,   Case No. _____

                                        Debtor

                                        Chapter _____ 11 _____

LIST OF EQUITY SECURITY HOLDERS

Following is the list of the Debtor's equity security holders which is prepared in accordance with Rule 1007(a)(3) for filing in this chapter 11 case.

Name and last known address or place of business of holder	Security Class	Number of Securities	Kind of Interest

None

<u>0</u>   continuation sheets attached to List of Equity Security Holders

Appendix B

Confidential Private Placement Memorandum

DRAFT 1799:1

_____ CORPORATION

CONFIDENTIAL PRIVATE PLACEMENT MEMORANDUM

This Confidential Private Placement Memorandum (this "Memorandum") relates to the private offer and sale (the "Offering") of 1.5 million units (the "Units") consisting of one share of common stock, par value $.01 per share (the "Common Stock"), and one warrant to purchase one half of one share of Common Stock (a Warrant) of _____, a Pennsylvania corporation (the "Company"), at a price of $ .00 per Unit.

The Offering is being made to _____(or a special purpose partnership to be formed by it,) and other selected "accredited investors" as defined in Rule 501(a) of Regulation D promulgated under the Securities Act of 1933, as amended (the "Securities Act"). The Company will sell the Units pursuant to definitive stock purchase agreements as described herein.

The primary market for the Common Stock is the NASDAQ SmallCap Market, where it trades under the symbol "_". The Common Stock is also traded on the Philadelphia Stock Exchange under the symbol "_" . However, the shares of Common Stock underlying the Units and any shares of Common Stock issued upon conversion of Warrants will be subject to restrictions and may not be resold or otherwise transferred except pursuant to registrations under or exemptions from the registration requirements of the Securities Act and applicable state securities laws.

An investment in these Units involves a high degree of risk. See "Risk Factors" on page __. Investors must be prepared to bear the risk of their investment for an indefinite period and be able to withstand a total loss of their investment.

These securities have not been registered under the Securities Act or any applicable state securities laws. Neither the Securities and Exchange Commission nor any state regulatory authority has approved or disapproved these Units and the Offering or determined if this Memorandum is truthful or complete. Any representation to the contrary is a criminal offense.

The information contained in this Memorandum and any other materials related to the Offering (the Related Materials) is confidential and proprietary to the Company. The Company is submitting this information to prospective investors solely for their confidential use. By accepting delivery of this Memorandum and any Related Materials, prospective investors understand and agree that, without the prior written permission of the Company, such investors will not release or discuss the information contained herein and therein with any person other than persons authorized by the Company. Prospective investors may not reproduce this Memorandum or any Related Materials or use them for any purpose other than evaluating a potential investment in the Company. Prospective investors further agree to return this Memorandum and any Related Materials to the Company if they do not subscribe to purchase any Units, their subscriptions are not accepted, or the Offering is terminated or withdrawn.

The date of this Memorandum is January __, 20__

Prospective investors should carefully review the following statements, as well as the remainder of this Memorandum, before making an investment decision.

- In making an investment decision, prospective investors must rely on their own examination of the Company and the terms of the Offering, including the merits and risks involved.
- The offer and sale of the Units have not been registered under the Securities Act or any state securities laws, in reliance upon exemptions from registration provided by Section 4(2) of the Securities Act, Regulation D promulgated thereunder and similar exemptions from registration provided by certain state securities laws. The Units are being offered only to accredited investors who have the qualifications necessary to permit the Units to be offered and sold in reliance upon such exemptions.
- This Memorandum constitutes an offer only to the prospective investor whose name appears in the appropriate space on the cover page hereof and to whom the Company initially provided this Memorandum. This Memorandum does not constitute an offer to sell to or a solicitation of an offer to buy from anyone in any state or other jurisdiction in which such offer or solicitation is unauthorized, or to any person to whom it is unlawful to make such an offer or solicitation.
- The Company reserves the right, in its sole discretion and for any reason whatsoever, to modify, amend, or withdraw all or a portion of the Offering or to accept or reject, in whole or in part, any prospective investment in the Units or to allot to any prospective investor less than the amount of Units such investor desires to purchase. The Company shall have no liability whatsoever to any person if any of the foregoing shall occur.

- Prospective investors should not imply from the delivery of this Memorandum or any sale made hereunder that the affairs of the Company and other information contained herein have remained unchanged since the date hereof.
- The Company has summarized certain provisions of various agreements or other documents in this Memorandum, but prospective investors should not assume that these summaries are complete. Such summaries are qualified in their entirety by reference to the texts of the original documents, which the Company will make available to prospective investors upon request.
- Prospective investors should not construe the contents of this Memorandum, any Related Materials, or any prior or subsequent communications from or with the Company or any professional associated with the Offering as legal or professional tax advice. The prospective investor authorized to receive this Memorandum should consult its own legal, financial, and other advisors as to matters concerning purchase of the Units.
- Prior to any closing for the sale of Units, the Company will give prospective investors and their advisors the opportunity to ask representatives of the Company questions concerning the Company and the Offering and to obtain any additional relevant information, to the extent the Company possesses such information or can obtain it without unreasonable effort or expense. Except for such information that is provided by the Company in response to such requests, no person has been authorized in connection with the offer or sale of the Units to give any information or to make any representation not contained in this Memorandum. Prospective investors should not rely upon information or representations not contained in this Memorandum unless they are provided by the Company as indicated above.
- The securities described herein may not be sold nor may any offers to purchase be accepted prior to the delivery to prospective investors of certain underlying documents including, among others, a stock purchase agreement reflecting the definitive terms and conditions of the Offering. Prospective investors should review the full text of such stock purchase agreements carefully prior to purchase.

TABLE OF CONTENTS
[to be supplied]

Cautionary Statement Concerning Forward-Looking Information

This Memorandum contains forward-looking information, including projections and forward-looking statements, that involve a number of risks and uncertainties. A number of factors could cause actual results, performance, achievements of the Company, or industry results to be materially different from any future results, performance or achievements expressed or implied by such forward-looking information. These factors include, but are not limited to, the competitive environment in the _____ industry in general and in the Companys specific target markets; changes in prevailing interest rates and the availability of and terms of financing to fund the anticipated growth of the Companys business; inflation; changes in costs of goods and services; economic conditions in general and in the Companys specific target markets; demographic changes; changes in or failure to comply with federal, state, local or foreign government regulation; liability and other claims asserted against the Company; changes in operating strategy or development plans; the ability to attract and retain qualified personnel; changes in the Companys capital expenditure plans; and other factors referenced herein. In addition, such forward-looking information included herein does not purport to be predictions of future events or circumstances and may not be realized. Forward-looking information can be identified by, among other things, the use of forward-looking terminology such as "believes," "expects," "may", "will," "should," "seeks," "pro forma," "anticipates," "or intends" or the negative of any thereof, or other variations thereon or comparable terminology, or by discussions of strategy or intentions. Given these uncertainties, prospective investors are cautioned not to place undue reliance on such forward-looking information. The Company disclaims any obligations to update any such factors or to publicly announce the results of any revisions to any of the forward-looking information contained herein to reflect future events or developments.

EXECUTIVE SUMMARY
INVESTMENT HIGHLIGHTS

The following is a summary of certain information appearing elsewhere in this Memorandum. Reference is made to, and this summary is qualified in its entirety by, and should be read in conjunction with, the more detailed information and financial statements, including the notes thereto, appearing elsewhere in this Memorandum or in the Companys annual and quarterly reports and other filings with the Securities and Exchange Commission.

The Company

_____ Corporation ("___" or the "Company") is engaged in the research, development, and commercialization of _____(" ") technology for use in _____devices. The initial markets for the Companys technology will likely be in the _____industry. The _____ has been estimated by___ to be $___ in 20__. The _____of this market was approximately $_____in 20__ and is rapidly growing.

The Company has the exclusive, perpetual, worldwide license to commercialize all_____. To date, ____ patents have been issued in the United States, more than ____ patent applications (with corresponding foreign protection) have been filed, and additional patents are being filed.

The Company believes that its _____ can have significant cost and performance advantages over existing technologies and provide it with an opportunity to gain significant _____ industry of the future. Some industry observers have compared the_____ industry to the _____industry, projecting a significant future growth opportunity, provided a new technology can be commercialized to meet the needs of the expanding information age. The Company believes that its _____ technology has the potential to fulfill the needs of this large and rapidly growing market.

_____Technology

Research Partners

Market Opportunities

Commercialization Strategy

Strong, Experienced Management Team

The Company has assembled a strong and proven management team with expertise in technology development and commercialization; strategic alliances; and licensing, finance, and marketing.

The Offering

Set forth below are the basic terms and conditions on which the Company proposes to sell the Units to ___ and certain accredited investors in a private placement, subject to definitive stock purchase agreements. The Company shall use the net proceeds from the sale of the Units to fund the start up of the Companys Development and Pilot Line Facility and for general corporate purposes, including to fund additional operating losses and product development.

Security:	A Unit, which consists of one share of Common Stock and one Warrant to purchase one half of one share of Common Stock.
Offering Amount and Size:	$6,000,000 for an aggregate of 1.5 million Units, consisting of an aggregate of 1.5 million shares of Common Stock and Warrants to purchase 750,000 shares of Common Stock.
Purchase Price:	$4.00 per Unit
Warrant Exercise Price:	$5.00 per share.
Expiration of Warrants:	Five years from date of issuance.
Anti-Dilution Provisions:	The conversion price of the Warrants is subject to adjustment in the event of____ [insert customary anti-dilution provisions].
Registration Rights:	[The holders (the "Holders") of shares of Common Stock underlying the Units and shares of Common Stock issued upon conversion of Warrants may require, on not more than two occasions after _____, _____ that the Company use its best efforts to file a registration statement covering the public sale of such Common Stock; provided, however, that the Company will have the right to delay such a demand registration under certain circumstances for a period not in excess of ___ days each in any 12-month period. The Holders will also have piggyback registration rights, [subject to underwriter cut back]. The registration rights expire ___ years after _____, ____. No Holder can exercise any registration rights for an intended sale that can be effectuated in compliance with Rule 144 under the Securities Act.]
Co-Sale Rights:	If _____ agree to sell any of their shares of Common Stock, they are required to first give the Holders the opportunity to participate in such sale on a basis proportionate to the amount of securities held by the Holders.

Board Representations:	The Company will expand its Board of Directors to eight members and elect the nominee of AW to fill the vacancy created by such expansion. The Company will form a Finance Committee consisting of three independent directors, which shall advise and provide recommendations to the Board of Directors on all major financings, acquisitions, divestitures, and other major corporate events. The Chairman of the Finance Committee shall be the AW nominee.
Offering Expenses:	The Company shall reimburse AW, on a current basis, for all out-of-pocket expenses, including, but not limited to, legal and due diligence related expenses, whether or not the closing of the Offering occurs. The Company shall be consulted on all budgetary estimates for the engagement of professional advisors for which it is providing reimbursement, and shall be entitled to an accounting of all expenses.
Fees:	The Company shall pay AW a fee equal to 3% of the Offering amount at closing. In addition, the Company shall issue to AW at closing warrants to purchase one million shares of Common Stock, each exercisable at $6.00 per share, at any time within five years of the closing of the offering (the AW Warrants). The Company shall also be responsible for all fees and expenses of any agent, broker or finder retained by the Company for the purposes of the Offering.
Lock-up Period:	All Holders will agree not to sell or to offer to sell any securities of the Company for up to one year following the date of the issuance of the Units.
Fully-Diluted Common Stock:	Shares % of Total Common Stock outstanding before the Offering[1] _____ _____ Common Stock underlying the Units[2] _____ _____ Pro Forma Common Stock Outstanding _____ _____
Exclusive Period:	AW will have an exclusive right to purchase the Units, for a period of 90 days from _____, 20__. The Company has the right to obtain up to $2 million of additional financing. The terms and timing of such additional financing, as well as the investors identity, are subject to AW's written approval, which will not be unreasonably withheld.

[1] At _____, 19 includes _____ shares of Common Stock outstanding, plus _____ shares of Common Stock underlying employee options outstanding with an average exercise price of $_____ per share, $_____ director options outstanding with an average exercise price of $_____ per share and outstanding warrants to purchase _____ shares of Common Stock with an average exercise price of $_____ per share.

[2] Based on an aggregate Offering amount of $6,000,000 [Includes the AW Warrants.]

USE OF PROCEEDS

The net proceeds (after deducting underwriting commissions and the estimated expenses of this offering) to be received by the Company from the sale of the securities offered hereby are estimated to be approximately $5,300,000. The Company expects to use the net proceeds approximately as follows:

Application of Proceeds	Approximate Dollar Amount	Approximate Percentage of Net Proceeds

Does not include approximately $5,000,000 which the Company would receive if its publicly traded warrants were exercised. There are approximately 1,495,000 warrants outstanding, which are exercisable at $3.50 per share of common stock and expire on _____, 20__.

The Company anticipates, based on management's internal forecasts and assumptions relating to its operations (including assumptions regarding the completion of the technology transfer facility, including capital equipment, the progress of research and development, both internal and at, relating to _____ technology) that the net proceeds of this offering will be sufficient to satisfy the Company's contemplated cash needs for twelve months following the consummation of this offering. If all or most of the public warrants are exercised in _____, 20__, the period the additional cash received available to satisfy the Company's working capital needs for at least an additional 12 months

Proceeds not immediately required for the purpose described above will be invested promptly in short-term investment grade debt obligations, bank certificates of deposit, United States government money market investments, or other short-term interest-bearing investments.

CAPITALIZATION

The following table sets forth as of _____, 20__ the Company's capitalization on an actual basis and as adjusted to give effect to the issuance and sale of the 1,500,000 shares of Common Stock and 750,000 warrants offered hereby and the application of the estimated net proceeds therefrom:

| | _____, 20__ | |
	Actual	As Adjusted(2)
Liabilities		
Short-term debt	$0	$0
Long-term debt	0	0
Total liabilities	0	0
Stockholders equity		
Preferred Stock, par value $.01 per share, 5,000,000 shares authorized, 200,000 shares designated Series A Nonconvertible Preferred Stock, 200,000 shares issued and Outstanding	$	$
Common Stock, par value $.01 per share, 25,000,000 shares authorized;_____ (actual) and_____ shares issued and outstanding (as adjusted)(1)		
Additional paid-in capital		
Deficit accumulated during development stage		
Total shareholders' equity		
Total capitalization	$	$

(1) Does not include: (i) 750,000 shares of Common Stock reserved for issuance upon exercise of the Warrants; (ii) an aggregate of 1,000,000 shares of Common Stock reserved for the issuance upon exercise of the_____ warrants; (iii) approximately _____public warrants, which are exercisable at $3.50 per share and expire on, 20__; (iv) an aggregate of_____ shares of Common Stock reserved for issuance upon exercise of outstanding warrants; (v)_____ shares of Common Stock reserved for issuance upon exercise of options granted and available for future grant under the 1995 Stock Option Plan.
(2) Gives effect to (I) the application of the estimated net proceeds of this offering of $5,300,000.

RISK FACTORS

The securities offered hereby are speculative and involve a high degree of risk. In addition to the other information contained in this Memorandum, investors should carefully consider the following risk factors before making an investment decision concerning the Units. An investment in the securities offered hereby should be considered a venture capital investment and the securities should not be purchased by investors who cannot afford the loss of their entire investment. Each prospective investor should carefully consider the following risk factors before making an investment decision.

1. Continuing and Future Losses

Since its inception, the Company has not generated any product revenues, and has incurred significant losses, resulting in an accumulated deficit of $

2. Significant Capital Requirements and the Need for Additional Financing

The Company's capital requirements have been and will continue to be significant. However, upon the conclusion of the Offering, the Company believes it has sufficient capital to complete the improvements to the technology transfer center, including the acquisition of capital equipment, and will have approximately $1,800,000 remaining from the offering in addition to approximately $2,000,000 it currently has on hand. The $3,800,000 will be adequate to meet its working capital requirements for at least 12 months. Completion from the closing date, completion of the research, development, and commercialization of the_____ technology for potential applications will require significant additional effort and resources. The Company will not obtain sufficient proceeds hereunder to meet all of its future obligations. Assuming exercise of the 1.45 million public warrants at $3.50 per share expiring _____, 20__, the Company will receive an additional $5,000,000, which the Company believes should meet its working capital requirements for at least an additional 12 months.

3. Uncertainty of Feasibility of _____ Technology for Product Applications

At this time, the Company is unable to determine the feasibility of its _____ for the commercial viability of any potential applications. While significant advances and developments have been made in the Companys technology, substantial advances in the research and development efforts must be made in a number of areas before products utilizing the technology are manufactured and sold including, without limitation: reliability, the development of more fully

The Companys research and development efforts remain subject to all of the risks associated with the development of new products based on emerging and innovative technologies, including, without limitation, unanticipated technical or other problems and the possible insufficiency of the funds allocated to complete such development. Any of the proceeding could have a material adverse effect on the Company.

4. Uncertainty Concerning Market Acceptance of the Technology

The potential size, timing and viability of market opportunities targeted by the Company are uncertain at this time. Market acceptance of the _____ technology will depend, in part, upon such technology providing benefits comparable to ___ and ___ technology (the current standard for display quality) at an appropriate cost, and its adoption by consumers, neither of which has been achieved. Many potential licensees of the technology manufacture flat panel displays utilizing competing technologies and may, however, be reluctant to redesign their products or manufacturing processes to incorporate the technology. Potential licensees may never utilize the commercially viable_____ technology.

5. Dependence on the Research Partners

Research and development of commercially viable applications for _____ technology is dependent on the success of the research efforts of the Research Partners conducted pursuant to its_____ Agreements. There can be no assurance that the Research Partners will make additional advances in the research and development of the_____ technology.

While the Company funds the_____ technology research, the scope of and technical aspects of the research and the resources and efforts directed to such research is subject to the control of the Research Partners.

6. Dependence Upon Strategic Relationships

The Company's strategic plan depends upon the development of strategic relationships with companies that will manufacture and use products incorporating its _____ technology. The Company has not yet entered into any such relationships. The Company intends to _____with the proceeds from this offering, and it believes such a facility and the increased capabilities the Company will then have will be advantageous to developing such relationships, but there are no assurances in that regard. The Company's prospects will be significantly affected by its ability to sublicense the _____tech-nology and successfully develop strategic alliances with third parties for incorporation of the _____ technology to be manufactured by others. Strategic alliances may require financial or other commitments by the Company. There can be no assurance that the Company will be able, for financial or other reasons, to enter into strategic alliances on commercially acceptable terms, or at all. Failure to do so would have a material adverse effect on the Company.

7. Uncertainty of Intellectual Property Rights

The patent laws of other countries may differ from those of the United States as to the patentability of the ____ technology and the degree of protection afforded. Other companies and institutions may inde-pendently develop equivalent or superior technologies and may obtain patent or similar rights with respect thereto. There are a number of other companies and organizations that have been issued patents and are filing additional patent applications relating to ____ technology and there can be no assurance that the exercise of the Company's licensing rights respecting its ____ technology being developed by _____ will not infringe on the patents of others, in which event the Company or its partners may be required to obtain a license, pay damages, modify their method of operation, or be prohibited from infring-ing the patents of others. If products incorporating the Companys ____ technology are found to infringe upon the patent or other intellectual property rights of others, it could have a material adverse effect on the Company.

The United States government, through the Defense Advanced Research Projects Agency (DARPA), has provided funding to _____ for research activities related to certain aspects of its _____ technology. If all or certain aspects of its_____ technology developed (if any) from the Companys funding to _____is deemed to fall within the planned and committed activities of DARPAs funding, the federal government, pursuant to federal law, could have certain rights relating to the _____technology, including a license to practice or have practiced on its behalf any such technology, or require the Company to grant licenses to other parties in certain fields of use.

8. Competition and Competing Technologies

The _____industry is characterized by intense competition. The market is currently domi-nated by, and in the foreseeable future is expected to be dominated by, products utilizing _____technol-ogy. Numerous companies are making substantial investments in, and conducting research to improve characteristics of, ____ technology. Several other_____ technologies have been, or are being, developed, including _____. In addition, other companies are engaged in research and development activities with respect to technology using _____. Advances in _____ technology or any of these developing technologies may overcome their limitations or become the leading technology for flat panel displays, either of which could limit the potential market for flat panel displays utilizing the Company's _____ technology.

Substantially all of these competitors have greater name recognition and financial, technical, marketing, personnel, and research capabilities than the Company. The Company's competitors may succeed in developing technologies and applications that are more cost effective, have them or have other advantages as compared to the Company's _____ technology. The Company may never be able to compete successfully or develop commercial applications for its _____technology.

9. Dependence on Key Personnel

The Company's performance is substantially dependent on the continued services and on the performance of its senior management and other key personnel. The Company's performance also depends on the Company's ability to retain and motivate its other officers and key employees. The loss of the services of any of its executive officers or other key employees could have a material adverse effect on the Company's business, prospects, financial condition, and results of operations.

10. Restrictions on Transferability

Potential investors should be aware of the potentially long-term nature of their investment. The offer and sale of the Units (and the shares of Common Stock underlying the Units) will not be registered under the Securities Act or under any state securities laws and are offered pursuant to exemptions from registration, which depend in part upon the investment intent of the investors. Each purchaser of the Units will be required to represent that it is purchasing such stock for its own account for investment purposes and not with a view to resale or distribution. No transfer of the Units (and the shares of Common Stock underlying the Units) may be made unless such transfer is registered under the Securities Act and applicable state securities laws, or an exemption therefrom is available and same will be noted on a restrictive legend placed on each Common Stock certificate and Warrant.

DESCRIPTION OF THE BUSINESS

General

The Company is engaged in

The Company's commercialization efforts are focused on

The Company believes that products i should have superior performance characteristics at lower costs than existing technologies for a wide variety of product applications. The Company's first products will likely be. The Company intends to move forward as quickly as possible to larger area full-color devices such as low-power, personal digital assistants and rugged, lightweight laptop computers. Goals of the Company's proprietary that could be attached anywhere.

The Company is incorporated under the laws of the Commonwealth of Pennsylvania and corporate headquarters are at

The Company's Technology

Commercialization Strategy and Market Opportunity
Initial Target Markets

Government Support

Development Activities

Competition

Employees   The Company has fifteen employees.

Facilities   The Company's corporate offices are located at

MANAGEMENT AND ADVISORS

Key members of the Company's management include the following individuals:

Mr._____ has been Chairman and Chief Executive Officer of the Company since its founding in _____.

Mr. _____ joined the Company as President, Chief Operating Officer, and Director in _____. He is responsible for _____, its strategic partnering program and overall day-to-day management. He was previously

Mr. _____ has been the Company's Executive Vice President, Chief Financial Officer, Treasurer, and Secretary since ____, and a member of the Board of Directors since ____. He is responsible for all internal and external financial, treasury, and administrative functions.

Key members of the Company's research and development team include:

Troubled businesses, symptoms of, 5-6
Turnaround Management Association, 79
Turnaround specialist, hiring outside, 76-82
  compensation requirements, 80
  finding, 78-79
  full-time, 81-82
  part-time, 80-81
  qualifications of, 79-80
Turnaround strategy. *See also* Financial turnaround
  business plan in, 11-53
  compensation schemes for employees in, 94-97
  completing, 282-85
  keys to performing successful, 6-7
  managing people in, 85-107
  steps to successful, 7-9

U
URL, 198

V
Values for business, 17
Vendors
  comparison of company with others in terms of quality, 174
  in funding turnarounds, 229
  informing new, of debt negotiation, 168
  meeting with, 9
  referrals in attracting and keeping customers, 187
  sending debt negotiation letter to, 164-66
  as source of marketing prospects, 116
  telling about layoffs, 157-58

Venture capital in financing turnarounds, 227-28
Venture consultants in financing turnarounds, 243
Venture leasing in financing turnarounds, 235-36
Verticals, 221
Vision for business, developing, 15, 16

W
Weber, Robin, 13
Web site
  address for, 198
  content recommendation, 200
  defined, 221
  hosting, 198
  internet connection for, 198
  launch schedule for, 200
  maintenance schedule, 200
  site map for, 200
  work schedule for, 200
Web site audit, 177-79
  competition, 178
  content checklist, 177-78
  customer interviews, 178
  internal interviews, 178
  marketing materials, 179
  technical functionality, 179
Web site development, 192-95
  competitive analysis in, 199
  copywriter for, 194
  external analysis in, 199, 203-5
  future changes in, 195
  glossary of terms in, 220-21
  in-house graphic artist in, 193
  internal analysis in, 199, 202-3
  maintenance of, 195
  management of, 194
  plan for, 198-200
    sample, 201-19

viewing site during construction, 194
Web site development software, evaluating, 196-97
Wilson, Charles E., 11
Witness, need for, in termination meeting, 154
Wooden, John, 85
Workout departments in banks, 78, 251

Y
Yeager, Chuck, 182

Find more on this topic by visiting BusinessTown.com

Developed by Adams Media, **BusinessTown.com** is a free informational site for entrepreneurs, small business owners, and operators. It provides a comprehensive guide for planning, starting, growing, and managing a small business.

Visitors may access hundreds of articles addressing dozens of business topics, participate in forums, as well as connect to additional resources around the Web. **BusinessTown.com** is easily navigated and provides assistance to small businesses and start-ups. The material covers beginning basic issues as well as the more advanced topics.

✓ **Accounting**
Basic, Credit & Collections, Projections, Purchasing/Cost Control

✓ **Advertising**
Magazine, Newspaper, Radio, Television, Yellow Pages

✓ **Business Opportunities**
Ideas for New Businesses, Business for Sale, Franchises

✓ **Business Plans**
Creating Plans & Business Strategies

✓ **Finance**
Getting Money, Money Problem Solutions

✓ **Letters & Forms**
Looking Professional, Sample Letters & Forms

✓ **Getting Started**
Incorporating, Choosing a Legal Structure

✓ **Hiring & Firing**
Finding the Right People, Legal Issues

✓ **Home Business**
Home Business Ideas, Getting Started

✓ **Internet**
Getting Online, Put Your Catalog on the Web

✓ **Legal Issues**
Contracts, Copyrights, Patents, Trademarks

✓ **Managing a Small Business**
Growth, Boosting Profits, Mistakes to Avoid, Competing with the Giants

✓ **Managing People**
Communications, Compensation, Motivation, Reviews, Problem Employees

✓ **Marketing**
Direct Mail, Marketing Plans, Strategies, Publicity, Trade Shows

✓ **Office Setup**
Leasing, Equipment, Supplies

✓ **Presentations**
Know Your Audience, Good Impression

✓ **Sales**
Face to Face, Independent Reps, Telemarketing

✓ **Selling a Business**
Finding Buyers, Setting a Price, Legal Issues

✓ **Taxes**
Employee, Income, Sales, Property Use

✓ **Time Management**
Can You Really Manage Time?

✓ **Travel & Maps**
Making Business Travel Fun

✓ **Valuing a Business**
Simple Valuation Guidelines

http://www.businesstown.com

About the Author

MARC KRAMER is president of Kramer Communications, a marketing, management, and communications consulting firm located in Downingtown, Pennsylvania. Marc has won such awards as the *Inc.* Entrepreneur of the Year, American Electronics Association Spirit of America, and Enterprise Award. Marc has a bachelor of science degree in broadcast journalism from West Virginia University and a master's in management from Penn State University.

Kramer Communications develops and implements business, sales, operating and marketing plans and Internet content and e-commerce strategies. Marc Kramer can be reached at marc@kramercommunications.com.